Northern Ireland 1968–2008

Northern Ireland 1968–2008

The Politics of Entrenchment

Cillian McGrattan
Government of Ireland Post-Doctoral Fellow, University College, Dublin

© Cillian McGrattan 2010

All rights reserved. No reproduction, copy or transmission of this publication may be made without written permission.

No portion of this publication may be reproduced, copied or transmitted save with written permission or in accordance with the provisions of the Copyright, Designs and Patents Act 1988, or under the terms of any licence permitting limited copying issued by the Copyright Licensing Agency, Saffron House, 6–10 Kirby Street, London EC1N 8TS.

Any person who does any unauthorized act in relation to this publication may be liable to criminal prosecution and civil claims for damages.

The author has asserted his right to be identified as the author of this work in accordance with the Copyright, Designs and Patents Act 1988.

First published 2010 by
PALGRAVE MACMILLAN

Palgrave Macmillan in the UK is an imprint of Macmillan Publishers Limited, registered in England, company number 785998, of Houndmills, Basingstoke, Hampshire RG21 6XS.

Palgrave Macmillan in the US is a division of St Martin's Press LLC, 175 Fifth Avenue, New York, NY 10010.

Palgrave Macmillan is the global academic imprint of the above companies and has companies and representatives throughout the world.

Palgrave® and Macmillan® are registered trademarks in the United States, the United Kingdom, Europe and other countries.

ISBN 978–0–230–23891–6   hardback

This book is printed on paper suitable for recycling and made from fully managed and sustained forest sources. Logging, pulping and manufacturing processes are expected to conform to the environmental regulations of the country of origin.

A catalogue record for this book is available from the British Library.

A catalog record for this book is available from the Library of Congress.

10 9 8 7 6 5 4 3 2 1
19 18 17 16 15 14 13 12 11 10

Printed and bound in Great Britain by

CPI Antony Rowe, Chippenham and Eastbourne

For my parents

Contents

List of Abbreviations	viii
Acknowledgements	ix
List of Principal Actors	x
Introduction	1
1 The Northern Ireland Conflict	7
2 Turning Points in the Troubles, 1968–71	34
3 Direct Rule and Power Sharing, 1972–74	58
4 The Politics of Entrenchment, 1974–85	89
5 The Northern Ireland Peace Process, 1985–97	121
6 The Politics of the Past, 1998–2008	156
Conclusion	181
Notes	189
Index	226

List of Abbreviations

AG	Attorney-General
CAB	Cabinet Office
CENT	Central Secretariat
CONV	Constitutional Convention
CPGNI	Consultative Group on the Past in Northern Ireland
DFA	Department of Foreign Affairs
DT	Department of the Taoiseach
DUP	Democratic Unionist Party
FCO	Foreign and Commonwealth Office
IDU	Inter-Departmental Unit on Northern Ireland
GAA	Gaelic Athletics Association
HMG	Her Majesty's government
IDU	Inter-Departmental Unit in Northern Ireland
IRA	Irish Republican Army
LVF	Loyalist Volunteer Force
NA	National Archives (Public Record Office, London)
NAI	National Archives of Ireland (Dublin)
NIC	Northern Ireland Committee
NIHCD	Northern Ireland House of Commons Debates
NIO	Northern Ireland Office
NIPC	Northern Ireland Political Collection (Linenhall Library, Belfast)
OE	Office of the Executive
PIRA	Provisional IRA
PREM	Office of the Prime Minister
PRONI	Public Record Office of Northern Ireland (Belfast)
PSNI	Police Service of Northern Ireland
RUC	Royal Ulster Constabulary
SDLP	Social Democratic and Labour Party
TD	Teachta Dála, member of the Irish Dáil
UKUP	United Kingdom Unionist Party
UUC	Ulster Unionist Council
UUP	Ulster Unionist Party
UUUC	United Ulster Unionist Council
UVF	Ulster Volunteer Force
UWC	Ulster Workers' Council

Acknowledgements

This book would not have been possible without the support and guidance of Henry Patterson, to whom I owe enormous personal and intellectual gratitude.

For their advice, encouragement, and help over the past few years I also wish to thank a number of others: Sahla Aroussi, Fidelma Ashe, Arthur Aughey, Carol-Ann Barnes, Brian Barton, Aaron Edwards, Adrian Guelke, Paul Hainsworth, Cathy Gormley-Heenan, Thomas Hennessey, Eamonn O'Kane, Patrick Roche, Carmel Roulston, Kirk Simpson, Jennifer Todd, Jonathan Tonge and Robin Wilson.

The book is partly based on my doctorial research at the University of Ulster, which was funded by the Department for Employment and Learning (Northern Ireland), and it draws on material from several institutions. As such, I extend my thanks to David Huddleston and the staff in the Access Section of the Public Records Office of Northern Ireland for their assistance in highlighting and tracking down pertinent files and their help in accessing previously closed documents. I also thank the staff in the University of Ulster's library at Jordanstown; the staff at the National Archives in Kew and in the National Archives of Ireland in Dublin. Thanks also to the staff in the Belfast City Central Library's Newspaper Library and in the Northern Ireland Political Collection in the Linenhall Library. The University of Ulster's School of Economics and Politics and the Social Sciences Research Graduate School provided funding for research trips and I am grateful to the staff in both schools for all their assistance.

Finally, I wish to thank my parents and family for their unstinting encouragement.

List of Principal Actors

Adams, Gerry, Sinn Féin, MP MLA, president of party 1983–

Ahern, Bertie, Fianna Fáil, Irish Taoiseach, 1997–2008

Allen, Dr Harry, former Presbyterian Moderator

Baird, Ernest, Vanguard Progressive Unionist Party, deputy party leader; later leader of United Ulster Unionist Party, 1975–82

Barr, Glenn, Vanguard Progressive Unionist Party

Blair, Tony, Labour Party, party leader, British prime minister, 1997–2007

Bloomfield, Sir Kenneth, cabinet secretary to Terence O'Neill, secretary to the power-sharing initiative; later Head of Northern Ireland Civil Service

Brooke, Peter, Conservative Party, Secretary of State for Northern Ireland, Thatcher and Major administrations, 1989–92

Boland, Kevin, Fianna Fáil TD

Bruton, John, Fine Gael, Irish Taoiseach, 1994–7

Burnside, David, Ulster Unionist Party MP

Carrington, Lord Peter, Conservative Party, Minister of Defence, Heath administration, 1970–4

Chastelain General John de, head of International Commission on Decommissioning

Chichester-Clark, James, Ulster Unionist Party, Prime Minister of Northern Ireland, 1969–70

Cooper, Frank, permanent under-secretary, Northern Ireland Office

Cooper, Ivan, Social Democratic and Labour Party, founding party member

Cosgrave Liam, Fine Gael, Irish Taoiseach, 1973–7

List of Principal Actors xi

Costello, Declan, Fine Gael, Attorney-General, 1973–7

Craig, William, Minister of Home Affairs, 1966–8, Ulster Unionist Party MP, Founder of Vanguard and Vanguard Unionist Progressive Party

Cubbon, Brian, permanent under-secretary, Northern Ireland Office

Currie, Austin, Social Democratic and Labour Party MP, founder party member

Devlin, Paddy, Social Democratic and Labour Party MP, founder party member

Donaldson, Jeffrey, Ulster Unionist Party MP

Donlon, Sean, Irish government liaison to Northern Ireland

Donoughue, Bernard, senior policy adviser to Harold Wilson

Duffy, John, Social Democratic and Labour Party, party chairman

Eames, Robin, Archbishop of Armagh and Church of Ireland Primate for All Ireland

Faulkner, Brian, Ulster Unionist Party, prime minister of Northern Ireland, 1971–2, Chief Minister of the Northern Ireland Executive, 1974

Fitt, Gerry, Social Democratic and Labour Party MP, party leader, 1970–9

FitzGerald, Garret, Fine Gael, Minister for Foreign Affairs, Cosgrave administration, 1973–7; later Irish Taoiseach, 1981–2, 1982–7

Flanagan, Ronnie, Chief Constable of the Royal Ulster Constabulary, 1996–2001, Chief Constable of the Police Service of Northern Ireland, 2001–2

Good, Rev. Harold, president of Methodist Church in Ireland, peace negotiator and joint overseer (with Father Alec Reid) of decommissioning of IRA arms

Hain, Peter, Labour Party, Secretary of State for Northern Ireland, Blair administration, 2005–7

Heath, Edward, Conservative Party, British prime minister, 1970–4

Hillery, Patrick, Fianna Fáil, Irish Minister for Foreign Affairs, Lynch administration, 1969–73

Holden, David, permanent secretary at the UK Ministry of Finance

Hume, John, Social Democratic and Labour Party, founding party member; later party leader, 1979–2001

Hunt, Sir John, chair of Northern Ireland Committee

Ingram, Adam, Labour Party, Northern Ireland Security Minister, first Minister for Victims, Blair administration

Lemass, Seán, Fianna Fáil, Irish Taoiseach, 1959–66

Lindsay, Kennedy, Vanguard Progressive Unionist Party

Lynch, Jack, Fianna Fáil, Irish Taoiseach, 1966–73

Maginnis, Ken, Ulster Unionist Party MP

Major, John, Conservative Party, British prime minister, 1990–7

Mallon, Seamus, Social Democratic and Labour Party, deputy leader; later deputy First Minister of Northern Ireland, 1999–2001

Mandelson, Peter, Labour Party, Secretary of State for Northern Ireland, Blair administration, 1999–2001

Mason, Roy, Labour Party, Secretary of State for Northern Ireland, James Callaghan administration, 1976–9

Maudling, Reginald, Conservative Party, Home Secretary, Heath administration, 1970–2

Mayhew, Patrick, Conservative Party, Secretary of State for Northern Ireland, Major administration, 1992–7

McAteer, Eddie, Nationalist Party, party leader, 1964–9

McGuinness, Martin, Sinn Féin, chief negotiator in Belfast/Good Friday Agreement; later Deputy First Minister of Northern Ireland, 2007–

McLachlan, Peter, Ulster Unionist Party Assembly Member

McLaughlin, Mitchell, Sinn Féin, senior party strategist

Mitchell, George, Senator, US Special Envoy for Northern Ireland and chair of all-party talks leading to Good Friday/Belfast Agreement

Molyneaux, James, Ulster Unionist Party, party leader, 1979–85

Mowlam, Marjorie, 'Mo', Labour Party, Secretary of State for Northern Ireland, Blair administration, 1997–9

Ó Bradaigh, Ruairí, former Chief of Staff of the IRA, Sinn Féin leader, 1970–83

O'Brien, Conor Cruise, Labour Party, Minister for Posts and Telegraphs, Cosgrave administration, 1973–7

Ó Conaill, Dáithí, former member of the IRA's ruling Army Council; later deputy leader of Sinn Féin

O'Hanlon, Paddy, Social Democratic and Labour Party, founding party member

O'Neill, Terence, Ulster Unionist Party, premier of Northern Ireland, 1963–9

Paisley, Ian, Democratic Unionist Party, party leader, 1970–2008; later First Minister of Northern Ireland, 2007–8

Patten, Chris, Conservative Party, undersecretary of state, Northern Ireland Office, Thatcher administration; later chair of the Independent Commission on Policing in Northern Ireland (Patten Commission)

Powell, John Enoch, Ulster Unionist Party; formerly British Conservative Party Housing Minister, Macmillan administration and Shadow Defence Minister, Heath opposition cabinet

Prior, James, Conservative Party, Secretary of State for Northern Ireland, Thatcher administration, 1981–4

Rees, Merlyn, Labour Party, Secretary of State for Northern Ireland, Wilson administration, 1974–6

Reid, Father Alex, priest, confidant of Gerry Adams and peace negotiator; later overseer (with Harold Good) of IRA arms decommissioning

Reynolds, Albert, Fianna Fáil, Irish Taoiseach, 1992–4

Robinson, Peter, Democratic Unionist Party, deputy party leader; later First Minister of Northern Ireland, 2008–

Smyth, Martin, Ulster Unionist Party MP, Head of Orange Order

Spring, Dick, Labour Party, Tanaiste (deputy prime minister) of Ireland in Fine Gael-Labour Party coalitions, 1982–7, 1993–7

Taylor, John, Ulster Unionist Party MP, deputy party leader

Thatcher, Margaret, Conservative Party, party leader, British prime minister 1979–90

Trimble, David, Ulster Unionist Party, party leader; 1995–2005; later First Minister of Northern Ireland, 1999–2002

Twomey, Seamus, former Chief of Staff of the IRA **West, Harry**, Ulster Unionist Party MP, party leader, 1974–9

Whitelaw, William, Conservative Party, Secretary of State for Northern Ireland, Heath administration, 1972–3

Wilson, James Harold, Labour Party, British prime minister, 1964–70, 1974–6

Introduction

Northern Ireland and the politics of change

The unfolding of history influences how we view the past. Changing events and circumstances affect the type of questions we ask about history, the chronologies we impose and the answers we reach: *'even the recorded past* changes in the light of subsequent history'.[1] Tony Judt has recently remarked how the events of the winter of 1989 – the fall of the Berlin Wall and popular uprisings in Czechoslovakia, Hungary, Poland and Romania – not only opened up possibilities for Europe's future, but also created a new perspective on its past: 'the years 1945–89 would now come to be seen not as the threshold of a new epoch but rather as an interim age'.[2]

In part, this book takes its impetus from the idea that the present influences how we see the past. A reliable estimate puts the number of deaths of the Northern Irish conflict at 3,704;[3] a further estimated 40,000 were wounded as a result of the hostilities. In the midst of this violence it became commonplace within the worlds of journalism, academia and the wider public sphere to claim – and dismiss – the 'Troubles' as a rerun of old Irish antagonisms: Catholics against Protestants, nationalists against unionists, Irish against British.[4] However, the signing of the Good Friday/Belfast Agreement in April 1998 and, more recently, the May 2007 Sinn Féin–Democratic Unionist Party (DUP) power-sharing détente suggest that Northern Ireland's Troubles have shifted to a less violent and more political sphere. This shift allows us to reappraise the Troubles and reflect on what the conflict was really about. This book engages with the questions that emerge from that reappraisal: Did the conflict arise and persist because of ancient and deeply embedded ethnic antagonisms? Was it an inevitable result of half a century of unionist domination and nationalist exclusion? What effect did the decisions and omissions of political leaders play in the evolution of the conflict?

The latter question points to the second main building block of this book: the idea that the past influences the present. I examine recently released archival material to ask why certain decisions were made and not others, why key decisions persisted across time and why accommodative alternatives to the violence and division failed to emerge. The primary material allows us to see that contingency and choice did exist in the early years of the conflict. However, it also allows us to identify how and why key choices coalesced to take on a greater solidity. These previously unavailable primary sources underpin the main argument of the book: namely, historical choices carried through across time to become entrenched policy frameworks and take on a structural, determinative force in themselves. The book locates the reasons for the persistence of the Troubles to decisions taken early in the 1970s and argues that key historical choices affected subsequent political developments. Put simply, identifiable choices carried through and established narrow paths of contention and antagonism once available routes to accommodation were left behind and became more and more remote as the conflict became ever more deeply entrenched.

The broadening of perspective and the release of archival material permit a critique of the prevailing assumptions regarding ethno-national antagonism and offer an opportunity to restore historical nuance to our analysis. Although an examination of political conflicts risks 'opening old wounds',[5] the implication of this book is that a failure to do so is to risk repeating the stories which inspired and fed the conflict. Unless these stories are tested and questioned, future generations will make up their minds about what actually happened based on received communal explanations.[6] Furthermore, the examination of the newly available primary material suggests that new theoretical frameworks are required in order to learn more about the political dynamics of this period. The book investigates how shifts in the political arena provided incentives to actors and emphasises how historical decisions had lasting effects. In particular, I emphasise how several key decisions – including the British intervention in August 1969, the decision by the Social Democratic and Labour Party (SDLP) to withdraw from the Stormont system in July 1971 and Northern Ireland prime minister Brian Faulkner's willingness to acquiesce in cross-border bodies in September 1971 – constrained later political negotiations and influenced the shape of the Troubles by giving rise to divergent historical 'paths'.

Specifically, therefore, the book concentrates on *change* and *continuity*. It examines the strategies and interaction of the two main communal parties, the SDLP and the Ulster Unionist Party (UUP) in the years after the prorogation of Stormont and the introduction of direct rule by London. The roles played by the two sovereign governments, Dublin and London, were instrumental in shaping events and influencing perceptions in the North; and the work stresses how, in many instances, their interventions had unintended repercussions. This is particularly true of British policy-making, which raised nationalist expectations of fundamental and radical change and ratcheted unionist fears concerning the constitutional link and the deteriorating security situation. The book points out that that ambiguity of British policy-making was 'constructive' only in the sense that it contributed to the complexity of the historical situation and influenced the growing entrenchment of political objectives. This early period of the Troubles has witnessed intense academic interest as a key historical moment in the development not only of the North, but also of the modern British and Irish states. This book is a contribution to that debate by outlining how the state policy-making apparatuses function on the basis of fragmentary and particularistic lessons learned about the past, and how the absence of decisive intervention may have as profound an effect on political developments as a coherent and cohesive strategy.

Northern Ireland and the politics of conflict

At the end of his history of the origins of the English Revolution, Lawrence Stone argued that 'It has not proved possible ... to identify any one cause and label it the decisive or even the most important one of all.'[7] Following his example, it may be useful to outline briefly the background 'precipitants' to the book's main area of inquiry – the evolution of conflict in Northern Ireland.

Northern Ireland's creation in 1920–2 was one of a number of uneasy ethnic and religious compromises that resulted in the aftermath of the First World War. The compromise in this case meant that nationalists, who aspired to a single, unified Irish state, would comprise about a third of the population. However, the nature of the majoritarian, first-past-the-post electoral system that was in place meant that of the 52 seats in the Stormont Parliament, nationalists could hope for no more than 10–12. From the 1930s onwards, they looked instead to the Irish Free State to improve their situation and formed what effectively became 'a state within a state'.[8] Correspondingly, Ulster unionists, who favoured retaining the constitutional link with Britain, saw little point in offering concessions to a minority that offered allegiance to a 'foreign' and 'hostile' government. This state of affairs was compounded by the fact that unionists were also a minority on the island of Ireland and, therefore, feared that any small-scale political or institutional change could increase the chances of a radical reconfiguration of the status quo. The outbreak of the Second World War widened these divisions as the Dublin government remained neutral while Stormont participated in the Allied campaign. In response to the South's neutrality, its declaration of being an independent Republic in 1948 and the wartime sacrifices of Northern unionists, the post-war Labour government passed the Ireland Act in 1949, which stated that Northern Ireland would remain part of the United Kingdom unless a majority within the province voted to leave. The transfer of constitutional change to the North from Westminster enraged Irish nationalists, who held that since Westminster had partitioned the country in 1920 it should retain the right 'unilaterally' to enforce reunification.[9]

A series of socio-economic and political changes coincided to transform this impasse. For instance, a broad international current of radical politics peaked in the late 1960s.[10] Again, the introduction of the welfare state had ramifications for political and economic life in Northern Ireland, as Catholic alienation and opposition was challenged by the range of tangible material benefits in education, health and social service provision. The introduction of the grammar school system has traditionally been pinpointed as a key factor in this 'embourgeoisement';[11] however, the historical record is more complex. Certainly, the emergence of articulate spokespersons such as Gerry Fitt (elected to the Westminster parliament in 1966) Austin Currie and John Hume raised expectations of political change. Together with local pressure groups such as the Homeless Citizens' League and Campaign for Social Justice, and the local labour movement, the rise to prominence of these politicians highlighted the inadequacy of the Nationalist Party's long-standing strategy of opposition and abstention.[12] Yet it is possible to overestimate the influence of the expansion in the Catholic middle class and overlook the fact that the civil rights campaign was a *mass* movement and that traditional nationalist forces played a decisive role in restraining and moderating some of the more radical tendencies within the civil rights movement.[13]

Four further factors influenced a shift away from the political stalemate. First, the republican movement initiated a policy rethink after the failure of its Border Campaign (1956–62) to mobilise Catholic support. This led to the emergence of leftist ideas and the strategy of using civil rights to create a broad-based, anti-Stormont movement. However, it is a mistake to overestimate the role the small cadre of republican thinkers played in the growth of the civil rights campaign.[14] Second, the election of a Labour government in 1964 provided a 'trigger' to civil rights mobilisation. Not only did Catholics expect direct intervention from the new government, but the Stormont administration also came under indirect pressure to move beyond the gradualist approach of the premier, Terence O'Neill, towards more radical political reforms.[15] Changes in unionist politics also added to the general perception of flux and possibility. Thus, O'Neill had expressed sympathy on the death of Pope John XXIII in 1963 and visited Catholic schools in 1964. In addition, in 1965, he entertained the Irish Taoiseach, Sean Lemass, for the first meeting between the heads of the two Irish states since the early 1920s. Third, the civil rights movement took inspiration from the Black mobilisation in the United States and consciously imported the tactics of Martin Luther King, including mass meetings, peaceful resistance and protest marches. This US model provided Northern Irish activists with inspiration and methods, but it also offered the British and Irish media a convenient and readily comprehensible narrative for explaining what was going on in Northern Ireland. In 1968 and 1969, television images of state forces attacking unarmed demonstrators in the North echoed previous reports from Paris, Prague and Selma, Alabama and resonated with political elites in Westminster and the general public across the British Isles. Finally, the rise to prominence of Ian Paisley and a new wave of fundamentalist politics directly influenced O'Neill's calculations and he resisted pressure from Westminster to engage the civil rights movement due to growing discontent among his backbenchers, cabinet colleagues and grass-roots supporters – evidenced in the Orange Order's warnings that the emergence of Paisley could precipitate British intervention and spell the end of the Unionist Party's control of the state.[16]

A key strategic factor behind why the civil rights movement threatened to break the historic impasse was that it was the first time that Catholics had abandoned traditional nationalist rhetoric in favour of a reformed Northern Ireland. Rather than looking to Dublin for change, the new idea was 'British rights for British citizens'. This objective ensured that Stormont could no longer resist pressure for reform based on the claim that it would threaten the Union. Instead, the civil rights campaign targeted the specific areas in which Northern Ireland diverged from Britain. The campaign demanded reform of Northern Ireland's security apparatus, the imposition of fair employment practices in local government and restructuring of electoral practices – including the introduction of the universal franchise and the ending of 'gerrymandered' electoral constituencies at the local government level. Currie has recently outlined the two main reasons behind the decision to escalate the campaign to include forms of mass protest in 1968. First, he had been told at the beginning of that year by the Labour Party MP Paul Rose that 'No British government ... will intervene to remedy injustice in Northern Ireland unless you people there force it to do so'. Second, the demand for 'British rights' undercut unionist resistance to granting rights available to the rest of the United Kingdom.[17]

The change of strategy from lobbying to street politics brought the civil rights movement into confrontation with state forces. The attacks by the police on a civil rights march in Derry in October 1968 and again by loyalists (and off-duty 'B-Specials') just outside Derry in January 1969 (described in chapter 2) are highlighted as possible triggers for the outbreak of violence.[18] The subsequent deployment of British troops on the streets of Northern Ireland in August 1969 is also depicted as a point of no return – certainly for the idea of Northern Irish devolution in its post-1920, majoritarian form.[19] Again, the general Catholic alienation from the state structures and the opportunistic decision by the Provisional IRA (PIRA) to attack the British army are also described as turning points in the history of the Troubles.[20] To this list of possible triggers, the book adds the decisions made by the SDLP and Faulkner in 1971. It argues that the abstention from Stormont by the SDLP and the approval of cross-border bodies by Faulkner effectively ruled out the (admittedly remote) possibility of political accommodation and set in motion a process of policy entrenchment that militated against dialogue and encouraged the pursuit of maximal, yet inward-looking visions of political change.

The main body of the book describes how these early years set the framework for later political relationships. As this brief overview demonstrates, while the social cleavage of Northern Ireland was structured around two poles – Irish–Catholic–nationalist on the one hand, British–Protestant–unionist on the other – these identities did not in themselves unleash conflict. Instead, a range of specific political and historical processes created the immediate background for the eruption and persistence of contention and violence. In other words, while pre-existing ethnic identities framed the outline of Northern Ireland politics, the Troubles were not simply a rerun of ancient antagonisms. Broad historical forces and key political interventions rather than simply the creation and mobilisation of ethno-national identities triggered and sustained the 30 or so years of violence and strife endured by Northern Ireland.

1
The Northern Ireland Conflict

Explaining Northern Ireland – the ethnic conflict model

The Northern Ireland conflict is often described in terms of the presence of two rival ethnic communities, two competing ideas about identity and belonging, and two antagonistic visions of political aspiration. As such, it is portrayed as a quintessential example of what can happen when two ethnic groups live close together in a territory.[1] This fundamental lesson underpins many others – in particular, the need to keep ethnic groups apart and the importance of viewing all aspects of the conflict through the prism of group rights and group demands. Since the signing of the Good Friday/Belfast Agreement in April 1998 and the gradual and uneasy movement away from violence an entire peace process industry has emerged, in which academics and political commentators, together with community sector leaders, ex-politicians and former paramilitaries, share these lessons with other troubled spots across the globe.[2]

This book tells a different story. First, I point out that the 'lessons' drawn and shared by dominant voices have little or no basis in reality. Rather than building on theoretical assumptions about the logic of ethnic antagonism, this book begins with the archival evidence. The increasing availability of primary source material relating to the early years of the Troubles gives rise to a radically different narrative from that propounded by theorists specialising in ethnic antagonism and questions the post-hoc explanations of political and paramilitary elites. The book builds on the cumulative insights of an emerging body of revisionist literature that is increasingly questioning received truths about the salience of ethnic antagonism in Northern Ireland.[3] Second, I argue that the narrative of ethnic antagonism is itself highly political and that the use of terms such as 'lessons', 'groups' and 'ethno-nationalism' not only eschews the empirical facts, it also upholds and perpetuates a whole series of assumptions about whose voices should be heard and whose can be ignored. By focusing on ethnic groups, theorists and politicians effectively silence questions concerning the importance of historical choices and responsibilities, the importance of social conflicts and civil rights, and the importance of gender, class, age and locale in people's experiences of the conflict.[4]

Even in a deeply divided society such as Northern Ireland, ethno-nationalism need not be the driving force behind political change and outcome. I argue that the prioritisation of ethno-nationalism as a key explanatory concept fails to capture historical nuances and may encourage anachronistic conclusions because the pursuit of a single (theoretical) idea – ethno-national antagonism – detracts from the wider historical context in which events occur, and decisions and interpretations are made.

Instead, this study argues that historical decisions (and omissions) drove the Northern Ireland conflict. The changing political context and the intervention of the British state inspired perceptions of opportunity or threat, influencing local decision-making. Thus, a situation of deepening communal division was created, not simply due to the existence of antagonistic communities, but also because specific decisions encouraged political entrenchment and communal polarisation. The decisions made in the early 1970s carried through (a) to constrain the choices available later by ruling out or leaving behind once-plausible alternatives; (b) to shape subsequent political proposals by encouraging the pursuit of further advance; and (c) to contribute to long-term division.

Conventional wisdom suggests that there is a strong causal relationship between ethno-nationalism and political conflict. For example, Donald Horowitz opened his influential *Ethnic Groups in Conflict* with the claim that

> The importance of ethnic conflict, as a force shaping human affairs, as a phenomenon to be understood, as a threat to be controlled, can no longer be denied ... Ethnicity is at the centre of politics in country after country, [and is] a potent source of challenges to the cohesion of states and of international tension.[5]

In a similar vein, Arend Lijphart argued that the presence of ethnic pluralism threatens state stability and so must be countered with rigid institutional arrangements, claiming that the stark choice was between the latter (what he termed 'consociationalism') and 'no democracy at all'.[6] Even historically-oriented scholars such as Anthony Smith have voiced similar concerns over the existence of antagonistic national identification:

> wherever ethnic nationalism has taken hold of populations, there one may expect to find powerful assertions of national self-determination that, if long opposed, will embroil whole regions in bitter and protracted ethnic conflict.[7]

The tendency to view ethno-nationalism as inherently unstable and dangerous continues to drive research analyses. Indeed, that wariness and suspicion form the basis of the consociational assumption that ethno-nationalist groups are resilient to marginalisation and, therefore, ought to be contained, regulated and controlled.[8] Despite such claims, what ethnicity actually means is never defined and at best it is assumed that ethnic division influences political and historical outcomes through quasi-psychological, emotive mechanisms.[9] As such, the ethnic-conflict model raises more questions than it answers. These include: How do identities become politicised or radicalised? How does ethnicity operate? What sets it in motion, what causes it to persist and what causes it to decline in salience? Do salient ethnic emotions trigger change or are they the result of political outcomes? If so, what accounts for those initial outcomes? Are there historical or cumulative aspects to psychology and, if there are, why with psychology in the first place? How does ethnicity affect politics and political change? In other words, rather than bringing any added value to the task of explaining political conflict, the concept ethno-nationalism tends to obscure historical context and ignores traditional concerns over explanatory factors such as differential power dynamics,[10] historical junctures and critical decisions[11] and perceived opportunities,[12] and assumes that political processes are informed and shaped by a fuzzy notion of ethnicity.

Despite the seeming causal potency of national identification and ideology, it does not necessarily follow that ethno-nationalism provokes political change. Ethnic groups, nations or races in themselves do not have specific attributes that can be identified as causing certain behaviours or political characteristics.[13] Rather, groups are continually created through and shaped by events and, specifically, through how those events are interpreted and framed. Thus, conflict is not ethnic in itself, but can be 'framed' in ethnic terms.[14] Groups do not contain identifiable determinative characteristics in themselves – race and gender do not 'cause' certain types of political or social behaviour any more than ethnicity does.[15] In other words, it is not 'nationalism' or 'ethnicity' that causes political processes, but historical choices, which are manifest in the framing of grievances, the 'coding' of differences or boundaries and the perception that change favours or disfavours certain groups.

Within this constructivist approach, ethno-national identification is something that 'happens' due to political interventions.[16] Thus, ethno-nationalism serves as a vehicle for specific political grievances, which are set in motion and constructed according to measurable and identifiable factors, such as triggering events and self-reinforcing processes.[17] In this perspective, ethno-nationalism is 'a subset of identity categories', which *assumes* characteristics such as commonality of culture, language, history, institutions and territory.[18] Importantly, these characteristics are not in themselves intrinsic to ethno-nationalism but are common to all forms of collective action and may be interpreted or described as 'ethnic' by politicians, journalists or academics.[19] For example, while history is not an intrinsic ethnic variable, historical events may often involve pre-existing ethnic identities and particular narratives may then emerge to 'justify' particular agendas.[20] In short, ethno-nationalism is not an independent variable; it only becomes a salient feature of political disputes through a specific and historical process of collective action.[21]

The ethno-national narrative is a superficially persuasive and easily comprehensible rendering of the 'Irish question'. Fundamentally, it reiterates the story of Protestant vs. Catholics; unionists vs. nationalists; British vs. Irish; in short, 'Northern Ireland is where British and Irish nationalism remain locked in a stand-off'.[22] Previous conflicts are held up as examples of the return of ancient antagonisms, regardless of the fact that in those cases also the decisions of political elites were crucial in shaping the course of events.[23] Scholars working from ethno-nationalist assumptions have developed complicated narratives that stress various dimensions of the Northern conflict, ranging across analyses of ideology and discourse, religion and identity, electoral results and institutional design.[24]

The problem is that much of this work treats ethno-nationalism as a determinative force without considering why and how this may be so or, indeed, even if it may in fact provide the causal impetus that it is assumed it bears. For example, although Stefan Wolff claims that Northern Irish politics is home to various conflicting viewpoints, his attempts to explain these are filtered through an ethno-nationalist lens in which ethnic belonging and ethnic antagonism bring about political change.[25]

In this view, groups are treated as concrete entities, shaped and maintained by a variety of psychological or rational choice processes; thus, despite references to constructivist theorists such as Rogers Brubaker and David Laitin, Wolff's approach is indicative of the belief that the very existence of those groups leads to conflict.[26] A similar tendency can be found in some 'conflict transformation' scholarship that is ostensibly sceptical of the elite, consociational approach. Kieran McEvoy and Peter Shirlow, for example, argue that 'strong and secure identities ... can also serve as the basis for political generosity' and that they may assist efforts at challenging 'sectarian attitudes and practices'.[27] Underneath such noble yet fundamentally asinine rhetoric lies the problem that if we do not ask how those 'strong and secure identities' are created and maintained we risk taking them at face value. Thus, political realities are obscured and scholars may simply reproduce the stories that elites use to uphold their positions within their communities.[28] In short, a major part of the consociational and conflict transformation approach is to deal with groups as reified entities, while ignoring the historical facts that contributed to division. In the end, the smuggling in of constructivist citations or the plea that it is pragmatic suggestions and not panaceas that are being offered amounts to a certain disingenuousness: consociationalists and conflict transformationists airbrush out of existence questions about political power or historical legacies because it suits their theoretical ideas about how conflicts can be regulated. As I point out, this is only possible as long as the historical evidence and the political implications of these approaches is ignored.

This essential primordialism underpins the consociational division of 'exogenous/internal' and 'exogenous/external' factors behind the conflict.[29] Thus, 'externally' oriented explanations of the conflict stress the antagonism that exists between republicans and the British state on the one hand, and unionists and Dublin on the other. 'Internalist' accounts, by contrast, focus on the 'implications of economic, religious, and/or cultural conditions in the province'.[30] The underlying message is that the Northern Ireland case is a classic example of an ethnic conflict. While religion, culture and economics may accentuate certain aspects of the conflict, the main driving force is ethnicity:

> Such conflicts are better understood as socio-psychological, rooted in historically established collective identities and motivated by the desire to be governed by one's co-nationals, both for security and for collective freedom.[31]

The general approach of ethnic conflict theorists has been to identify the main areas in which inter-communal antagonism is most salient and then to propose 'solutions' to how those areas can be regulated, contained or controlled. Bernadette Hayes and Ian McAllister allude to this circular reasoning:

> In Northern Ireland, religious affiliation, ethnic identity, national identity, and territorial allegiance are all intertwined in a complex way. It is these interlocking facets that not only provide the ethno-nationalistic basis of the conflict but also give rise to its reinforcing and recurring nature.[32]

Why those features should intertwine or where they emerge from is not questioned. Alternative experiences of the conflict or alternative bases of identity such as class, gender, age or local environment are marginalised from the dominant narrative. Applied to Northern Irish politics, the ethnic conflict model becomes totalising as the often contradictory nature of the historical record is subsumed within the overriding imperative of reducing all outcomes to the existence of 'two communities'. Questions of change, historical nuance or political agency are ignored in favour of sweeping assumptions regarding the determinative power of ethnic antagonism and highly tendentious (and in any case probably unverifiable) assumptions regarding the 'motivation' of the communal groups.[33] Such opacity and circularity are possible because ethnicity is not problematised or defined on the one hand, and the 'evidence' used to support what is therefore a rather vague concept tends to originate from elite interviews or secondary material on the other. As is pointed out in the next section, this 'evidence' is often deployed in a self-serving, decontextualised fashion. This is because the concept of ethno-nationalism is not used in any kind of critical or heuristic fashion, and long-term historical processes tend to be ignored in favour of short-term changes.

The primacy of ethno-nationalism as an explanatory variable or a causal, determinative force informs several strands of the academic literature on Northern Ireland, including analyses that look specifically at ideology, religion and institution-building. Despite the differing focus of such studies and sometimes heated debate between their main adherents, the prioritisation and pursuit of ethno-nationalist antagonism remains the primary, underlying concern. However, by chasing a single explanatory variable, these analyses deploy teleological methodologies that inevitably influence their conclusions. In other words, the initial assumptions heavily influence the form of the search and the end result.[34] The net effect is that even in empirically-oriented work, questions of change and outcome are glossed over or under-conceptualised;[35] while the more theoretical analyses ignore primary evidence in favour of reading assumptions back into the historical record, in the process reducing context to a series of snapshot observations.[36]

Strategic choreography

One strand of the literature on Northern Ireland is built around the idea that nationalist and unionist elites, or 'actors', act out ideologically informed 'scripts', which they tailor according to the 'audience' they are addressing – namely, their 'own' hardliners, the other 'side' or the British and Irish governments.[37] For Paul Dixon, political entrepreneurs speak and act the way they do because they are playing certain loosely defined, but intelligible ethnic roles.[38] Just as the message may be altered according to the audience, actors may 'improvise' on their core message and send 'coded' signals depending on whether they are speaking 'front stage' or before the media, or in 'backstage' closed negotiations.[39] A related body of work looks towards subtle shifts in rhetorical strategies or 'official discourses' in an effort to ascertain the basic character of Irish nationalist or Ulster unionist politics.[40] Politics is viewed as a 'struggle over meanings, labels, and identities' and scholars therefore focus on 'the social construction and organisation of language'.[41]

While much of this analysis is pitched against the dominant ethnic conflict model scholarship, in fact it often utilises similar 'essentialised' understandings of ethno-nationalist groups as coherent, unified actors. Thus, it overlooks the fact that there may not in fact be a clear-cut divide between leadership rhetoric and the aspirations of the party supporters – in other words, it is not wholly unreasonable to assume that party elites and the grass-roots believe in the same values. While its primary emphasis is on the tactics used by those elites, it also proceeds on the basis that unionist and/or nationalist ideologies simply 'resonate' or 'chime' with people without addressing questions relating to why this may be so. Quite why academics are able to understand these 'codes' while voters (the 'audience') simply buy into the scripts in an undiscerning fashion is unclear.[42]

These criticisms relate to more fundamental problems concerning how the choreographic or 'dramaturgical' approach handles primary evidence and deals with temporality. First, the idea that leaders strategically frame aspects of the dominant ideologies leads to a rather static presentation of how politics works. In other words, the strategic approach views politics as essentially elite-driven: leaders promote or advertise their parties to prospective buyers in a one-way fashion and are somehow able to ignore previous policies – the idea of continuity or consistency is airbrushed from the picture. A more nuanced view of the historical record suggests that political messages do not simply resonate with mass audiences, instead, political ideologies and perspectives on the course of change are derived from the particularistic lessons that people learn from the past.[43] Furthermore, taken to its extreme, the strategic approach cannot be articulated without self-contradiction because the view that political elites can construct 'reality' at will must itself be a product of some previously established interests.[44]

The fact that the strategic approach does not really conceptualise temporality or deal with the past in any coherent way leads to an anachronistic methodology and a lack of context in the conclusions reached. For example, the widespread idea that Sinn Féin has, since the mid-1990s, replaced radical constitutional transformation with (more easily achievable) equality and human rights-based concerns undoubtedly captures something of what has happened.[45] Yet no serious attempt has been made to conceptualise the process or explore the counter-factuals involved in why and how the Adams–McGuinness leadership somehow managed to bet on the right horse. The narrative of strategic shifts obscures the historical record: primary evidence from the SDLP archives reveals that equality concerns were at the heart of the party's project from the early 1970s.[46] That the empirical evidence suggests continuities within Northern nationalism means that scholars need to look again at the role of moderate influences and how they shaped the long-term trajectory of nationalist politics.[47]

Ethno-religious sociology

Given the deep religious divide in Northern Ireland, it is unsurprising that sociologists have placed questions of belief and cultural practice at the forefront of their investigations.[48] In this view, ethnic identity drove the North's conflict, but the primary motivating and definitional aspect of ethnicity in Northern Ireland is associated with religious differences. For example, Claire Mitchell describes how religion marks off social boundaries and affords meaning to ethnic identification – religion is therefore at the centre of ongoing communal division. The relationship of religion to the Northern Ireland conflict is, according to Mitchell, a nuanced one: politics is refracted through the prism of religion, and religion informs people's views about political change: 'Religion is not passive; it actively produces, reproduces and transforms social relationships. It is constitutive of political context and possibilities.'[49] However, as with the strategic approach, the sociological perspective fails to conceptualise how change and continuity occur across time. Thus, the sociological approach confuses causal relationships. In assuming that political outcomes follow from people's identities and beliefs, it ignores how historical events, power disparities and policy decisions may affect developments. While policy choices are influenced by people's beliefs, values or ideological preferences, policy choices in themselves may also shape identities and aspirations as well as constraining the range of options open to groups and individuals at later points.[50]

In other words, political groupings do not merely 'act out' ethno-religious identities; instead, they may also respond to perceived opportunities and the out-workings of previous choices. Sara McDowell, for example, has criticised Mitchell's contention that the ending of discrimination and the introduction of equality legislation has led to a weakening of Catholic attachment to traditional nationalist narratives. Instead, McDowell's empirically based research points to the fact that Northern nationalists continue to identify strongly with established narratives of victimhood and oppression, evidenced in the 'cultural landscape' of commemoration and the rejection of historical revisionism.[51] As McDowell points out, Sinn Féin in particular invests enormous effort into creating and maintaining carefully constructed stories about the Troubles and the wider Irish nationalist historical experience. Thus, the release of government files, which appeared to indicate that Adams' leadership ignored British offers of a resolution to the 1981 hunger strikes in order to maintain momentum prior to the election of the Sinn Féin proxy candidate in an August by-election, despite the deaths of six prisoners, sparked intense controversy among the republican leadership and grass-roots.[52]

By ignoring the effect that previous choices have in influencing ideas about the future and in constraining political capacity, the ethno-religious interpretation of the Northern Ireland conflict tends to exclude political relationships and historical dynamics from the analysis altogether. While political events, such as parading, do have important communal and religious aspects, they only become politically and socially important because of the context in which they occur. The importance of context is implicitly acknowledged in Steve Bruce's account of the emergence of Ian Paisley. While he correctly points out that an anti-modernist and anti-ecumenist spirit was prevalent among Ulster Protestants in the 1960s, Bruce admits that this was a response to the perceived threat posed by a resurgent Northern nationalism and the economic reforms proposed by the Northern Ireland premier, Terence O'Neill. In this view, the rise of Paisleyism was inextricably associated with the perception of communal loss, together with the mobilising opportunities presented by the rupturing of the Stormont elite in the mid- to late 1960s.[53] Despite the irruption of the historical narrative into his analysis, Bruce concludes that 'The Northern Ireland conflict is a religious conflict ... This is the only explanation that makes sense of Paisley's career.'[54] However, as with ideology, religion is only important in Northern Ireland because the specific context makes it so. More specifically, religion may intertwine with and reinforce ethno-nationalism because historical events and decisions set those processes in motion.

Institutionalism and conflict management

As with the assumptions underpinning religious sociology, to say that the conflict in Northern Ireland is about incompatible conceptions of nationality or national belonging has important implications for the types of questions that are asked and the conclusions arrived at. As with the above approaches, the main problem here is to do with a teleological understanding of history that is supported by an anachronistic and circular methodology. The logic runs as follows: if there are two contending national groups, then the most reasonable way to manage that division – or, at the very least, regulate the relationship between the two groups – is to devise some means of balancing the two agendas. Although strong interpretative and prognostic divisions occur within the institutionalist approach, it is still reasonable to subsume apparently divergent scholarly opinion under the one rubric given the primacy afforded to ethnic belonging and ethnic antagonism as determinative forces behind political change and outcome. In other words, despite different ideas over the durability or pliability of ethnic identification, scholars working within this broad approach all tend to view ethnic division as the main cause of the North's Troubles. At times this view comes close to claiming that it was only the inability to devise institutions that could successfully regulate communal division that fuelled the Northern Ireland conflict.[55] Linked with that claim is the idea that it was only when the governments were finally able to devise appropriate institutional incentives in the 1990s that 'progress' was finally made in bringing the conflict to a close.[56]

Therefore, from the initial premise regarding two antagonistic ethnic communities, there is a tendency among certain political scientists to read the Troubles as a long history of power-sharing failure. Briefly, the narrative runs as follows. The inability of the Stormont government to respond quickly enough to the civil rights movement radicalised Catholic politics and set in motion a downward spiral of ethnic outbidding, eventually precipitating the intervention of the British army and its violent conflict with the IRA. Future political interventions, such as the 1974 Sunningdale assembly, would be frustrated by this ethnic antagonism, allowing the British and Irish governments to draw the major lesson that an inter-governmental accord was necessary on a level that did not depend on local input for its administration. While this lesson accounts for the 1985 Anglo-Irish Agreement, the dominant ethnic conflict narrative goes on to claim that the negotiation process of 1994–8 was possible because the two governments had successfully learned how to manage the warring tribes. Finally, it claims that the governments were eventually able to devise an elaborate set of institutions in which mutual vetoes and different policy implementation layers existed to ensure inclusivity and communal balance – including the d'Hondt method of proportional representation voting, weighted or 'double' majorities and cross-border bodies.[57]

Together with an explanation of the 'causes' and trajectory of the conflict, the ethnocentric approach has given rise to two competing institutional 'solutions' or prescriptions. On the one hand, scholars such as Robin Wilson, Rick Wilford, Rupert Taylor and Paul Dixon have questioned the model's normative premises and claimed that strengthening civil society organisations, providing opportunities for cross-communal engagement or ending segregated education completely will reduce ethnic divisions.[58] They claim that bottom-up measures such as integrated education or a voluntary coalition administration may induce less extreme political views.

On the other hand, John McGarry and Brendan O'Leary defend the model's normative foundations and its democratic implications and argue that ethnic identities are in fact quite durable and that the emergence of a moderate centre is no more than wishful thinking.[59] McGarry and O'Leary draw their conclusion from the failure of power-sharing initiatives that the antagonistic ethno-nationalist groups can only be accommodated within a cooperative institutional framework, which recognises the validity of their claims, rather than attempting to dilute them. The main features of this consociationalist approach are executive power-sharing, proportional allocation of governmental resources and mutual veto powers. McGarry and O'Leary argue that such segregation is not intended to institutionalise sectarian attitudes or reward extremist politics. Instead, they claim that consociationalism fosters 'tolerance, mutual recognition, and respect for differences. Moreover ... power sharing is a route through which communal identifications can (eventually) be eroded peacefully.'[60]

The idea that the Northern Ireland conflict occurred due to the absence of appropriate consociational or power-sharing structures not only disregards theoretical insights into the fluidity of identity and the ongoing nature of group maintenance, it also overlooks the historical record. As I argue throughout this book, the Northern Ireland conflict was not simply about rival national aspirations, it was constructed by political groups and based on prior choices and rational perceptions of change, which were themselves coloured by nuanced lessons about the past. Ultimately, the ethnic conflict model amounts to poor history, for even if the Northern Ireland conflict occurred because of the existence of two antagonistic ethnic blocs, there is no reason to believe that the conflict persisted because of repeated power-sharing failures. Indeed, given the Protestant backlash against power-sharing and Dublin's involvement in 1973–4, there is sufficient reason to expect that imposed power-sharing would have actually exacerbated rather than ameliorated the situation. Yet, in the consociational faction of the ethnic conflict approach, such ideas are never tested – archival material is rarely if ever consulted (and when referred to, is decontextualised); instead, power-sharing theories are read back into the historical record via secondary sources and post-hoc interviews.[61]

A second problem relates to the ethnic conflict methodology. An anachronism arises from the fact that the approach identifies ethno-nationalist differences as the primary factor, before looking back to history to justify this assumption. In other words, the concept of 'ethno-nationalist antagonism' is not tested heuristically – its primacy is unquestioned and the problem of whether other factors, omissions or actions could have produced similar outcomes (such as polarisation and entrenchment) is never raised. Instead, secondary source material and elite interviews are deployed to demonstrate that certain outcomes existed (the perpetuation of the conflict) to fulfil societal needs (endemic ethnic antagonisms). The ethnic conflict approach tends to take a snapshot or stepwise view of political developments – the conflict moved forward in sequential steps leading inexorably to the triumph of consociationalism in 1998. Linked with this is the problem that political developments cannot be reduced to a series of 'moves or 'steps'.[62] Rather, rational decisions are made across time, often in a cumulative or layered fashion and are constrained, or at least shaped, by earlier decisions and unintended consequences. The constant resort to the language of 'ethno-nationalism' not only ignores the fact that other variables can affect political outcomes, but negates the traditional historical concern for the importance of context and specificity. Thus, it is unclear why strategic voting in Northern Ireland should be rendered 'ethnic' when it would not occur to scholars to describe similar calculations that way when they occur in, for example, Britain or the United States.[63]

Third, the ethnic conflict approach tends to recycle conventional narratives founded on the existence of two divided communities. Thus, while Northern Ireland may indeed be a deeply divided society, ethnonationalist analyses do not say how or why those divisions are mobilised or given political meaning. By overlooking the effect of early choices and historical processes, many current analyses of Irish nationalism, for example, simply do not recognise the importance of layered change and long-term continuity; instead, Irish nationalist political development is reduced to a series of strategic shifts and revisions.[64] When questions do arise as to why Irish nationalism failed so comprehensibly to accommodate Ulster unionism, ideological incoherence or official nuance is offered as an explanation.[65] Given its emphasis on reified groups, it is unsurprising that the narratives recycled by ethnic conflict adherents are intensely gendered. Thus, the Good Friday Agreement provided for equality legislation to reflect group rights and cultural sensibilities but ignored gender inequalities.[66] The problem is not simply that the devolved institutions channel women's (individual and collective) experiences through a strictly ethnicised party system,[67] a more fundamental problem relates to the fact that the prioritisation of ethnicity actively marginalises what are already liminal voices in the public sphere.[68] In short, the emphasis on group antagonism and political elites is indicative of deeper political assumptions, which, in remaining unquestioned, enable political scientists, community workers and politicians blithely to reproduce social and gendered inequalities.

A fourth problem with the institutionalist type approach is that it overemphasises the capacity of political elites to manipulate the past to their own ends. As several recent historical surveys have shown, political conflict erupted in Northern Ireland at the end of the 1960s because of specific circumstances and long-term trends.[69] The complexity of the situation in Northern Ireland meant that political power was severely diluted and that unintended consequences often had a greater effect on political outcomes than a simple instrumentalist perspective would suggest. As is pointed out in chapter 4, for example, the dilemma of the British government was that it had to deal not only with actors with multiple and divergent goals, but with the cumulative effect of historical decision-making. This had a self-reproducing effect in that nationalist and unionist actors drew their own conclusions from the government's ambiguous and evolving position, so adding to the complexity of the situation.

A final problem worth highlighting relates to the latter two points concerning the implicit *political* nature of the ethnic conflict model and the narratives it gives rise to. Despite the concerns of McGarry and O'Leary for an equitable constitutional and institutional settlement, their adherents often smuggle elitist assumptions about historical changes and ignore the constraints under which policy-makers were operating.[70] Thus Michael Kerr claims that, in part, a 'solution' was not possible in the 1970s because 'an advanced understanding of the complexities of the conflict *was not reached* by either administration [in London or Dublin]'.[71] The implication is that had governmental policy-makers been a little smarter or taken a broader perspective, then years of violence would have been avoided. A similar logic underpins Brendan O'Duffy's recent book, which claims that an inter-governmental approach, based on a symmetrical relationship between British and Irish sovereignty over Northern Ireland, would have regulated the conflict. Even if O'Duffy is correct that the conflict was about differing nationalistic aspirations, it is not sufficient to depict policy-making, for example, as a 'confused approach' without asking why Britain did not bring the Irish Republic more fully into play until the mid-1980s.[72] Again, contrary to Etain Tannam's idea that policy learning occurred as Britain somehow recognised that power-sharing was the only way to deal with the troublesome Northern natives, successive British governments could only work within what Eamonn O'Kane has called 'the parameters of the possible'.[73] As the next section demonstrates, O'Kane's conclusion reflects the archival material and the fact that, unlike certain ethnic conflict theorists, British policy-makers actually recognised that ideas such as imposed power-sharing or an increased role for Dublin would have exacerbated an already disastrous situation.

An alternative approach – path-dependency and political opportunities

These collective problems suggest that a radical overhaul of aspects of Northern Irish studies and ethno-nationalist research in general is required. This book tackles the unspoken assumptions of ethnocentrism. It asks how and when ethnic mobilisation occurs. It questions how political division persists. It examines the influence of state intervention in a divided society and asks how the British state contributed to the 'ethnicisation' of suspicion and expectation. It also examines the response of non-state political actors and asks how and why certain policies were adopted and how and why these persisted. In short, the book marks a return to the historical concepts of sequencing and periodisation, and the linking of variables within a specific, identifiable causal chain.[74] It suggests that political developments in Northern Ireland occurred in a path-dependent fashion – in other words, that early responses to constitutional uncertainty carried through across time and affected later strategic options. The constraining influence of initial choices encouraged communal polarisation, the entrenchment of maximalist political agendas and the long-term marginalisation of Northern Ireland's political parties. With specific regard to the Northern Ireland case, the book argues that temporal, path-dependent processes explain the persistence and resilience of ethnic conflict. It identifies how initial responses to change and uncertainty on the part of the British government, the SDLP and the UUP created unintended, downstream effects. In short, British government intervention changed the political context of Northern Ireland in the late 1960s and early 1970s. This precipitated a radicalisation of pre-existing ethnic identities and influenced the shape of later political developments in the province.

The book contends that policy-making and historical decisions are as important as institutional innovation in affecting political outcomes.[75] Recently released material demonstrates that actors' initial responses to political initiatives – including cross-border institutions (the 'Irish dimension') and forms of power-sharing – carried through across time, constraining later choices. Actors persisted with early policies in order to maintain credibility and present continuity of purpose and past policy decisions shaped and constrained later options. In this way, policies may be viewed as similar to more formal political institutions – they empower groups; they establish end-goals and political and cultural norms; they mobilise opinion and give people incentives to invest their interest. They may also be highly resistant to change and, through that investment and mobilisation, contain the powerful vetoing mechanisms as may be found, albeit in a more open and recognisable way, in formal institutions and procedures.[76] The cumulative effect of this meant that the communal parties pursued oppositional agendas dedicated to achieving maximal goals for their constituents.

Path-dependency refers to historical sequences in which later events, outcomes or choices conform in specific ways to initial occurrences or choices – namely, when first steps increase the likelihood of further steps in the same direction or on the same path.[77] Originally developed as an explanation of commercial growth and market disequilibria in economics, the concept chimed with attempts to explain institutional development and change and coincides with traditional historical intuition.[78] In this view, decision-making is an historical catalyst, creating causal sequences or historical 'paths' by delimiting the range of options available to actors downstream and encouraging further steps in the same direction. Although pre-existing ethnic identities and ideological beliefs provided a context for later choices, the central idea of this book is that, in themselves, ethnicity and ideology were not the driving forces behind political change in Northern Ireland.

The idea that policies exhibit similar characteristics to more formal political institutions is not new – Paul Pierson noted that policy-making creates similar lock-in effects to formal political institutions. The establishment of a policy may carry through to shape the range of later choices as downstream decisions fall within the parameters set by the initial choice, and policy 'paths' or trajectories may be difficult to reverse.[79] Early choices may persist because political power may accrue to popular agendas or owing to structural asymmetries.[80] The idea that policy choices may imply a self-reinforcing logic and, in precipitating counter-responses, take on a causal, independent force of their own is intuitive to historical analysis.[81] However, it is contrary to much of the accepted wisdom of political science, which tends to view policy choices as flexible and having little effect on political behaviour in comparison to voting or the establishment of governmental agencies. There may be several reasons for this. Unlike formal institutions, policies may be easy to change. They are often responsive in nature – reacting to changing events or fluctuations in public or elite opinion. Similarly, Pierson acknowledges that policies 'often confront fewer, or more modest, veto points, than do revisions of formal political institutions'.[82] Again, the varied nature of policy-making militates against simple classification or consensus on the type or distinguishing features of policies. These problems are not insurmountable. Indeed, if 'Historical change ... invariably results from the interaction of external determinants and human agency',[83] then decision-making plays a key and determining role in political outcomes. In this view, historical choices delimit or constrain downstream options and may act as one of many 'external determinants', including mobilisation potential, ideological preferences, an incomplete knowledge of opponents' goals, and the necessity of presenting continuity and consistency of argument.

Why do historical sequences arise and why do 'paths' endure across time? The path-dependent conceptualisation of change looks to critical junctures or tipping points that establish distinct historical trajectories. In this view, historical choices may constrain downstream options by ruling out once-plausible alternatives or through cumulative and self-reproducing logics – the reproduction explains why a particular decision or event was critical and defines the path. The idea that specific choices create 'knock-on' effects – making some outcomes more likely than others, or definitively ruling out the possibility of certain courses of action at a later point – is fundamental to historical understanding and practice and corresponds to the so-called 'historical turn' in key areas of political science.[84] As Niall Ferguson has pointed out, historians have tended to shy away from overt, counterfactual scenarios, despite implicitly using the idea of 'plausible alternatives' in assessing why certain outcomes occurred:

> by narrowing down the historical alternatives we consider to those which are *plausible* – and hence by replacing the enigma of 'chance' with the calculations of *probabilities* – we solve the dilemma of choosing between a single deterministic past and an unmanageably infinite number of possible pasts.[85]

In other words, historical explanation depends on assessing the realistic or plausible options open to decision-makers – an assessment that depends on explicitly posing and examining the question of why a certain option was chosen. The idea of 'plausible alternatives' not only guards against any tendency towards teleological or 'just-so' analysis. It also allows us to specify more accurately the nature of historical sequences or what Ian Kershaw has recently called 'chronological patterns',[86] and to raise the question of why an outcome at a certain point was more likely than it would have been earlier. Alternatively, the concept of alternatives and critical junctures allows us to explain why policy interventions at one point in time may significantly alter the range of available options later. This is because those options may rule out other once-viable alternatives, they may mobilise support or create incentives for certain types of action, and they may raise public expectations of further changes.[87] In short, historical sequences unfold due to prior choices, but those choices shape the range and even the type of options open at a later stage. While ideological preferences and forms of solidarity, such as perceived ethnic ties, may play a subjective role in influencing decision-making, ultimately, it is those historically conditioned constraints and opportunities that shape the range of options open and drive forward change. This idea of critical junctures corresponds with the social movement literature concept of 'political opportunity structures' – namely, watersheds that transform politics, or 'consistent ... dimensions of the political environment' that encourage or discourage collective action'.[88] For Sidney Tarrow, these include shifts in the prevailing political trends or institutions such as the opening up of governmental access to certain groups or the creation of political or economic resources through new avenues of interaction. Doug McAdam, who utilised the concept in his *longue durée* study of Black civil rights mobilisation,[89] offers four instances of opportunity structure changes:

1. the relative openness or closure of the institutionalised political system; 2. the stability or instability ... of elite alignments ... 3. the presence or absence of elites; 4. the state's capacity for repression.[90]

While the term 'critical junctures' implies large-scale, revolutionary events, as the social movement and path-dependency literatures point out, small events or modest beginnings may also have enduring consequences. A second point relates to the fact that it is not so much the post-hoc identification of changing opportunities that is important when analysing political changes, but the historical *attribution* or *perception* of those by contending groups.[91] Charles Tilly and Jack Goldstone argue that this attribution explains why protest and contention follow dynamic and unpredictable patterns.[92] In practical terms, they conclude, perceived opportunities mean that 'A group may decide to bear very high costs for protest if it believes the chances of achieving success are high; but the same group may decide to avoid even modest costs of protest if it decides the chances of succeeding are low'.[93] This book avoids a post-hoc imposition of reputed opportunities by interrogating the historical record. In short, that record reveals that British government intervention in the North in 1969, its assumption of direct rule in 1972 and willingness to consider power-sharing and cross-borderism opened up new avenues for participation and advancement for nationalist politics. In response, Ulster unionist suspicions and fears that politics were progressing in one direction were embedded long before the Sunningdale agreement of December 1973 and influenced the mobilisation efforts of the United Ulster Unionist Council (UUUC) and its maximalist policy direction after the fall of the power-sharing executive in May 1974.

These insights still leave open the question of how change occurs, and more specifically, how prior choices affect later options and events. Not only do early choices delimit the types of response available to individuals or groups later, they may also make similar choices more likely in the future.[94] Thus, political change may be 'layered' where groups that lack the capacity to affect wholesale revision of an institution or policy may attempt to add amendments or institutional reforms favourable to their goals.[95] This concept goes beyond the idea that groups can strategically shift their position according to changing public opinion or political events and implies an underlying continuity across long periods of time. In addition, Jacob Hacker points out that 'changes in the operation or effect of policies [may occur] without significant changes in those policies' structure'.[96] In other words, groups may resist policy implementation without having the structural power to reverse it at the level at which decisions are made or policies designed. Instead, they may effectively prevent the operation of policies at the ground or implementation level.[97] This suggests implicit rather than 'open' political conflict between asymmetrical groups; thus, power relations are important for maintaining policy trajectories[98] and policy choices may themselves exert independent causative effects.[99]

Path-dependency theorists also posit the possibility of constrained change occurring through *learning* in which 'dominant actors and ethnic entrepreneurs ... adapt new institutions to older patterns of conflict'.[100] The present book, however, argues that learning tends to occur in fragmentary, particularistic ways. The lessons that groups or individuals learn from the past may be based on the exigencies of the present; they may be subjective and partial or else complete 'fabrications' of what actually happened. Alternatively, historical lessons may be completely suppressed or directly ignored.[101] The past always impinges on later memories in unexpected and partial ways. As Paloma Aguilar points out:

> When a political decision is successful, the costs of that decision are rarely considered, nor is any consideration given to whether a different decision might have been able to produce better results. ... In many cases, few lessons are learned when the outcome is successful, given that nobody ever inquires into whether this outcome has really been achieved as a result of a political decision or whether, on the contrary, it has been achieved in spite of that decision.[102]

Perceived failures are likewise explained by inadequacies in policies that were considered the best possible options at the time. Thus, while the

Sunningdale power-sharing experiment failed because it excluded political extremes, it is wrong to say that this is the principal or even only reason for its collapse. As the book points out, given the polarised political climate it is unlikely whether any power-sharing deal would have succeeded in the early 1970s. A primary reason as to why policy learning is at best partial and fragmentary when it occurs is that there is an absence of any kind of moderating mechanism in complex political environments. In other words, unlike economics where price plays a moderating role, political interactions are typically based on incomplete information and rarely begin on a clean slate.[103] As such, it is not enough to say that perceived threats and opportunities influence political calculations. Those perceptions are themselves coloured by past events. Perceived opportunities, communal suspicions and entrenched policy-making shaped Northern Ireland's political trajectory in a more profound way than entrepreneurial innovation. In other words, political capacity was highly constrained during the Troubles and its effect was often indirect and unintentional. Indeed, even when elites sought to devise new mechanisms of institutional accommodation they quickly recognised the constraining influence of prior choices and the embedded distrust and expectations of their supporters.

Changing the script

The path-dependency and political opportunity approach not only highlights the theoretical shortcomings of ethnic-conflict analyses, it also provides radically new insights into political developments in Northern Ireland between 1972 and 1985. First, it suggests that the Northern Ireland conflict persisted because historical choices became ever more entrenched, and once-viable accommodative alternatives became ever more remote, as time progressed. Second, in stressing the importance of long-term continuities, the path-dependent approach offers important implications for the study of ethno-nationalism and, in particular, for the rationale behind the persistence and resilience of ethno-nationalist conflict. Finally, its emphasis on change as a gradual, cumulative process offers insights into how large-scale outcomes may result from apparently modest beginnings.

An important implication of the approach advocated by this book is that attention to temporal processes, the tracking of historical legacies, provides a potentially rich source for examining the forces that shape ethno-nationalist contention. Rather than proceeding from assumptions regarding the determinative basis of ethnicity, the path-dependent approach adopts a synthesising perspective in which the choices of contending groups create identifiable historical trajectories or chains of events. Although the idea of historical trajectories or paths explains how several variables (the actions of several contending groups) create specific outcomes, the historical processes identified in this work exerted powerful causal effects on the strategic planning, ideological development and policy direction of the SDLP, the UUP and the British and Irish governments. At the risk of anticipating arguments that appear later in the text, the following sub-sections briefly describe how the findings associated with this approach not only chime with recently released archival material, but overturn many of the conclusions inspired by the ethno-nationalist approach.

Irish nationalism and the hidden politics of policy entrenchment

Academic analyses of modern constitutional Irish nationalism tend to concentrate on its outward manifestations of change and continuity. In so doing, they fail to explain adequately the persistent salience of nationalist politics and the perpetuation of suboptimal strategies and end-goals.[104] This book questions why modern constitutional Irish nationalism continually failed to reach agreement with Ulster unionism during the Troubles. It argues that nationalist mobilisation, rather than simply unionist obduracy, contributed to the long-term polarisation of communal politics – nationalist policy decisions in the early 1970s carried through across time, raising Catholic expectations and heightening Protestant suspicions. More importantly, later strategies built on that early vision and on the gains accrued with each new political initiative. Moderation and reform were ruled out and nationalist politics became progressively more entrenched.

The decision by the SDLP to withdraw from the Northern Ireland parliament following the shooting of two Catholics by the British army in Derry in July 1971 set in motion a policy direction based on the pooling of gains, the glossing over of losses and the targeting of further concessions. The maximalism inherent in the original decision meant that the party would not return to political participation prior to radical concessions – in its view, an institutionalised role for Dublin (the 'Irish dimension') and executive power-sharing. These goals harmonised with the efforts of successive Dublin governments to gain political leverage in Northern Ireland and end the insurrectionary campaign of the IRA.[105] However, that maximalist perspective carried through in a path-dependent fashion to affect downstream outcomes, including the 'suboptimal' effect of heightening unionist fears, undermining potential allies such as Brian Faulkner and giving credence to the anti-power-sharing lobby led by Ian Paisley, Harry West and William Craig. The maximalist policy direction effectively ruled out mid-range alternatives, such as the reform of security structures or the targeting of moderate power-sharing proposals. Instead, constitutional Irish nationalism proceeded along a specific historical path characterised by the accumulation of gains and the targeting of further concessions. In contrast with several recent studies,[106] the picture that emerges is of a 'processual' Irish nationalism, which stresses that while personal and ideological preferences may condition choices, historical change is also the result of the cumulative effect of cross-time decision-making. The emphasis on historical choices extends beyond the ideologically-oriented approach to Irish nationalism.[107] In contrast to the tendency to ascribe strategic shifts to nationalist policy-making, the path-dependent approach emphasises a cross-time understanding of rational decision-making and points out that seemingly 'inefficient' or 'suboptimal' policies may in fact be the result of a series of quite reasonable, but ever-constraining, decisions.[108] In this view, Irish nationalism is less an 'incoherent ideology'[109] and more a product of perfectly comprehensible historical choices.

By focusing on 'open' changes in rhetoric and discourse on the one hand, or policy and strategy on the other, scholars of modern Irish nationalism have tended to overlook the gradual changes and deep-seated continuities. Without disputing the idea of ideological and rhetorical nuance, this book contends that nationalist policy direction remained remarkably consistent after the early 1970s. First, it claims that a process of policy entrenchment resulted from critical decisions made by nationalist actors in the early 1970s. Although these decisions followed a path-dependent or self-reinforcing trajectory, downstream entrenchment did not occur merely due to the absence of 'decision-making'. Instead, initial choices set the parameters for future decisions, which built on accumulated gains. Second, that entrenchment entailed a radicalisation of Northern Ireland's Catholic community and contributed to the long-term polarisation of the province's political parties and communal blocs. Recently released primary evidence reveals that this process, which began in the early 1970s, calls into question the traditional accounts of the period that describe constitutional nationalism's supposed late 1970s 'greening' as a reaction to obdurate unionism or as self-protection against potential outbidding from the IRA.[110]

Constitutional Irish nationalism remains an under-researched area of modern Irish history. The movement presented in this book suggests a greater degree of consistency with pre-Troubles, 'traditional' nationalism than is the case elsewhere.[111] Although Richard English is correct in pointing out that Irish nationalism is 'emphatically a story of *nationalisms* ... The terms and aspirations of nationalists have altered over time',[112] this book argues that those alterations occurred in a cumulative, incremental fashion: concessions were banked and new demands emerged to take their place. A remark attributed to the Irish diplomat Seán Ó hUiginn, captures this idea of incessant momentum: Irish nationalism is 'like a shark. It must keep moving or it dies'.[113] The image of the SDLP, in particular, to emerge from these pages is of an essentially conservative party which pursued a long-term agenda. The idea that constitutional nationalism was overwhelmingly driven by fears of being 'outbid' by the more radical republican movement is simply untenable once the archival evidence is taken into account.[114] That evidence suggests that rather than simply acquiescing to the violent campaign or the threat of nationalistic 'outbidding' by the IRA or Sinn Féin, the SDLP retained a gradualist or reformist bent – undoubtedly, due in part to the longevity within the party's hierarchy of key civil rights leaders such as John Hume, Austin Currie and Paddy Devlin and Gerry Fitt. While Hume and the SDLP emphasised for the first time the importance of recognising the need for unionist consent for constitutional change, I suggest that, placed within the perspective of the *longue durée*, the contribution of the SDLP to constitutional nationalism was one of upholding consistent principles based on civil rights and gradual progress towards closer links with the Republic.

Ulster unionism: resistance and agenda-setting

As outlined above, this book argues that policies establish historical sequences and are not merely reactive to events or responsive to changes in public or elite opinion. The book deals with two related aspects of unionist politics: the critical decision by Faulkner to agree to a cross-border scheme in September 1971; and the long-term effect of unionist resistance and agenda-setting activities on the operation of British policy in Northern Ireland.

First, Faulkner: this book highlights his decision made at the British prime minister's country residence, Chequers, to agree to cross-border cooperation as a key turning point in the political development of Northern Ireland. Faulkner's decision carried through across time and elicited various responses from his nationalist and unionist rivals. At the same time, it allowed the SDLP and the Fine Gael–Labour coalition to embark on a maximalist strategy in 1973 and 1974. On the other, it afforded Faulkner's unionist opponents an opportunity to adopt contradictory positions and mobilise support by emphasising the long-standing fear of Dublin involvement in Northern Ireland. Faulkner's subsequent attempts to forestall political progress were undermined by the expectations and suspicions of the Dublin–SDLP axis and the Paisley–Craig–West grouping respectively. Once-viable alternatives quickly became closed off for Faulkner, who attempted to manage the projected changes from a shrinking power base. The book charts the trajectory of that unionist mobilisation and concludes that, contrary to the accepted narrative, the Sunningdale experiment was not a 'missed opportunity' and that a power-sharing, Irish dimension settlement had virtually no chance of success from as early as when it was first proposed by the British at the end of 1972.[115]

As the empirical evidence reveals, key principles such as power-sharing and an institutionalised role for the Dublin government were part of the British approach even before Westminster assumed direct control of Northern Ireland in March 1972. However, Ulster unionist resistance to these principles, coupled with repeated calls for security and political guarantees effectively transformed the operation of government policy, culminating in recent political events. Unionist resistance and agenda-framing work profoundly affected the actual operation of British government policy towards the North, and re-oriented it to include protective guarantees. The basic *structure* of Westminster policy for restoring devolved power carried through with little change since the early 1970s – namely, an institutionalised Dublin involvement (the 'Irish dimension') and a power-sharing executive. However, decisive changes did occur at the ground or operational level of that policy's *direction*. The picture that emerges, then, is one in which unionism resisted British government interventions without being powerful enough to enact a preferred policy reform. However, by blocking repeated unfavourable initiatives – namely, those premised on radical structural changes with minimal security reforms – and by stressing the importance of constitutional protection, the unionist bloc slowly transformed the direction of political progress to take account of the underpinning concern with security. Continuity in this perspective does not mean inertia or simple, 'rejectionist' politics. Instead, by working outside the government-directed policy sphere for much of the Troubles, unionist politics created hidden but powerful changes in the political development of Northern Ireland. This perspective diverges from accepted wisdom concerning the opaque reductionism of unionism's obduracy;[116] indeed, those accounts highlight the overt weakness and the schismatic, reactionary nature of contemporary Ulster unionism.[117] Although unionist policy-making was indeed reactionary, the resistance, inflexibility and agenda-setting actually *did* precipitate gradual changes in both the British and nationalist appraisals of the security issue and in the environment in which reforms were proposed.

Again, this depiction has important implications for the characterisation of Ulster unionism. The evidence presented below supports the view of others that unionist unity was an essential component of the unionist project.[118] But I also argue that over the course of the Troubles, and despite its tendency to fissure, Ulster unionism was largely driven by conservative, moderate forces. The importance of physical and constitutional security effectively shaped the fortunes of other political groups – notably, constitutional and (eventually) physical force nationalism, but also the radical, fundamentalist and 'outsider' politics of Paisley. Emphatically, this argument does not go as far as saying that the O'Neillite period of the 1960s was a 'tragic missed opportunity' or that Catholics were 'on their way' prior to the mass mobilisation of the civil rights movement – arguments (as I point out in chapter 2) that fundamentally obscure the inadequate, patrician approach of O'Neill and the basic gradualist dynamic of constitutional nationalism.[119]

The British government: interventionism or arbitration?

As the previous sub-sections indicate, the British state is often the primary actor in Northern Ireland's modern political development. The view of the British state espoused in this work is starkly at odds with that of the ethno-nationalist approach. McGarry and O'Leary, for example, depict the British government as a force in Northern Ireland, 'arbitrating' incompetently between the warring ethnic factions.[120] The present approach is more nuanced – British intervention in the Northern state set in motion a radicalisation of ethnic tension and a mobilisation of pre-existing ethnic sentiments, aspirations and identities. On the other hand, that radicalisation and mobilisation also affected long-term changes in the operation of British policy in the North. A line can be drawn from the British decision to pursue power-sharing and Dublin involvement in October 1972 and the Anglo-Irish Agreement of 1985. This line is not, however, a simple institutional or legalistic one. Rather, it stems from the radicalised political forces that the initial state intervention set in motion. By 1985, those forces had established entrenched, communal and maximalist policies – the Anglo-Irish Agreement was but the latest effort to establish a degree of stability. Thus, British government policy-making was less a conscious effort at arbitration or 'coercive consociationalism',[121] and more a series of political initiatives that were constrained in several ways by the unintended effects of prior interventions.

Placing the Northern Irish policy interventions of the British state in a longer time-frame also significantly enhances its essential impact on political and historical outcomes. First, the ambiguity of the British state, as perceived by local actors, significantly contributed to the persistence and instability of the North, in effect belying genuine attempts to reach some kind of devolved settlement. For example, the IRA's perception that Britain was on the verge of withdrawing in the late 1970s did little to moderate its goals and, by continuing to negotiate with republicans and encourage those perceptions, Westminster effectively undermined unionist confidence and willingness to countenance political proposals. The key lesson that can be learned from this catalogue of errors concerns the tendency of ambiguity perpetuate itself. Second, and linked with this in an admittedly counterintuitive way, is the idea (discussed in detail in chapter 4) that the British capacity to effect real change was severely constrained. The problem was not that Britain did not have any policy; it was rather that a plurality of policies existed, yet none could be found that would not conceivably make the situation worse. This trend, which can be dated from at least Labour's victory in 1964,[122] continued throughout the period and, arguably, is still a major force behind party political decision-making in Northern Ireland today.

The international dimension

The narrative presented in the following chapters concentrates specifically on the political parties of Northern Ireland and their relationships with successive London and Dublin governments. The historical 'paths' described are primarily endogenous: they were created, shaped and sustained by the historical choices and omissions of those local actors. The 'international dimension' to the Northern Ireland conflict is, therefore, placed in the context of the perceptions, decisions and strategies of the local actors. For example, chapter 3 describes how it the international embarrassment of internment and the spiralling violence it precipitated operated as a major influence on British thinking prior to the decision to assume direct control of the North in 1972. Chapter 4 outlines how John Hume's attempt to apply the lessons of European integration to the North was refracted by Hume and Ulster unionists through the Northern Irish prism and the core constitutional question remained the same. Again, chapter 5 describes how the ending of the Cold War provided a manifest challenge to republicans' ideas about British imperialism and the nature of the British presence in Ireland. In other words, events on the ground and changes in the perceptions and thinking of local actors were essential to political developments rather than wider balances of power.[123]

The book also challenges the more normative aspects of international relations theory and Northern Ireland. Despite the emergence of a 'peace process industry' dedicated to exporting the 'lessons' of Northern Ireland to other troubled areas around the world, this book remains sceptical of simplistic theoretical models or typologies and of the self-serving rationale of their promoters.[124] Regardless of the normative and practical problems involved in meeting the consociationalist target of 'imposing power-sharing',[125] this book highlights a fundamental problem with the attempted internationalising of the Northern Ireland conflict: namely, that it tends to be based on a distortion of the historical record. Attempts to make Northern Ireland fit into some kind of conflict resolution parable can only succeed through careful manipulation of the empirical material – elite actor interviews are prioritised without asking in whose interests the statements are being made; secondary sources are preferred to the general exclusion, let alone interrogation of archival material; and, when all else fails, the historical record is simply ignored.[126] The peace process industry exports a range of platitudinous lessons from 'gradual policy learning' and 'coercive consociationalism' to societal reconciliation and the valorisation of 'storytelling'.[127] The evidence and the general narrative presented in this book stands in sharp contrast to these ideas, not least because it stresses how 'lessons' are always learned in a highly particularistic and fragmentary manner and are, therefore, often loaded with historical and political significance.

2
Turning Points in the Troubles, 1968–71

Critical choices

This chapter begins the process of charting how historical decisions exacerbated inter-communal rivalries, political polarisation and entrenchment. It explores the argument that policy choices and historical interventions had a downstream impact – certain choices carried through to constrain and shape later options; and the act of making decisions ruled out once-plausible alternatives, which became evermore remote. Which choices actually carried through? Which events, if any, set in motion the process of escalating polarisation and inexorable division? This chapter's central claim is that once-viable alternatives to maximalism and entrenchment were discarded in 1971 and that, from that date, Northern Ireland's political parties pursued divergent policy paths, making rapprochement increasingly unlikely.

Certainly, the conflict between the PIRA and the British army had been gathering strength from late 1969, and from 1968 even moderate, middle-class Catholic opinion was becoming further alienated from the Northern state. However, the decisions made by the main nationalist and unionist political actors in 1971 effectively established a political framework that lasted for over a quarter of a century. On the one hand, the prioritisation of an Irish dimension over and above power-sharing remained a central aim of SDLP policy articulation, frustrating dialogue during the 1970s and the 1980s. On the other hand, unionist opposition to executive power-sharing and to the idea of Dublin involvement hindered the emergence of accommodative proposals. In short, despite the violent conflict, the choices of the politicians did little to prevent inter-communal division but, on the contrary, encouraged long-term entrenchment. Later chapters focus on the implications of these choices;

but first this chapter examines what those choices were and why they persisted. The choices made were twofold: the SDLP's walkout from the Stormont system in July 1971; and Faulkner's decision to acquiesce in a cross-border project in September of that year.

Although these two decisions in the summer of 1971 may have foreclosed any possibility of alternatives being at the very least initiated, the fact that alternatives were effectively ignored meant that the implications of the early choices went unchallenged. As such, an omission also occurred in that the Stormont government did not seriously entertain alternatives to either of the proposals on the table, namely, an offer of policy committee seats for nationalists or the SDLP's principal proposal of fully-fledged executive power-sharing. A second point relates to the fact that inter-communal tensions pre-existed, and were heightened by, the emergence of the civil rights movement in the late 1960s.[1] This, together with the military struggle between the PIRA and the British army, suggests that political alternatives to the onset of violence were never likely to succeed. While this may be true, the existence of such alternatives prior to the prorogation and imposition of direct rule – that is, prior to the radical intervention of the British state in 1972 – implies that the movement away from constitutionalism and political dialogue did not occur decisively until 1971.

Was '68 (all that) important?

Conventional accounts of the origins of the Northern Ireland conflict tend to stress an inexorable slide into violence dating from the rise of the civil rights campaign in 1968. Broadly, the narrative runs as follows. The growing ethnic divisions, evidenced by the rise to prominence of Ian Paisley in the mid-1960s, began to spiral out of control following the attack by the police on civil rights marchers in Derry in October 1968. These clashes radicalised Northern Catholic opinion and turned a constitutional mobilisation into a nationalistic one. By the time that British troops arrived to restore order on the streets in August 1969, the province was lurching away from civil rights protests and towards an older style of politics in the form of inter-communal conflict.[2]

Within this basic framework, two variations have emerged. In an influential analytical history, Brendan O'Leary and John McGarry argue that the outbreak of sectarian conflict in the late 1960s and early 1970s was the result of the fracturing of what they call unionist 'hegemonic control'.[3] In this narrative, Catholics ended their uneasy acquiescence in the Northern state, which rapidly collapsed when Westminster refused to countenance a situation of open revolt. There are three historical problems with this. First, while Catholics were structurally disadvantaged under the majoritarian Stormont system, the idea that a monolithic unionist bloc existed in Northern Ireland between 1920 and the introduction of direct rule from London in 1972 does not correspond with the empirical evidence.[4] Second, while O'Leary and McGarry admit that increased Westminster interest created a perception of opening opportunities within Catholic politics,[5] they underemphasise the conservative strain of Catholic politics – evidenced in the first instance by the SDLP – which continued to acquiesce in the constitutional system as late as 1971. Third, as Paul Bew has pointed out, the British cabinet continued to support Faulkner into the autumn of 1971 and the final decision to impose direct rule proceeded from the international embarrassment that had resulted from the imposition of internment in August 1971 together with Faulkner's inability to deal with Catholic disaffection.[6]

These problems stem from the teleological methodology that lies at the heart of the ethnic conflict project. In other words, O'Leary and McGarry begin from the assumption that ethnic 'motivations' inspire unionist and nationalist actors. However, even if politicians do act from ethnic motivations, this is largely irrelevant since there is no guarantee that their actions would have the desired consequences. The so-called 'ethnic conflict model' in fact reads back ethnic assumptions into the historical record, while ignoring the importance of chronology and failing to appreciate the context. The teleological approach understandably contradicts the evidence, which points to a more nuanced picture of historical development in which real choices existed for key nationalist and unionist actors as late as 1971. In short, there was no ethnic imperative leading to the North's Troubles.

There is a 'strong' and a 'weak' version of the second main narrative, both of which stress the centrality of 1968, but place greater emphasis on the importance of the primary material than does the ethnic conflict model. Corresponding to a certain degree with O'Leary and McGarry's arguments, the strong version of the '1968 thesis' suggests that the clash between Northern state forces and the civil rights movement set in motion the series of events that culminated in the ethno-nationalist conflict that began in earnest in the early 1970s. The focus of this book, however, tends to be on the British state rather than reputed ethnic factions. Thus, Bew argues that the television coverage of the confrontation between the police and civil rights marchers in Derry on

5 October 1968 finally convinced Westminster elites of the need for direct intervention.[7]

Both Bew and Simon Prince have argued that local reaction to the events in Derry inspired the left-wing student movement, 'People's Democracy', to march from Belfast to Derry at the beginning of 1969. It was this decision, they argue, that marked 'the pivotal point at which the troubles changed from being primarily about civil rights to being about the more traditional disputes concerning national and religious identities'.[8] Marc Mulholland makes a similar point, but stresses the fracturing of unionism and the civil rights movement in the 1969 election campaign as marking the beginning of a more divisive climate.[9] Niall O'Dochartaigh employs a similar chronological perspective when he argues that it was the ending of 'Catholic quiescence' in 1968 and 1969 that spelt the end of Unionist Party dominance.[10] However, there is a less than direct line linking 1968 with later hostilities. First, as mentioned above, even after the introduction of internment in August 1971, the British government prevaricated over whether to prorogue Stormont. Second, the main Northern Irish political factions did not abandon the possibility of constitutional accommodation until the summer of that same year.

The 'weaker', more qualified, version of the 1968 argument claims that the civil rights movement's confrontation with the police moved the debate beyond political reforms and onto an issue that was much more meaningful for unionists – security: 'the Stormont regime had passed the point of no return'.[11] In this perspective, the decision to deploy British troops on the streets the following August irrevocably changed the political context: 'With two governments [Belfast and London] now very directly involved, there was a clear division and a potential confusion of responsibility.'[12] In other words, the very ambiguity of the British response – direct intervention by the army, but with devolution still in operation – created governmental confusion, did little to quell the civil unrest and facilitated the emergence of paramilitary factions. The available evidence complements this view, but suggests that, while the mobilisation of pre-existing communal identities from 1968 onwards played a key role in establishing the context for the subsequent violent conflagration, the possibility of constitutional and political progress existed until the second half of 1971. In other words, the SDLP's abstentionism, together with Faulkner's decision to acquiesce in cross-border proposals, effectively exhausted the possibilities of constitutionalism by establishing the parameters of the political stalemate that characterised the Troubles.

The civil rights movement and the unionist counter-responses may indeed have reawakened the 'old conflict over national and communal identities';[13] however, the choices made in 1971 initiated the long-term process of entrenchment at the level of unionist and nationalist policy-making. Despite the growing communal antagonism, the choices made in 1971 precipitated the process of *political* polarisation and effectively set the terms of the marginalisation of the North's constitutional representatives for over two decades. As such, Bew is correct in arguing that the civil rights marches in late 1968 and early 1969 transformed the political context by raising the profile of nationalistic grievances to the detriment of issues concerning civil liberties;[14] however, the fact remains that constitutional politics still continued after the marches. It is, therefore, going too far to argue that the civil rights march from Belfast to Derry which began on 1 January 1969 marked a watershed in the history of the Troubles. Again, although Thomas Hennessey is correct to point out that July 1971 marked something of a 'watershed [that] altered the parameters of political debate', this was not merely because the Catholic population reacted to British security measures by withdrawing further from the Northern Ireland state.[15] Faulkner's offer of participation at the level of governmental committees was no longer an option for Catholic politics. The logic of the SDLP withdrawal was that it would only return to government if it was guaranteed executive responsibilities – and if there were closer links with Dublin. The implication was not only the targeting of gradual reunification, but also a policy direction that was self-reinforcing and that therefore moved away from unionist sentiments and down a more nationalistic path. In other words, Northern nationalist politics were not simply reactive, but sought to take advantage of a changing political environment.

While the civil rights era heightened pre-existing communal tensions, it did not exhaust the various historical opportunities or 'plausible' political alternatives that would render it a true critical juncture of 'pivotal point' on which subsequent events turned.[16] Simon Prince claims that by raising communal tensions in Derry, a contentious relationship emerged between the civil rights movement and the Northern Ireland state which meant that 'the likelihood of bringing the crisis to a peaceful resolution was virtually non-existent'.[17] However, as is the case with all historical inquiries, any assessment of the civil rights movement – and the decision by PIRA to wage war on the British army – must also acknowledge what did not occur, as well as attempting to assess what did.[18] That is to say, there is a certain teleological reasoning underlying any inextricable linking of the civil rights era to the political contention of the 1970s – the civil rights movement did not negate *all* the possibilities of political progress. True, the civil rights era raised inter-communal tensions and *intra*-communal fears and suspicions; but in addition, it afforded a new respectability or credibility to extra-constitutional or extra-parliamentary politics for the Northern nationalist community. However, neither the civil rights era nor PIRA's armed struggle exhausted the possibility for political progress. Again, British intervention in the form of troop deployment in August 1969 radically transformed the political scene, but it was the response of the Northern Ireland political parties to Westminster's increased interest that set the parameters on what was and what was not politically possible. British intervention influenced political decision-making and played a crucial role in shaping 'events on the ground', but it was the interpretations of that intervention and the subsequent decisions and obfuscations by nationalist and unionist parties that set in motion the long-term process of political polarisation. The decisions made in July 1971 ruled out once-viable alternatives, and informed and constrained subsequent options – in short, it was the summer of 1971 that marked a key turning point in the political dynamics of Northern Ireland's recent past.

The SDLP and abstentionism, July 1971

Formed in August 1970, the SDLP emerged from the Northern Ireland civil rights movement as a party dedicated to the internal reform of the province. Although it professed a preference for an eventual united Ireland solution, Gerry Fitt announced at its first press conference: 'We support the maintenance of Stormont at the present time as it is the only institution which can bring about the reforms we desire.'[19] In contrast to the rhetoric of the Provisional IRA, for example, the idea of the abolition of Stormont began to enter the SDLP's agenda in a meaningful way only *after* the July 1971 abstentionist decision.

Abstentionism itself had a long history in Northern nationalism – hence Paddy Devlin's later condemnation of the decision as being 'the old nationalist knee-jerk'.[20] However, even before Faulkner succeeded James Chichester-Clark as Northern Ireland prime minister in March, the SDLP was increasingly aware of the limitations of the Stormont system. Hume had stated that 'reform, reconciliation, and reunion' were the party's goals on 3 March 1971.[21] Yet by the end of the month, the *Irish*

Press was reporting internal discontent with the Stormont system: 'Privately, a couple of members of the Opposition have been admitting recently that there seems to be little more that they can secure through Parliament, except to "hold the fort," or act as watchdogs.'[22] The SDLP refused to go as far as calling for outright abolition, which would have placed it close to the position of the Provisionals; instead, it argued that sectarianism, 'the key-stone of the Unionist Party', and polarisation must be addressed.[23] Seemingly, the party still harboured the belief that it could build up a middle ground by contrasting itself with both the IRA and the unionist government.[24] The army shootings of two Catholics, Desmond Beattie and Seamus Cusack, in Derry on 8 July, however, removed any lingering doubts in Hume's mind, and he later commented:

> Stormont had no real part to play in resolving our problem since it was based on majority rule and on what I call the Afrikaner mindset ... Unionism was about holding all power in their own hands ... It was becoming quite clear that Stormont itself was not going to bring about any change. Therefore, a necessary part of the strategy was to try to bring it down and have it replaced – that was the thinking behind the withdrawal factor.[25]

Certainly, a threat of Provisional 'outbidding' influenced the withdrawal;[26] however, the evidence suggests that a growing frustration with the Stormont system also informed the decision and that the spiralling summer violence lent a degree of inevitability to the walkout.[27] The July decision also chimed with the party's (and indeed the civil rights movement's) earlier strategy of looking to Westminster rather than Stormont for reform. Given these historical precedents, it was arguably a matter of 'when' rather than 'if' the SDLP would withdraw from Stormont.

On the other hand, the fact remains that while nationalists may have expected more of Faulkner, Hume and the SDLP were prepared to support the committee proposals at that point. Despite growing Catholic militancy, the decision to walk away from parliamentary politics during the summer of 1971 was a high-risk strategy, for it meant that the SDLP would be forced to criticise unionism without being able to offer any tangible returns for its opposition. Devlin and Fitt recognised the dilemma at the time.[28] However, the central implication regarding the timing of the decision is that it had effectively changed the terms of debate *prior* to the introduction of internment. For the SDLP, the set-up at Stormont was no longer acceptable. Piecemeal reforms such as Faulkner's committee proposals were no longer negotiable; instead, it believed that radical change was necessary. In effect this meant full, executive participation in the running of the Northern state by the SDLP, and an increased recognition of nationalists' political aspirations through an as yet undefined official mechanism. These ideas were implicit in the July 1971 decision and were quickly fleshed out from September 1971 onwards, indicating that despite the alienation of Catholics following internment, the SDLP did not merely react to this through an outright radicalisation of its stance, but instead sought to plot a political and constitutional means out of the impasse.

Traditional accounts of the SDLP's formation and early strategy ignore the varied historical constraints and perceived opportunities that conditioned the SDLP's policy-making after the July 1971 decision. Concentrating, instead, on the party's relationship with the Provisionals, they tend to characterise the SDLP as a reactive and pragmatic party.[29] Within this perspective, the SDLP abandoned its early reformism after Bloody Sunday (31 January 1972) and became further radicalised due to unionist obduracy during the Sunningdale experiment (1973–4) and the Constitutional Convention (1975–6). When Hume and Seamus Mallon became leader and deputy leader respectively at the end of the 1970s this ratified the 'greening' of the party. A cross-time analysis of the party's decision-making and careful attention to the internal party papers, however, critiques those assumptions and challenges the conclusions. In short, two consequences followed from the July 1971 walkout. First, the 'greening' of the SDLP occurred as the party embarked on a maximalist policy agenda in 1971. The SDLP's abstentionist decision created a critical juncture that carried through across time: subsequent choices proceeded according to the parameters established by the initial decision. This trajectory had little to do with ideological incoherencies,[30] but arose from a series of rational, yet cumulative choices. Second, the accumulation of concessions rather than simply Protestant reactions conditioned nationalist radicalisation during the 1970s. Although the threat of Provisional outbidding influenced SDLP policies to a much more salient degree, the party mobilised support due to its emphasis on accumulating gains. The 'greening' of the SDLP occurred as the party embarked on a maximalist policy agenda in 1971.

Although internment and the near-total alienation that it produced in many Catholic areas quickly overtook the July abstentionist decision,[31] the SDLP's choice implied that the party would not return for less than it had achieved in June 1971. This was apparent to the party as early as

September, when the first of several internal policy position papers set out the guiding principles of full power-sharing and an institutionalised Irish dimension. The paper had four main proposals:

1. To mount a challenge to 'the right of the Unionist Party to claim more than mere equality, there is no *right* to veto'.
2. A 'solution' that ignored the inter-dependence of the two parts of Ireland would be meaningless.
3. Any new arrangements must take into account the interests of Britain, Ireland, the unionists and the nationalists, and be underwritten by the international community.
4. Stormont to be replaced by 'a 100-member Commission broadly representative of the Northern Ireland', chosen jointly by the SDLP, the Unionist Party, Dublin and London.[32]

Further evidence of the SDLP's move to a long-term approach is contained in the revised 'second draft' of the September paper.[33] This paper ostensibly offers a more considered approach in relation to Protestant opinion:

> Any changes directed towards establishing a period of co-existence leading towards a more integrated community must at one and the same time guarantee the Catholic community against continued or renewed repression while relieving the Protestant community of their apprehension of being coerced into an all-Ireland Republic.

Quite how this could be achieved is left open. Instead, the paper describes how a conference to discuss the future should operate: it should consist of the 'four interested parties' – the SDLP, Dublin, London and the Unionist Party. In addition, the paper states that the 'Westminster model of government' should be abandoned in favour of proportional representation. Most importantly, it offers more detail on how a Council of Ireland would operate – it would provide for cross-border economic and social cooperation, arbitrate on the infringement of human rights and 'provide the machinery for … [joint] policing of the border'. Finally, the paper envisages the end of Stormont and argues that the North 'should be administered by a Council of State'.

Both the SDLP's long-term strategic vision and its tactical response to internment chimed with the Dublin government's thinking, which recognised an opportunity to widen its influence in the North and subdue republican violence. Whereas Irish government policy towards the North was previously split between ad hoc conciliation and irredentism,[34] the SDLP's assertive nationalism gave it an (albeit unreliable) ally and instituted a new nationalist strategy of 'banking' concessions and pursuing further gains. Much to London's disapproval, The Irish Taoiseach, Jack Lynch, aligned himself firmly with the SDLP's civil disobedience campaign, telling the British prime minister, Edward Heath, that it must

> be obvious to you that solutions require to be found through political means ... In the event of the continuation of existing policies attempting military solutions, I intend to support the policy of passive resistance now being pursued by the non-Unionist population.[35]

Although the SDLP immediately became 'greener', that is, more nationalistic, from the summer of 1971, it did so on its own moderate or conservative terms. While the broad thrust of its policy development was at odds with unionist sentiments, the party was careful not to appear to be playing into the hands of the PIRA. Its nuanced approach to the civil disobedience campaign, for instance, belies any notion that it was simply reacting and pragmatically seeking any proposals to protect itself from republican 'outbidding'.[36] In fact, internal party papers reveal that the SDLP was dissatisfied with the so-called 'Dungiven assembly', which met in October 1971 as an alternative to Stormont. Internal briefings indicate that the party believed the assembly would need to meet regularly and 'convey a sense of dignity, competence, and power'.[37] Unionists had criticised the notion as a nationalist 'debating society',[38] and the SDLP was apparently less than enamoured with the participants of the first session: the assembly, it said, needed 'more abundant talent and more authority'.[39] However, it also recognised that it did not have the resources to stage 'elections' to the assembly, which in any event 'at present would be irresponsible'. The party refused to become too closely associated with the assembly, which it recognised could reduce its influence at a higher, governmental level. In short, its half-hearted approach indicated that it believed the assembly to be fatally flawed given the outright hostility from unionist rank-and-file and Catholic apathy: 'if ignored by the anti-unionist population [the assembly] would be disastrous ... [it] may become at best useless, at worst a source of friction and bitterness'.[40]

The SDLP also sought to channel Catholic alienation away from ad hoc protest and towards a more structured form of support for itself. Again, as regards the dynamics of Catholic politics in the aftermath of internment, this project was essentially conservative and moderate.

Thus, although it recognised the anti-internment 'rent and rates strike' as a success – quoting government figures of between 26,000 and 30,000 families participating[41] – it also warned that it was 'important that all civil disobedience activities be explained and understood as an alternative to violence rather than as a concomitant to it'.[42] Rather than being simply a reaction to the Provisional campaign or to the widespread Catholic militancy 'on the streets', the SDLP sought to bring nationalist opinion round to a coherent policy agenda and political strategy based on a Council of Ireland and the (interim) replacing of Stormont with a proportional system of executive power-sharing. This was the logic of its July abstention, and while that logic may have been copper-fastened by internment, party papers reveal that the SDLP quickly ascertained the implications of that decision and sought to align Northern nationalist opinion with its vision as early as September 1971. In short, the SDLP was not simply reacting to Provisional or popular (Catholic) alienation. That near-total alienation occurred after internment and Bloody Sunday in January 1972 is beyond doubt, but it was the July 1971 walkout that established the basic framework of SDLP policy direction and fundamentally influenced the shape of political developments in Northern Ireland.

As its internal position papers reveal, the SDLP's policy formation over the period following internment was a cumulative and fundamental process rather than the reactive pragmatism described in recent histories.[43] In other words, the party sought to channel Catholic opinion around its own agenda and did not simply strike out for the first available policy in response to changes 'on the streets' or in the Provisional campaign. Second, the chronology points to an early radicalisation of policy – September 1971, not simply post-January or post-March 1972. Finally, it is important to recognise that at the heart of this process was the SDLP's recognition that constitutional politics were in a state of flux and that any new proposals would depend on its support. Understandably, it sought to make the most of this situation by accumulating concessions leading inexorably to ending partition – or, rather, to a political environment in which, through a Council of Ireland, reunification in effect would be in operation. However, it also recognised that its boycott of the British government frustrated its ability to achieve substantial concessions, as pointed out in an internal paper following the prorogation of Stormont:

> If [we] refuse absolutely to enter into negotiations at any time ... it is very likely that the Westminster government will decide on complete

integration as the only possible solution. It should, therefore, be born in mind throughout that our decision on the question of negotiation may well influence the nature of that eventual solution.[44]

Brian Faulkner and the Irish dimension, September 1971

Faulkner defeated Craig to assume the premiership of Northern Ireland at the end of March 1971. Security, the issue that precipitated the resignation of his predecessor, James Chichester-Clark, would prove to be the touchstone of Faulkner's period in office.[45] As such, he initially held that any resolution of the deteriorating situation should take priority over political proposals.[46] During his first meeting with British government ministers on acceding to the premiership, he agreed with Heath that internal reform was important, but claimed that 'the main immediate question was that of law and order and in particular the activities of the IRA', and stated that 'he viewed internment as a practical security matter, not a political issue'.[47] Faulkner's chief political innovation was to try to enhance the system of democratic accountability through the allocation of policy committee chairs to the SDLP.[48] Faulkner had decided to set up three new committees with responsibilities for scrutinising and proposing policy in the areas of social, environmental and industrial provision. He indicated that the chairs of the committees would be allocated according to the composition of the Stormont Commons – thus, allowing the SDLP to take up those positions. Faulkner argued that such a proposal would encourage greater involvement within the Stormont system and that 'Short of asking the Opposition to run the country, this is the best means of participation for them'.[49]

Although Devlin of the SDLP described the proposal as Faulkner's 'best hour',[50] the general tenor of the SDLP response was one of circumspection. The initial assessment of the SDLP leader, Gerry Fitt, was that they would 'look at the proposals and [that they] hoped to be able to cooperate'.[51] Furthermore, his deputy, Hume, followed with a sceptical assessment of the limited nature of the proposals:

> What has failed in Northern Ireland other than the system no one wanted? Surely that is the lesson that is staring us in the face, and are the confines of our discussion on the problems of Northern Ireland not too narrow? Should we not be discussing the system itself rather than tinkering with it any further?[52]

Hume pointed out, 'There will still be a majority of Hon. Members opposite on each committee and this ... will effectively, perhaps, negative the workings of the committees.'[53] Indeed, the leader of the DUP, Ian Paisley, also questioned the practicality of Faulkner's plans: 'I wonder how many would be present at a committee of nine if, with the membership of the present House, we can sometimes hardly have a quorum on certain committees.'[54] Thus, rather than what Faulkner called a 'lost opportunity',[55] the plans were received with a mixture of scepticism and reticence. However, the fact remains that even given the rising levels of paramilitary violence and the increasing Catholic disillusion with the Northern state, the proposals were stillborn. Despite the longer-term perspective of, for example, Hume, both he and the SDLP represented a conservative element within Catholic politics which served to restrain the more radical urges during the late 1960s and early 1970s.[56] In other words, even within a context of increasing Catholic popular militancy – detached from the Provisional project – a definite strain of conservative or moderate politics is detectable. This is evidenced in the fact that the SDLP actually agreed to support the proposals because they might serve to reduce sectarian violence.[57] However, understandably, the SDLP's scepticism over Faulkner's intentions was heightened through press coverage of his meeting with the Orange Order the following week.[58] The extent of Hume's doubts over the efficacy of the Stormont system was fully revealed in the wake of the shooting of two unarmed Catholics following a riot in Derry on 8 July.[59] He issued an ultimatum – an inquiry, or the SDLP would withdraw from Stormont – and this, in practical terms, marked the end of the party's participation in the Northern Ireland governmental system.[60]

Understandably, the pivotal point of Faulkner's period in office is often held to be his decision to introduce internment in August 1971. Indeed, the evidence suggests that it was that decision – rather than simply the catastrophe that was Bloody Sunday (30 January 1972) – that led directly to the prorogation of Stormont the following March.[61] Faulkner made his decision on internment following extensive discussions with the British government.[62] He had been advised that there were around 1,500 Provisionals and 500 Officials in Northern Ireland (800 and 300 respectively in Belfast) and that internment carried the definite risks of 'further disorders' and that 'the possibility of securing the cooperation of the minority may be lost'. Despite this, officials advised Faulkner that, given the level of intimidation, the fact that 'the ordinary law places the terrorist at an advantage', particularly in relation to the security forces, 'the time has come when [the] risks are outweighed by the greater risk that without internment there may be an irreversible drift towards civil strife'.[63]

While the internment decision itself precipitated unionist discontent – entailing as it did a ban on Orange marches[64] – the process that actually led to the mid-1970s unionist schism and the subsequent entrenchment of the North's constitutional politics was in part set in motion by Faulkner's attempt to secure Dublin security and economic cooperation through an institutionalised Irish dimension. Paisley and Craig had displayed ambivalence towards the benefits of a devolved parliament.[65] However, their ability to mobilise support during 1973 and 1974 depended on their opposition to power-sharing and a Council of Ireland. Faulkner's willingness to examine the possibility of cross-border arrangements (and latterly executive power-sharing) provided his opponents with that mobilising opportunity. While O'Neill had encouraged closer links with the South during the 1960s, he had sought to balance concessions to nationalists with militant propaganda and a strategy dedicated to exposing the differences between 'moderate' nationalist leaders such as Eddie McAteer and 'firebrands' such as Currie and Fitt.[66] Faulkner's decision to pursue cooperation on terrorism, however, placed the idea of cross-border institutional links at the heart of his policy articulation. He first enunciated that position in talks with Heath and Lynch at the end of September 1971.[67] Although Faulkner repeatedly resisted Lynch's pressure for executive power-sharing, he 'suggested that there might be room for greater economic cooperation between the North and the South of Ireland'. The minutes conclude that both Heath and Lynch

> agreed to take positive steps to promote closer cooperation between the two parts of Ireland ... For this purpose an intergovernmental body will be established for the discussion of such items of concern as the governments of the Republic and of Northern Ireland may agree to remit to it.

Faulkner's suggestion of a prototype Council of Ireland was not in fact taken up immediately at an intergovernmental level; rather, it resurfaced as a public policy statement in the Unionist Party's submission to the Darlington conference on Northern Ireland's future the following September.[68] This 'blueprint' envisaged closer security cooperation between Southern and Northern security forces in return for a

> joint Irish intergovernment[al] council to be formed with equal membership from the governments of Northern Ireland and the Irish

Republic. Such a council could discuss matters of mutual interest, particularly in the economic and social field.[69]

Between the two dates, Faulkner utilised the idea of an intergovernmental council as a way to offset power-sharing demands. He had used this, for example, during the final rounds of negotiations with Westminster prior to the introduction of direct rule. In February 1972, Faulkner again rejected the idea of full power-sharing; however, he pointed out that, in return for a commitment by Dublin to 'act with total firmness' against the IRA, 'an attempt should be made to seek a realistic measure of agreement which takes into account the declarations by Mr Lynch and others that unity must be sought through agreement'.[70] Should Dublin agree, he stated, 'we would hope it would be possible to deal at the same time with two other matters – (a) a common policy and action on the suppression of illegal organisations; (b) provision for intergovernmental machinery'. Ultimately, however, Faulkner's opposition to Westminster's decision to assume control of law and order in the province brought the question of direct rule to a head.

Certainly, since at least the autumn of 1971 Faulkner's inability to meet London's expectations of extensive Catholic involvement in the Stormont cabinet contributed in large part to his downfall.[71] However, this inability to move Unionist Party policy towards London's demands merely reflected the multilayered constraints under which the Northern prime minister operated during the last months of the Stormont system. One major constraint stemmed from what the unionist daily, the *Newsletter*, referred to as the 'savagery of the reaction' to internment.[72] Security remained central to unionist politics during these months as Faulkner came under increasing pressure from Paisley and Craig, who called for a more aggressive strategy. Claiming that Faulkner was weak on security, Paisley claimed it was time he 'took the handcuffs off the army.'[73] Both Craig and the *Newsletter* meanwhile called for the governments to 'harness [unionist] anger or be overwhelmed by it'[74] and for Stormont to introduce police reforms to deal with the IRA threat.[75]

A second set of constraints operating on Faulkner's policy-making during the latter half of 1971 stemmed from the changing relationship with the British government – specifically, from the relationship between Stormont and Westminster. The British cabinet was broadly supportive of Faulkner's stance on security and political reform in the immediate aftermath of internment. Thus, in a meeting between Faulkner and the Westminster cabinet (including Heath) on 19 August, the UK ministers

> accepted that the [SDLP] had acted precipitately and unwisely in their withdrawal and subsequent actions, and they agreed with Mr Faulkner that any moves to give the minority a greater say in the affairs of Northern Ireland could only be within the framework of normal, majority-rule democracy.[76]

Despite this, Heath counselled that 'the man in the street in Great Britain was now looking to the governments ... [to] bring back the Parliamentary Opposition and somehow remove the fears of the minority'. Having placed itself in opposition to broad international opinion and human rights concerns, with its acquiescence in the internment decision, Westminster however quickly began to recoil. Although Faulkner intended once again to attempt to seize the initiative and avoid 'having solutions thrust upon [Stormont]'[77] by publishing a Green Paper, the British government still ascertained that his proposals would fall short of what they believed was needed. Thus on 6 October, while Faulkner intended to reiterate his June ideas, Heath's cabinet secretary, Burke Trend, inquired whether this could be 'supplemented by a broadening of the government at Stormont? Would the recruitment of non-militant republican Catholics be made more palatable if it were agreed there would be [no] change in the border without a referendum?'[78] However, the Stormont cabinet had already pre-empted this train of thought and had decisively ruled out 'appeasement'.[79] In other words, even if Faulkner had desired to move towards a more inclusive parliamentary set-up, he would have met with strong opposition from his party.

In the event, he did not diverge from the Stormont cabinet consensus. Despite further pressure from Heath to implement a 'broadening of the bases of government', Faulkner reiterated his unwillingness to move beyond Westminster-style, majoritarian practices. He argued that he 'could not countenance persons with republican views as members of his cabinet'.[80] In addition, he rejected the idea of allocating seats through proportional representation. In neither case, he explained, 'could a workable government be formed since its component parts would be too disparate. On the one issue which united the members of the present administration, such a coalition would be fundamentally divided.'[81] As a concession, Faulkner claimed to favour 'widening' the government by establishing 'some form of minority council, representative of Roman

Catholic opinion, whose Chairman might become a member of the cabinet'. This was arguably as far as Faulkner was able to go in meeting the wishes of Westminster. His correspondence with Heath at the beginning of 1972, for example, reaffirmed his belief that it would be 'wrong in principle to single out any particular element of the community' for special treatment such as the allocation of seats in an executive.[82] In this, he reflected not only the consensus opinion of unionist political elites, but echoed with the editorial comments of the *Newsletter*, which remained deeply suspicious of power-sharing. 'Concessions' such as policing and electoral reforms, the paper argued, had already been made, 'but [they] have come from one side only. On the other side [they] have been matched by deeper intransigence'.[83] In addition, the paper claimed, the ongoing security threat rendered meaningless 'words like "initiative," "package deal," "reform," [and] almost the word "politics" itself'.[84]

Given Faulkner's limited room for manoeuvre in either the security or political field, the question remains as to the effect his September decision had on his unionist rivals. As suggested above, while Craig and Paisley concentrated on Faulkner's perceived weaknesses on security, initially neither had a credible political alternative – Craig's ideas on unilateral independence were frequently attacked by the unionist press and Faulkner, while Paisley retained an ambivalent attitude on staying with the Stormont system. As Faulkner's belief in the security and economic efficacy of North-South links became apparent in 1972, however, new ground began to open for his rivals. Certainly, Craig's estrangement from the Unionist Party was all but complete by the time the Faulknerite 'blueprint' was published in September 1972 – he disavowed the document and rejected the idea of talks with the SDLP and the Alliance Party at the planned conference at Darlington. The crucial factor, however, in tying Faulkner to a distinct policy trajectory was the open espousal of an Irish dimension by the British government, Dublin and the SDLP from its first official appearance in the October 1972 Green Paper. On the one hand, having previously made known his views, Faulkner found it impossible to outmanoeuvre Craig or Paisley – his problems compounded by their long-standing claims that he 'sold out' Stormont and was 'soft' on security. On the other, the growing emphasis on the Irish dimension and power-sharing in both London's thinking and the SDLP's strategy tied Faulkner into a policy agenda that he could only hope (from a unionist perspective) to ameliorate or delay. The pace of change, however, served to undermine Faulkner's position within the Protestant community and simultaneously afforded credibility to the anti-power-sharing, anti-Irish dimension alternative offered by his unionist critics.

Political alternatives

Did Westminster underestimate Faulkner's difficulties? Was it unrealistic of the British government to expect Faulkner to develop substantial power-sharing proposals in the light of SDLP abstentionism and backbench pressure? Again, why did Westminster expect Faulkner to move so far towards fully-fledged power-sharing in 1971? Alternatively, was Faulkner over-reluctant to consider alternatives to his committee proposals? Correspondingly, did he underestimate the possibility of a radical intervention by London? It is difficult to avoid the conclusion that Faulkner forced the British hand in rejecting a diminution of Stormont's law and order responsibilities – particularly since Faulkner's predecessor, Chichester-Clark, had suggested such a possibility in 1969.[85] However, alternatives were in fact open to the Northern Ireland premier during the autumn of 1971 as regards Catholic participation in government. These included institutional changes, ranging from executive power-sharing to the establishment of a 'minority council' chaired by a minister without portfolio, and the idea of a Council of Ireland.[86]

It is probably incorrect to conclude that even if Faulkner had attempted to 'broaden the bases of government' he could have avoided the showdown with Westminster over the division of security. However, by undercutting later SDLP and loyalist radicalism, a more accommodative approach at that early stage would arguably have forestalled the anti-Faulknerite mobilisation that gathered strength during 1972 and 1973. As with nationalist politics, an underlying moderation and conservatism are detectable within Ulster unionism during the late 1960s and early 1970s. Despite the prognostications of Paisley and Craig's penchant criticisms, the unionist right failed to mount a direct challenge to Westminster during this time.[87] Instead, Paisley and Craig, conscious of the changing political context, sought to articulate a credible alternative message to the one Faulkner was espousing. While the unionist right (and undoubtedly Craig from within the Unionist Party) would have remained a threat to Faulkner regardless of the unfolding of events, an alternative and accommodative policy by Faulkner at an earlier point might have undercut the potency and urgency of the loyalist mobilisation of 1974. That alternative might have been a more astute approach to the idea of cross-border institutions, or, on the other hand, the development of a stronger cross-communal approach vis-à-vis the SDLP. The

Westminster and backbench constraints that inhibited Faulkner (and the unionist right) from pursuing more radical alternatives also bore a secondary implication – namely, that the SDLP's growing radicalism was not substantively challenged. Obviously, the exploration of these alternatives creates unanswerable questions and hypothetical scenarios; what is important, however, is that the very existence of plausible alternatives demonstrates that once-viable paths were open and real choices were made while others were ignored. The importance of identifying these alternatives is that their rejection was one factor in establishing the divergent policy trajectories pursued by the SDLP and Ulster unionism during the 1970s and beyond.

Certainly, from the time he assumed office, Faulkner was constrained in his actions by the pressure from the unionist right and the growing alienation of the SDLP from Stormont. However, given that even his own officials were proposing a fundamental revision of the parliamentary and electoral systems, it was reasonable for Heath to press Faulkner in October 1971 to consider the possibility of establishing a 'National Coalition cabinet to deal with the present emergency'. Faulkner's reluctance to countenance the proposal was based on his idea that not only would it have to include the Paisleyite faction, but that, in any event, 'Such a step would only be possible when firmer action had been taken ... He believed that the majority of Roman Catholics ... were as keen as he was to see the gunmen and intimidators put down.' In response, Heath warned that

> There was a difference between the assessment made by the Northern Ireland government and the United Kingdom government of the views and mood of the Roman Catholic community at the moment, and their likely reaction to tougher security measures.[88]

Following the withdrawal by the SDLP, Stormont officials began to develop their own ideas on affording the Catholic minority a legitimate presence in government. The possibility of establishing a 'minority council' was one such proposal that aroused some interest in the British cabinet.[89] In an August 1971 memorandum, for instance, the permanent secretary at the Ministry of Finance, David Holden, pointed out that establishing such a body would demonstrate 'greater solicitude for the minority than has been shown by its own elected representatives. It [would ensure] that minority views can be properly considered'.[90] Holden followed up this line of thinking in a later memo in February 1972 in which he argued that 'The real question is "How can majority rule be made acceptable to the minority without paralysing or inhibiting the machinery of government?"' Whereas Faulkner had stressed the practical political implication that affording Catholics executive seats would also entail extending similar rights to Paisley's supporters, Holden argued that 'In Northern Ireland, institutional checks and balances would tend to formalise the differences between communities and work against long-term integration'. Instead, he envisaged a minority council as a separate body that would provide a 'general sounding board for Catholic opinion'. Chaired by an *ex officio* cabinet minister without portfolio, the council's 'main objective would be ... to provide a channel of communication and an assurance that there will be no going back or slowing down on reform'. Despite possible short-term benefits of affording Catholics an institutional means of expressing their grievances, Holden argued that 'In the longer run, it would only seem desirable if participation cannot be secured through changes in the structure and working of parliament'.[91]

A second proposal that officials put to Faulkner concerned the idea of establishing some form of power-sharing executive, or 'community government'. In line with Holden's concerns, however, the Northern Ireland permanent secretaries advised that 'Politicians on the two sides ... represent very different and perhaps incompatible interests, and in doing so might not be able to work effectively together, even in a government deprived of law and order responsibilities'. On the latter point, the permanent secretaries agreed that 'direct rule would be preferable to an administration emasculated by the loss of law and order powers'. Indeed, the view was expressed that even opening a channel of communication to ascertain the SDLP's thinking 'would be seen as an act of weakness by the government, especially when there was a widespread view among the minority that the present Stormont system could not last longer than a few months'.[92]

Whereas the proposals for additional institutional layers or the introduction of a form of executive power-sharing proved problematic, another strand of more radical thinking emerged during the consultation process. This was based on the reasoning that 'more effective participation is the best and possibly the only way of preserving the existing devolutionary arrangements' and that long-term communal polarisation meant that it was 'impossible to see a return to normal political life within the context of the status quo'.[93] The 'study group' of 'young officials'[94] pointed out that security remained a priority. However, they warned that the division of security between Westminster and Stormont, coupled with the fact that army officers in Northern Ireland were not answerable to Faulkner, necessitated a fundamental reappraisal. Although the report advised against 'disturbing the existing constitutional arrangements' for fear of fuelling PIRA propaganda, they were notably reticent as regards concrete proposals for dealing with the anomalies. The group challenged Faulkner's basic arguments for resisting executive power-sharing on two counts. First, their report said, 'the unification of Ireland is a legitimate political aspiration, provided that it is pursued by constitutional methods and not by violence'; second, it envisaged a role for nationalists within the Stormont system 'if they are prepared to make a genuine and positive contribution':

> There is no necessary contradiction in a member of the minority being prepared to make every effort to improve the lot of the people of Northern Ireland within the present constitutional framework while at the same time hoping that eventually the majority will come to agree with his view that the constitutional position should change.

If anything, the sentiments expressed in the report were too late to be practicable simply because the SDLP had already withdrawn from the Northern Ireland system. To a certain extent, the officials misread the changes in nationalist politics:

> the emergence of articulate minority representatives who devote more attention to immediate social and economic issues than to traditional border politics means that ... [they] should be able to consider and help deal with these immediate issues without involving any questioning of the present constitutional position.

The importance of the study group in the context of the period lies precisely in the radical alternatives they proposed as regards political accommodation. These alternatives were framed within the constitutional status quo: 'It is our firm belief that more effective participation is the best and possibly the only way of preserving the existing devolutionary arrangements.' Thus, they argued that, in fact, the allocation of executive seats would not be enough to restore political normality. The report instead suggested that the Westminster-style system be completely jettisoned in favour of a full proportional system. The officials claimed that in the case of Northern Ireland, majoritarianism only encouraged extremist politics, militated against the emergence of a 'middle ground' and that 'Proportional Representation is not merely a desirable improvement but an absolute essential if a viable system of devolutionary government is to survive'. In short, they argued, only under a proportional system would there be the prospect 'for a coming together of moderates and it is in this that we see the only hope for stability and progress'.

Again, the argument could be made that, given the upsurge of violence and the concomitant downturn in community relations, these recommendations were redundant; however, they remained an alternative to Faulkner's actual proposals and, crucially, untested. The implication of this latter fact is that the accommodative proposals may have undercut the anti-Faulknerite mobilisation of the proceeding years and may have forestalled the radicalisation of the SDLP in its initial stages. Despite the almost total Catholic alienation from the Northern Ireland state, the proposals fitted within Westminster thinking as regards the need for inclusion and the manifold problems involved in outright withdrawal. As the evidence from the SDLP archive reveals, the party was not simply reacting to PIRA violence but sought to plot a path towards some form of parliamentary politics – envisaged as initially four-way negotiations between itself, the Unionist Party and the British and Irish governments. Indeed, while the SDLP aspired to a united Ireland, their short-term strategy included something akin to an internal power-sharing accommodation. It is, therefore, by no means certain that the kind of ideas being discussed by Stormont officials would have proved totally unacceptable towards restoring some form of political dynamic in the period between internment and the prorogation of Stormont.

Conclusion

As the primary evidence demonstrates, alternatives to political polarisation and policy entrenchment existed as late as the second half of 1971. The chapter began to draw out some of the implications of this. First, it pointed out that neither the civil rights movement in the late 1960s nor the Provisionals' pursuit of an armed campaign from 1970 necessarily exhausted the potential for political progress. Second, it suggested that it was the decisions of the SDLP and Faulkner in the summer of 1971 that effectively led to the abandonment of that political path and thereby reduced the chances for any form of accommodation taking root. As later chapters document, that abandonment became in effect irrevocable as the SDLP sought to mobilise support based on an incremental and radical programme, while Faulkner's prospects of securing an internal accommodative settlement were quickly undermined by the counter-mobilisation of his intra-bloc rivals. Although the SDLP and Faulkner decisions were coloured by prior events, political alternatives existed until late 1971. While the worsening situation as regards paramilitary violence and inter-bloc sectarianism may have militated against those political alternatives succeeding, the fact remains that neither the SDLP nor Faulkner considered the other options that were available: after 1971, the main Northern Ireland actors pursued divergent and often-maximalist policy agendas. The decisive factor in shaping those choices was the intervention of the British state, influencing as it did the perception of opening opportunities on the part of the SDLP, and ambivalent and unrealistic expectations by Faulkner. Alternatives to that polarisation not only became more remote and less likely to succeed in engendering accommodation. In short, the decisions made in the summer of 1971 acted as turning points or critical junctures in the history of the Troubles insofar as they established an identifiable historical sequence of long-term entrenchment.

The choices made by the SDLP in July 1971 and by Faulkner in September – although apparently unimportant at the time – left historical legacies that shaped the subsequent political history of Northern Ireland in profound ways. Faulkner's decision to acquiesce to a form of institutionalised cross-border cooperation set in motion a train of events that culminated in the Sunningdale initiative and fracturing of unionism in 1973 and 1974. The SDLP's decision to withdraw from Stormont in July 1971, on the other hand, reversed its earlier reformism and established a maximalist policy agenda that contributed to the radicalisation of Catholic politics and the undercutting of Faulkner's credibility within the Protestant community. Collectively, both the SDLP and Faulkner's decisions followed a self-reinforcing, path-dependent logic in that subsequent options were likely to conform to the parameters set by the initial choice. In Faulkner's case, his intra-bloc rivals took up policy alternatives and began to accrue credibility and support due to the perceived growth and success of Irish nationalist politics. By the autumn of 1973, Faulkner's choices were either to go along with the Whitelaw negotiations (the 'castle talks') or to withdraw from political life. His late 1973 conversion to fully-fledged power-sharing was, in this perspective, the logical result of his earlier choices. Faulkner's narrative cannot, however, be separated from the decisions made by his cross-communal opponents/allies, the SDLP. The decision by the SDLP to abstain from Stormont carried the implication that it would not return for less than the minimalist participatory scheme Faulkner had offered in June 1971. In practice, this coincided with Dublin's long-held desire to gain greater authority as regards the North – the idea of an institutionalised Irish dimension facilitated both groups' goals. Both Dublin and the SDLP embarked on a strategy of 'banking' gains and downplaying losses, which led to the emphasis on maximalist goals – power-sharing and the Council of Ireland – and the rejection of more mid-range concessions. Following the accession to power of the Fine Gael – Labour coalition government in Dublin, the choice set of constitutional nationalist politics dramatically decreased – as was the case with Faulkner, once-viable alternatives had disappeared and the SDLP and Dublin pursued complementary, but ultimately suboptimal, maximalist policies. Irish nationalist maximalism and Ulster unionist reactions contributed to the entrenchment of constitutional politics after May 1974 and the long-term communal polarisation that characterised the ensuing years of the Troubles.

3
Direct Rule and Power Sharing, 1972–74

Introduction

The prorogation of the Stormont parliament and the introduction of direct rule from London in March 1972 transformed the political context in Northern Ireland and contributed to the further radicalisation of the North's politics. Westminster's intervention in removing Northern Ireland state structures established the essential factors that framed the long-term marginalisation of the North's politics and its protracted political impasse. It profoundly influenced the mobilisation of embedded ethnic identities, the entrenchment of political policy-making and policy direction and the polarisation of communal relations. It was the very lack of long-term planning and the absence of an articulate vision of what would replace the Northern Irish state apparatus that was instrumental in that mobilisation as both nationalist and unionist actors reacted to perceptions of changing opportunities and new threats to their status. Those reactions quickly radicalised each community, whose knock-on effects tied politicians to specific agendas and, in the process, entrenched communal division.

Imposing direct rule

The decision to introduce direct rule in March 1972 was not merely a reaction to Bloody Sunday, but can be directly traced to the international embarrassment and near-total Catholic alienation that internment created. Indeed, the decision cannot be understood outside the context of the series of events beginning (at least) with the revived civil rights movement in 1968. However, as was the case with the internment decision, the final decision to prorogue Stormont was made in the absence of a long-term plan. Thus, on 7 March 1972 the Home Secretary, Reginald Maudling, reported to the cabinet that the defeat of the IRA was not achievable by military means alone: the 'only hope for the future of Northern Ireland lay in the creation of a united community in the Province, which could be tolerated, if not supported, by the majority of the people of the Republic'.[1] Maudling argued that that this necessitated a reduction in 'the dominance of the Unionist faction' and the assertion of the 'overriding authority of the United Kingdom Government and Parliament'. In practical terms, he proposed that

> responsibility for law and order should be transferred from Stormont to Westminster; that a plebiscite should be held on the question of the Border ... and that consultations should be initiated in order to seek ways of making consultations for the proper participation of the minority community as of right not only in the Parliament but also in the Government of the Six Counties.[2]

Maudling said that such a scheme would involve 'a clean break with the past', since it might not be possible to 'establish constructive consultations with all political elements in Northern Ireland so long as Mr Faulkner remained Prime Minister'. However, the cabinet preferred to avoid decisive action due primarily to the 'serious risks' such measures would entail – for Northern Ireland and for the government in Westminster.[3] In his summation of the discussion surrounding Maudling's ideas, the prime minister acknowledged that there was a consensus on the need to 'assume responsibility for law and order'. Heath had also begun to favour a radical initiative:

> The suspension of Stormont might be less unacceptable to the government's supporters, however, if it appeared as a necessary consequence of a refusal by Mr Faulkner to maintain his administration following a decision by the United Kingdom Government to transfer responsibility for law and order to Westminster.[4]

The decision to assume Stormont's law-and-order responsibilities was taken by the cabinet on 14 March, together with a commitment to 'inject substantial additional finance', a decision to hold periodic referenda on the Province's 'continued membership of the United Kingdom' and to establish a cabinet office of a Secretary of State for Northern Ireland. In putting these proposals to Faulkner, the cabinet agreed that Heath should not give 'any indication of the consequences of a refusal of cooperation'.[5]

The British position was 'to concentrate on what is now required to transform the political situation in Northern Ireland ... by this test, it is clear that Mr Faulkner's proposed reforms do not go far enough'. In this assessment, Faulkner was seen as expendable.[6] The British believed that Faulkner's rejection of community government was a 'significant' decision, which implied that 'he does not accept that 50 years' rule by the Unionist Party calls into question the appropriateness of the Westminster model for Northern Ireland'. Furthermore, the government believed that Faulkner's position was impractical: concluding that although the Catholic G. B. Newe had been brought into the Stormont administration, it is doubtful now whether [Faulkner] could get any Catholic to join his government'.[7] Crucially, the British government's view of internment and the responsibility for law and order conflicted strongly with Faulkner's: 'Since Mr Faulkner rules out any radical political initiative he seems prepared to contemplate the present situation continuing indefinitely and the numbers interned increasing, at least for a long time yet.' In contrast, the cabinet desired that 'a start ... be made in running down internment as an act of policy'. Underpinning this was the fact that the government saw Faulkner's interpretation as disingenuous – while he had called for the introduction of internment as a security and political measure, he now saw it in security terms only.[8] In short, the problem was that the government was 'answerable both at Westminster and internationally for what we cannot control. This is particularly the case as regards internment.'[9]

Despite his efforts to formulate a workable policy, Faulkner fell a long way short of the British expectations in the areas of security and Catholic participation. For example, following their meeting on 22 March, Heath concluded that,

> As regards the longer term, Mr Faulkner had not seemed fully to realise the nature of the problem either of persuading the representatives of the minority to resume active participation in the political life of the Province or of re-establishing law and order.

He believed that Faulkner's idea of joint ministerial authority 'would merely increase the responsibility of the United Kingdom Government without giving them any significantly greater control over public order and security in the Province', and as a result the cabinet would 'need to take the final decision'.[10]

The prorogation of Stormont ended the dominance of the Ulster Unionist Party in Northern Ireland and 'reduced overnight the Unionist

Party from a party of government with patronage at its disposal, to a body of incoherent and ineffectual protest'.[11] However, Faulkner was able to retain his leadership of the party by adapting his rhetoric to the concerns of his audience. It was the very lack of political opportunities and the reluctance of the new Secretary of State, William Whitelaw, to take any immediate initiatives that allowed Faulkner to avoid setting out any clearly defined policies.[12] In addition, his consistent avowal of the need for unionist unity contrasted with William Craig's militant outbursts and the perception that, for Ian Paisley, the ending of Unionist Party dominance was a welcome bonus.

Despite an initial consensus, unionist divisions became more pronounced during the summer as Whitelaw began to target political dialogue, and while unanimity continued around the issue of security, fragmentation grew over political strategy.[13] In an attempt to tackle the growing fragmentation and dissension, at the end of May Faulkner invited Craig to join the party's policy committee on future strategy.[14] Around this time, he also began to advocate an increasingly hard-line approach to future negotiations. Thus, Faulkner pointed out that should the necessity arise, 'we shall be absolutely immovable in defence of our democratic rights of veto', and that unionists would use this veto against any imposed settlement.

Following the breakdown of the IRA ceasefire on 13 July and 'Bloody Friday' when nine people were killed and over 100 injured in more than 20 indiscriminate bombings in Belfast city centre on 21 July, Faulkner hardened his approach and demanded that the IRA be defeated: 'Effective military action is absolutely essential. "No-go" areas everywhere must be ended. The IRA ... must be sought out at once.'[15] Moderates in the party, however, increasingly viewed Faulkner's new emphasis as too close to Craig's position, precipitating the defection of several members to the Alliance Party.[16] This, coupled with the publication of a position paper for an inter-party conference Whitelaw had planned to be held in Darlington, brought the divisions into the open in September 1972.

In fact, the September 1972 blueprint, *Towards the Future*, did not greatly exceed Faulkner's proposals to the British government at the start of the year, which in themselves were largely a reworking of his Green Paper of October 1971. The kernel of the proposals for a new parliament was a Westminster-style committee system. The prime minister of Northern Ireland would still appoint members to the committees – in contrast to the SDLP and British government's preference for governmental participation 'as of right' – and again, the party's ideas on restoring law-and-order responsibilities conflicted with the British government's desire to have total control over security. Under the Unionist Party proposals, security responsibilities would be split between Westminster (army) and Stormont (policing and intelligence-gathering). The paper also raised the issue of the North's relations with the South and called for Dublin to declare acceptance of the 'right of the people of the North to self-determination' and to offer greater cooperation in ending terrorism in Northern Ireland. In return, the blueprint document claimed that a joint Irish inter-governmental council could be formed to 'discuss matters of mutual interest, particularly in the economic and social field'.

While it took almost a year before Faulkner's Irish dimension decision began to bring about a splintering of unionist politics, no such lag is discernible in the political development of the SDLP. Although the party was constrained by its earlier decisions on non-participation and non-negotiation while internment lasted, on the other hand, its decision to pursue a more nationalistic strategy continued to affect its later options as it sought to mobilise Catholic support through a gradual and cumulative 'pooling' of concessions.

The Provisionals' response to direct rule was categorical: 'These people are going around seeking for peace [sic]. They are wasting their time. We are fighting on. We are not stopping until we get a united Ireland.'[17] The SDLP discussion paper of March 1972 was prepared in direct response to the changed political context.[18] It begins by asking two basic questions:

> A. What is our attitude to negotiations about the future of Northern Ireland after the one-year interregnum? B. What do we want to propose about the future of Northern Ireland? What is our attitude to the several alternative proposals likely to be made by the various parties concerned?[19]

The paper argued that the two questions were related and that the party's attitude during the prorogation would in part determine the outcome of any future settlement. It warned that a continuation of abstentionism could lead the British government to decide 'on complete integration as the only possible solution', and unlike the situation under the Home Secretary, Maudling, when Westminster wanted an 'active, permanent, and guaranteed' role for the minority, the paper claimed that the prorogation of Stormont rendered that possibility 'superfluous'; instead, the future administration of Northern Ireland was open for debate: 'in considering our attitude to negotiations, we must be absolutely clear that we are not morally committed by previous promises; these promises are related to different, i.e., Maudling negotiations'. The paper posed a basic question: 'Are we still committed to the absolute condition that every last man be released before we go to the Conference table …?'

The policy subcommittee of the SDLP decided to act on the March paper's proposals at its meeting on 26 April, when it was agreed to 'launch a campaign to make its position clear [on] the short, medium and long-term future of Ireland', and that this campaign should follow the publication of a policy paper, 'possibly entitled "Blueprint for a new Ireland" '.[20] Any fear of republican 'outbidding' effectively disappeared from the SDLP's public discourse and private discussion following the killing by the Official IRA of a Derry soldier, William Best, at the end of May. Party members such as Hume and Cooper ignored the problem of being accused of 'selling out' the internees, and now began to question the motivation behind the PIRA's continued campaign. Cooper was perhaps the most outspoken in the attempt to capture the moral high ground, arguing that it was necessary to tackle sectarianism in order to prevent Northern Ireland being overtaken by a 'lunatic fringe', and that 'in this sort of climate, it was impossible for demands to remain inflexible'.[21] On 18 July, the SDLP's standing committee agreed to convene a meeting of the policy committee and parliamentary party to discuss future policy so that 'our members should know the policy for which the party intended to fight'. It also decided to enter into negotiations with Whitelaw to deal with the issue of internment, because 'the Provos did not seem interested in a new ceasefire'.[22] The party raised its anti-republican campaign and challenged its supporters to make a 'clear choice between their elected representatives and the men of violence'.[23]

Together with this public disavowal of PIRA tactics, the SDLP also drew up internal discussion documents around the idea of joint sovereignty or a Northern Ireland 'condominium'.[24] For instance, the proposals drawn up by SDLP adviser Ben Caraher were concerned with the constitutional make-up of a future Northern Ireland state. His paper describes a state whose citizens could claim British or Irish citizenship, and which would be governed by two high commissioners, appointed by Britain and the Irish Republic.[25] Cooper's submission was markedly more nationalistic in tenor.[26] It reiterated the desire for a distinctive SDLP negotiating position, but argued that this position should be based on the party's nationalist credentials and support base. This nationalistic feeling culminated in the party's September publication, *Towards a New Ireland*.

For Cooper, the conflicting aspirations of nationalism and unionism meant that 'we must look seriously at making Northern Ireland into a territory pertaining to the sovereignty of the parliaments of Britain and the Irish Republic and having two recognised citizenships ...'. Cooper argued that these aspirations should be tackled in the political sphere, thereby eliminating religion 'as the criterion of division'. He stated that the proposals were 'an extension' of the party policy to be 'radical, left-of-centre', anti-sectarian and 'dedicated to the achievement of the national ideal by peaceful means'. However, in terms of selling the proposals and of the party's approach in general, he claimed that 'We should stop talking in mealy-mouthed terms of the anti-Unionist population or the minority but should play the card of Irish nationality as hard as the Unionists play the British national card'. A condominium, he insisted, would enable the party to match its nationalist claims on the same grounds as unionism; therefore, the party should 'as Irishmen and not British ... claim the right for those we represent to be Irishmen in their own country'.

From the end of July, the Dublin government and, in particular, its Minister for Foreign Affairs, Patrick Hillery were instrumental in bringing the SDLP into talks with the British government.[27] At the first meeting between Whitelaw and the SDLP on 7 August, Fitt began by arguing that 'the euphoria created in the Protestant community [by the British Army's actions during "Operation Motorman"] could be used to remove some of the grievances of Catholics'.[28] The SDLP, he said, was 'under pressure to come away with something on internment'. However, Whitelaw's position was that internment had to continue because of the ongoing violence and that the army had to remain in 'Catholic areas because that was where the IRA attacks came from'.

The SDLP held further discussions in private with the British government during August and September in which it continued to complain about internment. For his part, Heath argued that 'It was unrealistic of the SDLP to demand the fulfilment of all their objectives before attending the conference'. Further, he pointed out that 'If they had reservations about the structure of the Conference it would be more helpful if they would say so and attend. The interests of the Republic would in fact be dealt with between the two sovereign governments.'[29] Arguably, neither Whitelaw nor Heath was particularly concerned about SDLP non-attendance as Whitelaw previously confided to Hillery that 'he did not expect [the conference] to come up with any solution or in effect to do serious negotiating. Its purpose was to enable each group to hear at first hand the views of the other groups'.[30] However, given the lack of movement on internment, the SDLP declined the invitation to the Darlington conference,[31] allowing it to appropriate what it believed to be a moral authority:

> Strong as our objection to internment was, it really served as an excuse for us to remain on the political high ground. We felt that we held the whip-hand in the situation and that by holding out we could minimise the concessions we would have to make and maximise the gains.[32]

On 26–27 August, the SDLP's parliamentary party, executive and policy subcommittee met in Bunbeg, Co. Donegal, to finalise its position paper. The meeting examined not only the Caraher and Cooper proposals, but also party chair John Duffy's 'Notes' on the proposals.[33] Duffy pointed out that what Caraher and Cooper were proposing was not in fact a 'condominium' since they were suggesting that power be shared three ways (Britain–Northern Ireland–Republic of Ireland) rather than two. Instead, he described their ideas as leading to 'an entirely new type of constitutional arrangement'. Duffy argued that the party should try to 'devise a tidier, more credible alternative, which, he suggested, might include a dual nationality, 'community government ... which excludes security' and a 'Council of Ireland'. In order to provide for reunification, Duffy included the proposal that a conference should be held after a period of five years to review the arrangements.

Towards a New Ireland reiterated the call for Britain to declare its support for a united Ireland.[34] It also called for the creation of an 'interim system of government' for Northern Ireland. Under this system, two commissioners would be appointed to sign legislation, an 84-member assembly would be elected by proportional representation and a national senate should 'plan the integration of the whole island by preparing the harmonisation of the structures, laws and services ... and to agree on a constitution'. Although the Irish government was suspicious of the constitutional changes the latter proposals might entail, it concluded that the document 'would ... seem to be in line with general policy to encourage the coming together of the fundamental views of the Government and those of the most active minority political party in the North in relation to the national issue'. In addition, officials noted that the document was devoid of any socialist 'polemic', and that it gave 'considerable support to the idea that the Irish government has a *right* to be consulted by Britain' (emphasis in original).[35]

Devolution proposals and the anti-power-sharing mobilisation

The October 1972 Westminster Green Paper left open the possibility of what it termed the 'Irish dimension' together with a devolved assembly which would involve 'the whole community ... [with] a wider consensus than has hitherto existed'. Although Craig remained within the Unionist Party following the publication of the document, together with Paisley, he continued to push for a retraction of this Westminster framework. For his part, Faulkner found little solace in any protection that vanguard ostensibly offered from the Paisleyite right.[36] Thus, in December he pleaded with Basil McIvor not to resign:

> I know you are concerned about the activities of fringe elements in the party – so am I. But I am quite certain that the right way forward is to argue the case within the organisation. All the evidence coming to me indicates massive support for that.[37]

He reiterated these sentiments to Whitelaw at the beginning of December,[38] although, he said, he consented to an Irish dimension that could only follow Dublin's recognition of 'Northern Ireland's right to run its own affairs'. For his part, Whitelaw believed that a Council of Ireland could promote economic cooperation and assist in 'joint action against terrorists in border areas'.[39]

Paisley and Craig met separately with Whitelaw the following week and urged a reconsideration of the Green Paper proposals. While Craig argued that Northern Ireland would be 'better off as an independent state';[40] Paisley warned that were Whitelaw to impose such ideas, 'elements in Northern Ireland ... led by people like William Craig would resort to violence'.[41] Both Paisley and Craig emphasised the importance of enhanced security measures as an alternative to political initiatives. In addition to the complaints made by Craig and Paisley, unionist Westminster MPs made representations to Whitelaw decrying the Green Paper proposals. James Kilfedder, for example, claimed that 'on no account and under no name would he take a Council [of Ireland]; it was unacceptable and would be looked upon as an IRA propaganda victory'.[42] At the same meeting Captain William Orr argued that the introduction of a proportional power-sharing system would represent another psychological blow since it pushed Northern Ireland further away from Westminster practices. A lack of sufficient constitutional safeguards and guarantees seems to lie at the heart of the unionist case against power-sharing and a

Council of Ireland. Thus, the press release following the Whitelaw meeting actually left the door open for a council, should certain conditions be met:

> Until such time as the Irish Republic recognise[s] the constitutional position of Northern Ireland within the United Kingdom, and adopt[s] policies consistent with good neighbourliness, a Council of Ireland would be unacceptable and unworkable.[43]

Despite the protestations by Paisley and Craig and Faulkner's reluctance to countenance serving in an executive with the SDLP, the British government pushed ahead with concrete institutional suggestions in its White Paper of March 1973.[44] The paper retained the principle of Dublin's involvement and proposed an inter-governmental conference to discuss ways to achieve 'effective consultation and co-operation in Ireland for the benefit of North and South alike'. In addition, it proposed a new devolved assembly and envisaged legislation being enacted to enable the Secretary of State for Northern Ireland to appoint an executive, which, it said, could 'no longer be solely based upon any single party, if that party draws its support and its elected representation virtually entirely from only one section of a divided community'. Faulkner, however, presented the White Paper as a vindication of many of his aims since the fall of Stormont: it 'secured almost all of our fundamentals', namely, the principle of consent, a 'worthwhile ... executive government, the chance to obtain recognition by Dublin, and a commitment by Westminster to pursue the elimination of terrorism as its highest priority'.[45] Yet despite the ambiguities and discrepancies over Faulkner's interpretation, in essence, his position remained that of an arch-constitutionalist, preferring close proximity to Westminster's preferences. Thus, he presented the proposals as an opportunity to safeguard the Union and articulated what the *Belfast Telegraph* identified as a 'centrist' willingness to 'work the system'.[46] As he later explained:

> There was much talk of 'negotiating' further with Mr Whitelaw, but as far as I could see, the die was cast and the post-White Paper situation was a completely new one ... the constitutional framework was decided, it was essentially workable, and we needed now to prepare for the elections to the new assembly.[47]

Many unionists, however, did not share Faulkner's vision of the British proposals as a 'constructive document'. The *Newsletter* sought to influence the anti-White Paper campaign by claiming that it must be 'the final stage' in the 'concessions that have been made in response to the minority's political militancy over the past years'. Apart from this, the paper argued that 'any unionist worthy of the name' would have 'serious reservations' about many of the White Paper's proposals.[48] Again, the paper complained that for the SDLP the White Paper was being touted as an interim step, decrying the party's 'cautious welcome', and asking, 'What more, we wonder, can the main minority party want?'[49]

Unionist division over power-sharing was the defining feature of Faulkner's assembly campaign. He attempted to blur those differences with semantics, (in)famously claiming that he would not share power with those 'whose primary object is to break the union'.[50] Following the assembly election at the end of June, the Faulknerite faction amounted to 22 of the 78 seats, although, as Henry Patterson and Eric Kaufmann point out, the Unionist Party retained a strong residual support and that 'the party's vote was not necessarily a vote for the White Paper'.[51] The SDLP's gain of 19 seats surprised many observers and led the *Newsletter* to question what its next steps might be: 'The party would be running true to form if at this stage, it were to attempt to gain further concessions as a prerequisite for full and early participation in the assembly.'[52] Whereas for Faulkner power-sharing was the means to achieve a devolved government, for his opponents and the *Newsletter* it signified the possibility of further concessions and that unionist interests would be best protected by other means, such as full integration or a restored Stormont.

The Northern Ireland Constitution Act ratified the assembly in July and empowered the Secretary of State to establish an executive 'having regard to the support it commands in the Assembly and ... is likely to be widely accepted throughout the community'. Garret FitzGerald's statement on the eve of the executive talks proved instrumental in mobilising anti-Faulkner opinion as it allowed unionists an insight into the Irish government's aspirations. The Council of Ireland, he argued, 'would hold out to the majority of the Irish people a prospect of progress towards the unity that is their aspiration. At the same time, the power given to a majority in Northern Ireland to determine the pace of this evolution would provide them with the guarantees they seek against being forced unwillingly into a united Ireland.' The *Newsletter*'s succinct verdict was that 'What we are being offered, in effect, is a one-way ticket to Dublin, the only question outstanding – the date on which we are to be coerced into using it'.[53]

Doubts over whether Faulkner could achieve his goal and whether the assembly would affect IRA violence influenced the *Newsletter*'s growing scepticism over power-sharing. By mid-October, it had also begun to point out that enforced power-sharing was foreign to Westminster parliamentary democracy. It argued that while both Heath and Wilson

> are opposed to sharing power with those with whom they do not agree, they look to unionists in Ulster to do just that with men whose record as wreckers of constitutional and democratically elected government is appalling. And men who have made no secret of their desire to achieve a united Ireland.[54]

Faulkner met the Dublin officials Dermot Nally and Séan Donlon following his victory on power-sharing before the Unionist Party Standing Committee on 23 October.[55] Having insisted on 'absolute secrecy', Donlon reported that Faulkner would not report the meeting to his party and that 'there were obviously precautions in operation to see that no one saw us with him'. Faulkner also stressed that he wished to remain the only channel through which the government would communicate with the Unionist Party.[56] The meeting itself commenced with Nally outlining the four considerations that informed the government's Council of Ireland proposals. These consisted of the need to achieve a reconciliation of the Irish people; security; economic advantages; and 'the need to ensure that a Northern Ireland majority would in effect have a veto on the decisions taken by the council', including its evolution. In contrast to the various assertions made regarding Faulkner's lack of preparation at the beginning of October, he outlined a detailed vision to the Irish delegation. First, he argued, the Council should be inter-governmental and have executive functions from the outset. However, these functions 'would be exercised on the basis that Ministers would decide on a course of action at the council, go back to their respective governments for approval and ... the decisions would then be carried out by the council's secretariat'. Faulkner rejected the suggestion that the Council itself could veto ministerial plans, and argued that 'wreckers on both sides' would make a parliamentary level 'totally unworkable, no matter what type of voting system was devised'.

In effect, Faulkner was suggesting a dual Dublin–Belfast veto over all executive decisions, that is, apart from the Council itself – hence the need for a unionist majority on the Belfast executive. Despite Nally and Donlon's interjection that the Council needed to provide a basis for the 'aspirations of the Northern Ireland minority', which could more easily identify with a parliamentary level, Faulkner argued that the suggestion would lead to a 'political-social talking shop' that would impede ministerial decisions. Although he agreed with the possibility of devolving policing to the Council, he pointed out that legislative harmonisation would be difficult and rejected the need for the Council to have a human rights commitment. He also argued that words such as 'reconciliation' and 'Council of Ireland' limited his ability to sell the concept – that 'reconciliation' equalled 'reunification' for unionists and that they linked the Council concept with the '1920 idea'. The meeting concluded with Faulkner claiming that his party 'would give a definite commitment to move rapidly towards setting up a Council of Ireland' following a decision on the executive. He argued that this sequencing was crucial in that 'Unionists could hardly be expected to attend a conference where they were not on an equal footing with London and Dublin representatives'. Finally, Faulkner pointed out that he had 'not had enough time to sell the power-sharing concept to the party but that ... he hoped to win a decisive victory at a special meeting of the Unionist Council which would be held probably within a month'.

In the event, Faulkner was able to mobilise enough support for slim victory by promising a unionist executive majority and threatening that if such an executive were rejected, 'Northern Ireland's link with the United Kingdom would also be thrown out and the constitutional future of the province would be [put] into the melting pot'.[57] Following Faulkner's 379:369 victory, the anti-White Paper parties decided to put their coalition on a more formal footing. Paisley outlined the thinking behind this initiative and stressed that 'a new grouping of loyalists, united to save democracy in Northern Ireland would shortly be formed to secure the defeat of power-sharing in the assembly by constitutional means'.[58] Both the coalition and the *Newsletter* believed that the executive was powerless to end the violence.[59] It concluded that the loyalist coalition's arguments in this regard posed a degree of credibility: 'Opposition to power-sharing, still seen, understandably, by many, as the reward for violence, cannot be brushed off completely'.[60] Despite Faulkner's victory at the Ulster Unionist Council meeting, the *Newsletter* pointed out that the 'problem still remains ... [but the] people of Northern Ireland will try anything that has the faintest hope of bringing them peace and prosperity'.[61] The paper also implicitly endorsed the argument made by anti-Faulknerite politicians such as Harry West or Kennedy Lindsay concerning the composition of the agreed executive, warning that:

> One of the major weaknesses of the new executive is that the public has formed its own opinion on the men who will serve on it. This is particularly, the case in respect of the SDLP team which is associated

in the minds of many people with the origins of the troubled period that began five years ago.[62]

By the autumn of 1973, Faulkner's options had narrowed considerably. His decision to acquiesce in a cross-border arrangement resurfaced in September 1972 and crucially differentiated his position from that of his intra-bloc rivals. The extent to which he genuinely believed that the British proposals were necessary to secure the Union can only be surmised – certainly, his memoirs suggest that weariness and resignation brought him so close to government policy in 1973.[63] What matters though is that Faulkner continued to push forward the White Paper agenda despite mounting unionist unease. That he did so was because his earlier decisions carried through to delimit his later options in an increasingly constrained fashion – his opponents articulated anti-White Paper positions and, realistically, the only political alternatives open to him were to carry on or resign. As the implications of the White Paper became clearer towards the end of 1973, so also did the mobilising potential of his opponents' arguments. In short, Faulkner's dilemma became starker. In more general terms, what this suggests is that the likelihood of Sunningdale succeeding was negligible. Insofar as Faulkner enjoyed no real political options, it is unlikely that he could have carried the institutional agenda within the unionist community. Prior to the December Sunningdale conference, for example, the *Newsletter* questioned the executive members' aspirations: 'Is the ultimate object of the Stormont power-sharing operation a united Ireland or a united Ulster?'[64] In short, Faulkner's 1971 decision set in motion a sequence of events that irrevocably altered the power balance within unionism, and the pace and extent of change between that date and 1973 meant that the power-sharing accord was stillborn.

Nationalist policy-making, 1972–73

Following the publication of the October Green Paper, both the Irish government and the SDLP initiated policies of banking perceived concessions. In Dublin, plans proceeded from the premise that a 'meaningful North–South link' would form part of an 'interim solution', which would be 'sufficiently dynamic and evolutionary to create a climate which ultimately might lead to Irish unity'.[65] Officials in the Inter-Departmental Unit on Northern Ireland (IDU) argued that Faulkner's acceptance of the concept at Chequers in September 1971, together with an implied approval from both Heath and Wilson, meant that such a council was feasible. The IDU envisaged a two-tier structure – consultative and executive – and concluded that the SDLP's affinity with Dublin marked an 'important new factor in the situation … [since] the probability of active minority representation at both levels … would give the whole council a definite bias in favour of Dublin's point of view'. An obstacle would occur over 'unionist intransigence', but this could be overcome through safeguards and 'a momentum towards eventual political unity … [which would] gradually establish an alternative focus as regards the unionists, oriented towards an all-Ireland identity'. Heath's comments to Lynch at the end of November indicated that a council should be limited to the social and economic spheres. Yet, as was the case with the Fine Gael–Labour coalition which took over from the Lynch government in March 1973, those warnings were effectively ignored by Dublin officials, who were apparently convinced of the logical 'momentum' of this incremental scheme.[66]

The SDLP also campaigned for strong cross-border institutions, with Paddy Devlin claiming that the imminent White Paper must 'introduce institutions and structures that respond to a minority's need to be administered impartially and to have a built-in evolutionary element to their life-span'.[67] Despite a guarded welcome of the White Paper, it claimed that the proposed assembly meant that 'Stormont as we have known it is gone forever'.[68] Within the new Dublin government – a Fine Gael–Labour coalition headed by Liam Cosgrave, which won a precarious one-seat victory in the March 1973 elections – the Minister for Posts and Telegraphs, Conor Cruise O'Brien, advocated a cautious approach:

> There may be a case for delay in order to have the British determination to have power sharing sink into the Protestant population, and to allow them also to realise the disasters which attempts to wreck the White Paper policy could bring upon themselves.[69]

Regardless of this advice, the Department of Foreign Affairs (DFA), headed by Garret FitzGerald, began to draft plans for a Council of Ireland as early as May 1973 – plans which gained cabinet approval the following month.[70] Arguing that it 'is, of course, in no way committed to the agenda set out in the white paper', the government based its plans on the need for a 'strong Council of Ireland with real functions to perform'. The Council, it said, must be 'open-ended' and able to 'evolve with the consent of both sides', and that it 'should be as comprehensive and authoritative as possible'.[71] The draft acknowledges that neither the unionists nor the British would be receptive to the idea, and that, although Northern nationalists would favour a strong institution, 'they may not be able to contribute a great deal of thinking' as to how it could be achieved. Accordingly, the Paper stated that the 'onus' of producing workable proposals lay with Dublin and that it was desirable to produce such proposals, even if they 'do not succeed in winning general acceptance'. Like the December Paper, it viewed the Council as 'a premier means of working towards the growth of reconciliation'; however, its second goal was more concrete: 'it should also be an embryo and symbol of our working towards unity based on consent'. The Paper suggested immediate steps should be taken in this programme, including consultation with government departments whose responsibilities would be affected by the Council and consideration of the legislative and constitutional implications that would be posed by the Council's structure and functions by the IDU.

The decision to plan for a strong, meaningful cross-border institution carried through to the Sunningdale talks in a self-reinforcing fashion that excluded alternative or more moderate agendas as the planning process actually subsumed dissenting viewpoints in the belief that the final structure would be accommodative and could 'contain within itself the seeds of evolution'.[72] Indeed, the cabinet believed that its agenda could outmanoeuvre unionist dissent over executive functions. For example, the Attorney-General, Declan Costello, pointed out that 'the unionist viewpoint would be in a minority' at any inter-governmental meeting, during which a recommendation could be endorsed for 'future powers to be given to the council'.[73] The Dublin government was in many respects ahead of the SDLP in its conceptualisation of the Irish dimension and power-sharing. The 'apparent drift' of Dublin government policy, which concerned Hume in mid-July,[74] was resolved in the consensus reached between the two groups the following month, setting the foundations for a (largely) coordinated effort to maximise gains in future negotiations.[75]

However, before executive talks could begin, in private discussions with British and Irish officials Fitt conveyed an apparent willingness to agree to an executive prior to movement on the other issues. The question of whether the SDLP had changed tack was the subject of a busy two-day trip by the government's Northern liaison, Séan Donlon, at the end of September.[76] Donlon's first port of call was Hume, who stated that there was no change in policy. Hume spelt out clearly to Donlon the SDLP strategy. First, he said, there could be no agreement on an executive without 'firm, detailed commitment on a Council of Ireland' from London, Dublin and the other executive parties. Furthermore, he said, 'there would have to be some visible movement on internment and policing'. Finally, Hume believed that negotiations should quickly commence, and that

> Now that Faulkner was at his weakest ... it [was] more important than ever that he should be inextricably tied to a fully worked out and agreed council before the executive was formally established.

This timescale was vital, since once the executive was formed, Hume reasoned, the pressure from London would be 'turned down, if not off'. He was, however, willing to countenance agreement on a provisional executive, which would be 'frozen ... until the other matters were resolved'. This scenario, he claimed, would transfer any blame for delay from the SDLP and increase the pressure on the British to agree to a Council of Ireland. Donlon also visited Currie, who emphasised a residual resentment against Faulkner: 'there could never be any question of their committing themselves finally on an executive until Faulkner had been copper-fastened on the Council'. Donlon reported that Currie – who 'had absolutely no trust in Faulkner and would never accept his word for anything' – was perhaps willing to 'risk toppling Faulkner and thereby reduc[e] the prospects for forming an executive' if the issues were not 'fully and openly thrashed out and resolved'. Currie has subsequently reiterated these sentiments, claiming that during the Castle talks in November:

> We had already decided that, in view of our gains on other matters, particularly on the Council [of Ireland], we could not allow a breakdown on [the constitution of the executive] in circumstances where the whole agreement would come crashing down and Faulkner would have credibility for his position.[77]

In other words, there was zero-sum logic at work in the negotiations between the SDLP and the Faulknerite faction of the Unionist Party during 1973. While neither side wished to be associated with the collapse of the talks, both groupings sought to maximise their potential gains. For the SDLP, this meant securing the Council of Ireland and the principle of executive responsibility, while Faulkner targeted a unionist majority on the executive as a way of securing a veto over any changes.

The SDLP's desire to maximise its gains and its reluctance to yield ground to Faulkner appeared during the talks with Faulkner and Whitelaw. For example, Fitt warned the Dublin government that Faulkner was 'backtracking' on promises and that he had told the SDLP that he was 'only giving [the Council of Ireland] to them "as a sop" '.[78] Likewise, Currie said that Faulkner was 'using his weakness deliberately to get concessions from the SDLP and the British were doing the same'. In addition, Devlin claimed that

> Faulkner was using the SDLP as an insurance policy. Now was not the time to be generous ... [because] deep down, Faulkner was more interested in the failure of power sharing and sought total unionist control once more.

Meanwhile, in Dublin, O'Brien remained sceptical of the SDLP's analysis. In a letter to the Taoiseach following the SDLP meeting, he argued that its strategy would place Faulkner and under 'heavy additional strain'.[79] O'Brien pointed out that,

> From a unionist point of view, tripartite talks without an executive are equivalent to intrusion of the Republic into the affairs of Northern Ireland without any recovery by the unionist community of a say in the running of their own province. Faulkner is good at survival but he would find it very hard to survive that.

He went on to argue that the Dublin government should exercise caution in its own proposals: 'for us to make an unreasonable demand ... would be to play in to the hands of those who might like to suggest that we are behaving so unreasonably as to endanger the whole fabric of the White Paper'. At the beginning of November, the Department of the Taoiseach, however, began to take control of strategy development from the hands of the Department of Foreign Affairs.[80] Although the Department of the Taoiseach was arguably less radical than that of Foreign Affairs, it did not fully share O'Brien's concern for caution. Indeed, it believed that the Council's 'structures and institutions should be regarded as instrumental in relation to political purpose'. That political purpose ranged from the 'maximum national aspiration [of] an all-Ireland parliament and government ... [to the] fallback position [of] any broad arrangements which would encourage eventual unity'. As part of its final deliberations, FitzGerald suggested that the government should consider whether the Council was 'to be the nucleus of a future government and parliament of the entire island or whether the council is to be the agent through which the two administrations are to be brought together'.[81] In the end, the government opted for a mix of both options: while it envisaged the Council having economic, security and reconciliation benefits, it believed that it should also have 'the ultimate objective of unification with the consent of a majority in Northern Ireland'.[82]

The SDLP and Faulkner eventually agreed to a six unionists to four nationalists ratio on the executive. The intervention of the British Defence Secretary Lord Carrington proved instrumental in persuading the SDLP to accept this lesser role who told Hume that Dublin's proposals on policing and a common law enforcement area were 'from the moon'.[83] The final meeting between governmental officials prior to the tripartite conference took place at the end of November.[84] Since meeting Irish ministers at Baldonnel air base in the Republic in September, British officials were – certainly, in comparison to the Irish – ambivalent about many of the Council proposals. The British officials warned the Irish about expecting too much from the Council on several occasions during the course of the meeting. For example, they advised against the perception that the Council would 'harmonise' legal, cultural and political practices – the unionists, the British claimed, 'are highly allergic to the word "harmonising"'. Again, the British informed the Dublin officials that they should have modest hopes regarding the transfer of responsibilities to the Council. Although the British were 'not too receptive', they envisaged that reserved functions might devolve 'in the first instance' to the Northern Ireland assembly. The British were also reluctant to allow the Council to agree on devolved powers in the absence of Westminster input, although the two sides were content that the mechanism for achieving this would be a form of private or separate meetings, apart from the Council. The British clarified their position on law and order for the Irish officials: '[We] see no possibility of committing [our]selves in any way on the achievement at any time in the future of a common form of policing for the whole island.' The British were content to allow the Secretary of State for Northern Ireland to consult the Council of Ireland regarding policing appointments, but that 'Under no circumstances could any change be envisaged in the present statutory functions reserved to the Secretary of State in relation to the Northern Ireland Police Authority'. The Dublin delegation left with the impression that they should not pressure the unionists and 'accept whatever is the best that we can get'. Despite this, the Irish government's agenda for Sunningdale did not significantly change. At the beginning of November, the Department of the Taoiseach called for a 'unified approach', with the primary aim being to agree to a Council that would be subordinate to the two sovereign governments, but that would still possess evolutionary elements, 'with no restrictions on its development' as an 'embryonic all-Ireland government'. This could be achieved, it believed, if the 'council possess[es] maximum authority and flexibility at the earliest possible date'.[85] Similarly, the SDLP went to the conference with a broadly similar goal, as both actors continued along a nationalist trajectory.[86] In this regard, both groups agreed the status that the government should accord to the North, which would confirm that the government would work the agreed institutions for as long as a Northern majority desired – or, as the internal memorandum put it: it should 'meet the minimal requirements of responsible Northern Protestant opinion'.[87]

The Sunningdale experiment

The Sunningdale conference afforded the anti-White Paper coalition a concrete target around which consensus could be formalised and the various unionist factions headed by Paisley, Craig and West came together under the umbrella organisation the United Ulster Unionist Council (UUUC) on the first day of the talks, 6 December 1973. The counter-responses of the UUUC to the communiqué established a pattern that challenged the Westminster-inspired movement towards power-sharing and Dublin involvement and limited the room for manoeuvre open to the pro-Sunningdale factions. As the range of options open to the executive supporters narrowed, the UUUC increasingly presented itself as a credible alternative to Faulkner, power-sharing and the Council of Ireland. The first motion passed by the UUUC in its inaugural meeting illustrates the fact that the central concern remained power-sharing:

> It is imperative that all unionists and loyalists should act together to reject the new form of administration provided for under the [Northern Ireland] Constitution Act, 1973, and seek a constitution that effectively safeguards our heritage and right to democratic government.[88]

Faulkner, on the other hand, placed his faith in Dublin's recognition that 'there could be no change in the status of Northern Ireland until a majority of the people of Northern Ireland desired a change in that status' and that a Council of Ireland could combat terrorism.[89] The *Newsletter*, however, turned Faulkner's logic on its head by reasoning that rather than a Council of Ireland facilitating counter-terrorist measures, such a body should be superfluous in a situation where the Southern government would willingly cooperate in law enforcement.[90]

To detach the criticisms of Faulkner and the Council of Ireland from the embedded fears and mistrust of the SDLP-Dublin axis and the power-sharing arrangements is to lose sight of processes behind the formation of the anti-Faulknerite consensus. The reactions to Faulkner's position came to a head at the beginning of January when he lost an Ulster Unionist Council vote on the Council of Ireland by 427 to 374.[91] Although his adviser, Peter McLachlan, had anticipated defeat, Faulkner told the Secretary of State that he 'would be surprised if the result ... differed dramatically from the last council meeting', apparently believing that the 'Sunningdale safeguards' would carry the vote.[92] Regardless of the outcome, Faulkner reported that the rules of the party would allow him to continue as Assembly rather than Party leader and was succeeded in the latter role by Harry West. Faulkner attempted to paint the assembly faction as the main unionist grouping, claiming that

> I believe that the policies of the Assembly Unionist Party are policies that the bulk of unionists up and down the country support ... We believe we are the true Unionist Party and that the decision of the Unionist Council [in rejecting Sunningdale] does not reflect the feelings of unionists.[93]

In contrast, McLachlan told Irish officials that the meeting 'had been worse than in fact has been reported publicly ... the middle ground group found it very difficult to take the Council of Ireland'. Furthermore, he 'would like to see more selling by [Dublin] of the Sunningdale agreement bearing in mind their problems'.[94]

Meanwhile, the appeal to the Irish High Court by Fianna Fáil TD Kevin Boland that the Sunningdale communiqué was unconstitutional added to Faulkner's difficulties. The January verdict that the communiqué was 'no more than a statement of policy' belied Faulkner's interpretation; in addition, the government was constrained from offering further explanation as Boland immediately appealed the decision.[95] Faulkner met Cosgrave on 16 January in an effort to clarify Dublin's position.[96] While Faulkner said that he was willing to participate in the formal conference that would ratify the December communiqué, he maintained that this could not occur until the issue of recognition had been clarified. In a pointed and prescient remark, he inquired 'whether if the government won the Boland case would that not mean that the Sunningdale declaration was all washed up'. On his return to the Northern Ireland executive, Faulkner circulated a memorandum suggesting the need for consideration of the next stage in the ratification process.[97] The memorandum pointed out that the 'reality of the situation' was that the issues involved in the Council of Ireland 'are not primarily administrative or technical ... but political in character'. He suggested 'carefully phased progress on all the major fronts', to be accompanied by action on terrorism by the South. However, in contrast to his unionist opponents, Faulkner continued to advocate the course of action suggested by the Sunningdale communiqué. Unable to assert an alternative strategy, Faulkner opted to attempt to manage the pace of change.

For the SDLP, on the other hand, the power-sharing executive was but a means to an end – the overriding priority was the Council of Ireland. Despite the retrospective claims by Devlin and Fitt that Hume and FitzGerald inspired a strategically mistaken emphasis on the Irish dimension,[98] the primary material reveals that in fact, with the exception of Fitt, the policy direction was unanimously supported. Although the SDLP faced internal criticism, the leadership convinced its members that it should attend the Sunningdale conference despite the persistence of internment and its ongoing commitment to the rent and rates strike. While Basil McIvor's assessment that 'power sharing and the Council of Ireland were a fatal mixture' is substantively true,[99] it underestimates the importance of the latter concept to the SDLP and ignores the political pressure the party found itself under due to internment. Indeed, Devlin hinted at the unease within the party in December when he complained that it had settled for less than they could have had at Sunningdale.[100] Donlon related the unanimity of the SDLP and isolation of Fitt to the Dublin government at the beginning of January 1974.[101] He reported that both Currie and Devlin emphasised that they had no reason to believe that the leadership's view contradicted the general party consensus on the Council of Ireland. The 'exception' among the leadership was Fitt, who was regarded as 'being too close and too much under the influence of Faulkner'.[102] This consensus, they reported, held that 'Faulkner must now be pushed by both Dublin and the SDLP to conclude the formal stage of Sunningdale as soon as possible'. Despite Faulkner's setback at the UUC meeting, they argued that his 'support in unionist circles ... is solid and last week's meeting did not accurately reflect that'. At the beginning of 1974, the suspicion remained that Faulkner would stall or renege on his December promises.[103] This, coupled with the inability to make progress on ending internment, suggests the oft-cited comment by SDLP backbencher Hugh Logue that the Council of Ireland would 'trundle unionists into a united Ireland' reflects an underlying sense of urgency. Indeed, the *Irish Times* interpreted the formation of an internal anti-internment pressure group the following day as marking the 'first significant departure from the policies and practice of the leadership and will no doubt create resentment and accusations of rocking the boat at a crucial time'.[104] Michael Canavan, a member of the group, echoed party policy from 1971 to 1972: 'we will never be satisfied until the last internee, Protestant and Catholic, is released'.[105]

Suspicions of both the SDLP and Faulkner fuelled the UUUC's election rhetoric and continued as the basis of its policies after its landslide victory of eleven of the twelve Northern Ireland Westminster seats at the end of February when the Labour Party headed by Harold Wilson's defeated the Conservatives. Faulkner had spelled out the precarious position of the executive to the Dublin government during a meeting at Hillsborough Castle on 1 February. Although the meeting was ostensibly to agree progress on the Council of Ireland, Faulkner complained that the South's 'recognition' declaration was 'ambiguous and even worthless' in the eyes of unionists, and pressed the government on the need for action on the issue of fugitive IRA volunteers. He warned that 'Too much haste or too grandiose a scheme could damage or destroy power sharing itself'.[106] Like the SDLP, however, the Dublin government was wary about the possibility of Faulkner's proposals becoming preconditions to a joint North–South ratification of the Council's remit.[107] Donlon reported that diffidence towards Faulkner influenced the SDLP's reluctance to enter into an electoral pact with the Unionist Assembly Party.[108] Indeed, prior to the election, the party was more concerned over the Council of Ireland and internment than the fate of power-sharing and Faulkner. Thus, Fitt complained to Donlon that 'if the current mood within the SDLP was anything to go by, he might well refuse to ratify Sunningdale until there was some further evidence of British intentions to phase out internment'.[109]

Faulkner made his personal thoughts about the election known to NIO officials and the new Labour Secretary of State, Merlyn Rees, at the beginning of March. Faulkner reported that his executive team was 'shattered about the extent of feeling against a Council of Ireland', and in the way that 'moderate opinion … had gone over to the loyalists'.[110] Although he expressed disappointment with the Dublin government and the SDLP, he believed that, even at this stage, a statement from Cosgrave 'could have a real impact'. Without progress, Faulkner said that he 'could see no possibility of a Council of Ireland being saleable'. He reiterated several of these points to Rees a couple of days later, claiming that to attempt ratification would mean an end of the executive.[111] Although he said that Sunningdale could still command the support of around 80 per cent of the population, a commitment from Dublin to amend the constitution and 'positive evidence about something being done on extradition' were, he said, 'essential' because he 'did not have a single card to play'. Roy

Bradford was also shaken by the election result, but told supporters that it was 'not a clear-cut message to go into reverse. It was a signal to slam the breaks on.' He believed the agreement was still salvageable but that the vote was an indication of the fact that while Protestants 'have accepted changes on a scale which in 1969 was inconceivable' they had seen no corresponding improvement in security.[112]

Detailed security matters took up over half the meeting between Rees and the UUUC leadership on 18 March.[113] Turning to political matters, Craig expressed incredulity at Rees's determination to continue with Sunningdale. Such action, Craig said, would increase tensions and yet still fail to appease the 'small minority'. Paisley claimed that 'if the British government pressed on with Sunningdale, there would be civil war. People would say that there was no future for their community.' He continued by arguing that the first Council of Ireland 'was a consultative mechanism between two equal partners, both of whom would be in the United Kingdom', but that this was not the case with the present arrangement. Paisley added that 'the people of Northern Ireland had never accepted power-sharing and that the workers of Northern Ireland are straining at the leash'. All three UUUC leaders repeatedly reminded Rees of the election result. Rees, however, replied that the result entitled them to express their views in the House of Commons and that Sunningdale was 'not equivalent to a united Ireland'. Craig elucidated what he perceived to be the link between Sunningdale, power-sharing and the SDLP, and accordingly outlined its mobilising potential, arguing, 'it was a minority which had succeeded in overthrowing the structures of the last 50 years, and the majority view was now being disregarded'. The coalition meanwhile turned its attention to the assembly at the end of March, with the introduction of a motion that called for a 'renegotiation of the constitutional arrangements'.[114]

It was at this time that Faulkner began to press for a phased implementation of the Council of Ireland. For instance, during a meeting with Rees, the pair discussed the possibility of ratifying Sunningdale 'as it stood and then proceed by agreement on the basis that the council would in practice only operate on a consultative basis until it was subsequently agreed to extent to executive functions'.[115] The new Labour government, however, remained to be convinced as to the continued value of the experiment. Briefing papers prepared for a meeting with Faulkner describe him as 'by nature a somewhat solitary figure and his only real confidants are members of his immediate family'. He had, in London's eyes, 'little experience of "open" politics' under the Stormont system, and that although he has 'tried to overcome his natural reserve and forge links with his backbenchers ... there are increasing signs that he has got very far ahead of his assembly supporters let alone unionist public opinion'. Indeed, according to the papers, Faulkner had become so isolated that, 'Ironically, he is in many ways closer to his SDLP ministerial colleagues' than to his executive party, with the result that 'there is a real risk of defections from his backbench party which ultimately could lead to the whole constitutional arrangements being upturned'.[116] The brief describes the executive in equally frank terms and offers a bleak forecast for Sunningdale's future. Given the extent of Faulknerite disillusionment with the Council of Ireland combined with the Republic's handling of the status question, the papers claim that only 'a clear demonstration of greater Irish interest in improved cross-border security' could save the council. The briefing also set out the extent of executive division by spelling out the SDLP's position: not only did the SDLP consider the Council of Ireland to be 'essential' and believed in early ratification, but also influential members refused to support the police until the establishment of both the Council and a new police authority.

Faulkner used the meeting itself to reiterate his idea that Dublin would agree to phased implementation on condition that the SDLP agreed first.[117] Complete ratification was presently impossible, he said, because unionists now considered the Council to be an 'embryo of an all-Ireland government'. As was the case with his 1971 post-internment London meetings, Faulkner presented an optimistic assessment to his Belfast colleagues, claiming that the administration would be supported and allowed to serve its full four-year term, and that the UUUC MPs had little support at Westminster.[118] Following a meeting with the SDLP, Faulkner appeared to be more upbeat, telling Rees that he had left with the 'firm impression that the SDLP would not allow problems over the Council of Ireland to break up the executive'.[119] He claimed that any agreement on phasing would not be a victory for either side since it was still the SDLP 'who had got almost everything they wanted'. In contrast, the SDLP had a very different appraisal of the meeting, which was, according to officials, 'much more gloomy than the account that Mr Faulkner gave'.[120] The SDLP delegation (Fitt, Hume and Devlin) told Rees that ' "wee Brian" was losing his nerve ... he was exaggerating his difficulties with his own party ... [and] that if he would just screw up his courage and ratify, the SDLP would immediately throw their weight behind moves to gain the acceptability of the police'.

In fact, the SDLP remained in the dark as regards the nature of the changes envisaged by Faulkner until late April as Fitt held back a letter from the unionist leader in which he detailed his proposals.[121] Indeed, to Fitt's chagrin, the party executive passed a motion at the end of the month calling for the ratification of Sunningdale 'in its entirety and at once'.[122] Faulkner advised Fitt that only a staged progression from consultative to executive responsibilities could avoid a 'collapse of the executive'; but that such a progression could only proceed following a referendum or an assembly election.[123] However, as he outlined in a letter to the prime minister, Rees's priorities did not mirror those of the executive groupings. Thus, he told Wilson that his main aim was 'to avoid being faced with a crisis which hits us unexpectedly' – though he saw this coming from Faulkner's executive party rather than any other source.[124] The upshot of Rees's assessment was the cabinet's decision to establish a contingency planning committee. This consisted of an elite group of ministers assisted by their department officials. The group's remit specified the importance of secrecy – it would 'meet in special sessions and with severe restrictions on the circulation of paper'.[125]

Faulkner had party problems of his own: Peter McLachlan, for instance, complained that despite his own efforts, 'no real dialogue' existed between the leadership and the backbenchers, since 'Mr Faulkner's personality made it extremely difficult for a frank exchange of views'. McLachlan claimed that morale among the party's supporters 'was at rock bottom. Not only was there complete antipathy towards the Council of Ireland, but power sharing had now become a dirty word. The party organisation in the constituencies was in disarray.' Added to this was the serious problem of finances and the real threat that the party's main benefactor, Fred Tughan, was reconsidering his options. McLachlan also stated that the idea of ratification was unthinkable because it would provoke 'total defection'.[126] In contrast, the West faction of the Unionist Party had defined a set of policies that they took to the UUUC conference in Portrush at the end of April, which precipitated Faulkner's final break with the party.[127] Their 'immediate' objective was to 'prevent the creation of a Council of Ireland having (a) executive powers; (b) a permanent secretariat; and (c) a parliamentary tier'. Although the assembly itself would be retained, ministers would be 'responsible to the assembly and no longer hold office at the political whim of the Secretary of State'. Second, although the party upheld the principle of power-sharing, 'those whose objective is an all-Ireland Republic should not be involved in government' – apart from serving on committees. Around 70 delegates attended the three-day UUUC conference, which produced a series of agreed proposals, including 'Ulsterisation' of security to combat the IRA, immediate assembly elections and the maintenance of unionist unity against Sunningdale.[128]

Despite Dublin's apparent desire to push ahead with ratification, it had in fact begun to reassess its options immediately following the election result – over a month ahead of the Westminster officials.[129] The paper claimed that the government had agreed to the communiqué because it believed that a 'Council of Ireland was needed for reasons intrinsic to the situation'. Although, it said, Faulkner had originally spoken for broad unionist interests, the settlement 'no longer commands quite the same moral authority as a point of equilibrium between all the major forces in the island'. The paper argued that the 'setback' had occurred due to the failure to secure unionist support, the undermining effects of the court case undertaken by the former Fianna Fáil TD Kevin Boland in challenging the Communiqué's constitutionality, the delay in the Law Commission report and 'the fact that Faulkner ... spent more time calling for further action on security from Dublin than in selling the package'.[130] Nevertheless, it claimed that the agreement would have succeeded but for the intervention of the February election. Turning to the question of ratification, the paper argued that Faulkner's attitude was crucial, while suggesting that the SDLP might accept a pared-down version of the Council. The report suggested that five options were open to the government:

1. forget Sunningdale;
2. renegotiate the package;
3. accept that accommodation was impossible and prepare for a continuation of direct rule;
4. implement the package and hope that unionist support could be rallied in due course; or
5. ratify Sunningdale after electoral approval.

The paper rejected the first option due to the fact that 'internationally [it would seem to be] a cynical manoeuvre'. In addition, it would alienate the unionists and the British, and undermine the SDLP. A similar credibility question influenced its decision to reject the second option, though it admitted that 'While the council is a necessary condition for a power-sharing executive it may be the latter and not the former which in the event will prove the most potent force for change'. While option 3 was almost a complete non-starter, the paper suggested that option 4 'is the one we should go for', despite this entailing a less powerful council than had originally been envisaged, the postponement of the consultative assembly and a reduced secretariat. The paper concluded that although even this proposal might not win approval from the

Faulknerites, 'there is no alternative to the principle of an accommodation like that of Sunningdale ... the actual settlement, though weakened by election results ... cannot and should not be substantially changed'.[131]

The continuing tensions among the pro-Sunningdale elites undoubtedly precipitated the UWC strike, which ended the debate over immediate or staged ratification. Given the gulf between the SDLP and Faulkner's vision of the Council of Ireland, coupled with additional pressures such as the lack of movement on detention and the escalating violence, the strike actually gave the executive the impetus to reach a belated agreement, and therefore prolonged the life of the Sunningdale experiment.[132] That the timing of the strike was contingent or that it established itself through violence and intimidation is not in doubt. However, after its first few days, the strike benefited from the entrenched anti-power-sharing and anti-Irish dimension sentiments. The support that underpinned the strike's success originated from the long-term increase in unionists' fears and suspicions over the nature of political change. Faulkner's decision to agree to a cross-border body in September 1972 and his subsequent acquiescence in power-sharing hastened that process. The executive's attempt to alleviate those fears and suspicions during 1974 had brought it to the point of collapse, with the SDLP threatening to walk out and Faulkner facing a near-total absence of confidence.

As the strike continued, however, the SDLP apparently 'blinked first' or, in Currie's words, 'capitulated' and agreed to Faulkner's step-wise proposals.[133] Actually, even this apparent conversion proceeded from the party's established practice of maximising concessions. Thus, during a visit to Dublin on 21 May, the party continued to argue that the Council of Ministers' role would not be merely consultative, but should include responsibilities for 'cooperation and coordination of action' between the executive and Dublin.[134] In addition, the party would agree to Faulkner's phased plans following 'evidence that the British army have taken on and broken the UWC control of geographic areas ... [and restored] normal electricity supplies'. Furthermore, the party claimed that it had not reached agreement on this scheme, and that while the six administration members accepted it, up to six backbenchers, led by Paddy O'Hanlon, would be prepared to reject it.[135] The fractious and fragmentary meeting of the executive the following day concluded with the agreement that the Council of Ministers would 'provide the forum for consultation, cooperation, and coordination of action' and that further steps towards the fully-fledged Council of Ireland would proceed 'only after a test of opinion of the Northern Ireland electorate'.[136] From Faulkner's point of view, this scheme weakened the Council of Ireland. However, the Council did retain an evolutionary function and in fact the SDLP had gained the concession that the Council of Ministers become more than simply a monitoring or review body to one that had responsibility for overseeing the implementation of decisions.

Cosgrave conveyed the Irish government's displeasure at the outcome of events to Wilson in a strongly worded letter on 23 May, pointing out that the latest agreement represented 'a considerable departure' from the December communiqué. The Taoiseach warned that if the strike continued, 'the SDLP may find their support diminished to the point where the minority population might swing over to the IRA' and concluded, somewhat optimistically, that the 'first meeting of the Council of Ministers and of the Council of Ireland should be held without delay in a matter of days'.[137] Although cabinet ministers met with the executive at Chequers on 24, the attempts to save the power-sharing experiment were increasingly recognised as futile. This was evidenced in Roy Bradford's handwritten comments on his copy of the press release that followed the meeting: '1. Sunningdale – a dead duck; 2. Assembly elections'.[138] Bradford, who had previously come under pressure from his constituency association, had urged the executive and the Secretary of State to open up a dialogue with the UWC,[139] and it was this issue that ended the executive's final vestiges of collective responsibility on 28 May.[140]

Narrating Sunningdale

The Northern Ireland 1973–4 power-sharing experiment did not fail solely due to an over-powerful 'Irish dimension'. The decisive, but often overlooked, factor was an embedded unease amongst grassroots unionism with affording the SDLP an executive voice in the North. An emphasis on the Council of Ireland and the events that occurred after the communiqué was signed in December 1973 shapes both the academic[141] and the autobiographical literatures.[142] Roy Foster recently alluded to the ubiquity of that narrative:

> It is now generally agreed that insistence upon a high-profile "Council of Ireland" linking North and South was a bridge too far for the Northern majority and a decisive element in the sabotaging of the Sunningdale executive by industrial militancy in Northern Ireland during the summer of 1974.[143]

However, the widespread, long-term and deep-rooted disquiet over the perceived direction of political events within the unionist community meant that even the *idea* of power-sharing was most likely a 'bridge too far'; while for nationalism, the perception of opening up opportunities meant that power-sharing by itself – or even a purely 'consultative' Council of Ireland – would not go far enough. This was because, by the end of 1973, an anti-Faulknerite mobilisation based on suspicions over power-sharing had permeated all levels of the unionist community. Linked with this was the fact that for unionists the Northern state had been decimated by over five years of inter-communal conflict and perceived Northern nationalism as building on that uncertainty by further undermining the link with Britain.

The policy decisions made by Faulkner and the SDLP in the summer of 1971 established the parameters of future options and set the direction of downstream political developments. On the one hand, Faulkner's willingness to countenance a cross-border dimension increasingly locked him into a narrow policy agenda as concrete proposals began to surface from the autumn of 1972 and the agendas of his intra-bloc rivals, Paisley, Craig and West, began to limit his room for manoeuvre. Together with pressure from Westminster, that counter-mobilisation effectively tied Faulkner into a power-sharing and Council of Ireland agenda towards the end of 1973. On the other hand, for the SDLP no such time lag existed. The party's abstentionist decision implied that it would not return to government for less than it had achieved in the offer of committee seats in June 1971 and led it to mobilise Catholic support around the promise of further concessions. This maximalist and long-term strategy led the party to ignore the possibility of 'settling' for moderate goals such as internal power-sharing – that is, without an executive role for Dublin – or security reform. As this chapter points out, this created a situation where the SDLP actively sought to take advantage of Faulkner's difficulties to accumulate additional gains.

Through both its overt political initiatives and, more ambiguously, on other occasions, through its apparent reluctance to act, the presence of the British government played a crucial role in shaping the context in which these choices played out. Increased pressure from Westminster raised unionist suspicions and reduced the possibility of Faulkner being able to carry through the kind of radical power-sharing initiative favoured by Heath's cabinet. Again, state intervention played a decisive role in radicalising nationalist politics as the SDLP perceived a new political context that would be more open to achieving maximal goals. Unionist opposition to executive power-sharing was broader and more deeply embedded than is generally appreciated and it was this opposition – as Faulkner himself later recognised[144] – rather than simply an over-ambitious Council of Ireland project that fatally undermined the Sunningdale initiative. This account raises the problem of why, given that growing unease, did Faulkner persist in his course of action – the first section tackles this key question and argues that Faulkner's September 1971 decision carried through to delimit his later options. Although Faulkner stuck closely to Westminster proposals during 1973, the historically important changes were occurring elsewhere – namely, the gradual coalescing of the anti-Faulknerite groupings. Faulkner's decision also had implications for nationalist politics and, as the second section demonstrates, a merging of SDLP–Dublin government policy-making occurred around the idea of capitalising on perceived unionist divisions in order to achieve a maximalist remit for the Council of Ireland.

The very irreversibility of Faulkner and the SDLP's policy trajectories followed a path-dependent logic in which once plausible or potentially less divisive alternatives were left behind or ignored and instead early decisions carried through across time to produce essentially suboptimal or inefficient agendas. In this historical perspective, the ostensible irrationality of the SDLP's maximalist policy agenda[145] is actually revealed to be the outcome of a series of quite reasonable choices. A self-reinforcing process or path-dependent sequence, which began in 1971, saw the SDLP's desire to maximise gains culminate in an undermining of the party's only cross-communal ally. A similar path-dependent logic affected Faulkner's decision-making. Although his subsequent choices conformed to and proceeded from his 1971 decision, those choices were increasingly constrained by the expectations of the Westminster government and by the seizure of alternative positions by intra-communal rivals such as Paisley, Craig and West. As time progressed, the realistic alternatives open to Faulkner became fewer and more restricted.

4
The Politics of Entrenchment, 1974–85

Westminster policy-making and Northern Irish political entrenchment

This chapter examines the policy direction of the British government and the Northern Irish parties between the collapse of the Sunningdale executive in May 1974 and the Anglo-Irish Agreement in November 1985. The unfolding of historical processes played a determining role in the events of these years. As previous choices continued to work themselves out, the Northern Irish parties became further entrenched within their stated policies and the British government struggled to develop any kind of initiative that would not actually worsen the communal polarisation. Yet, as in previous years, by failing to challenge the inward-focused perspective of the main Northern parties, the absence of consistent or coherent governmental initiatives had the effect of encouraging the pursuit of maximalist goals. For example, Westminster attempted to contain and demoralise the IRA by prolonging 'secret' talks during 1975–6. While there is some evidence to suggest that this was successful, it also encouraged republicans to believe that Britain was contemplating immediate withdrawal and heightened tensions within the unionist community which remained highly suspicious of the long-term intentions of London policy-makers.

The main theme of the chapter, therefore, relates to the absence of a long-term or consistent policy vision on the part of the British government. Importantly, this absence of consistency did not indicate an absence of policy-making *per se*; instead, it reflected an overabundance of competing voices within the decision-making apparatus. The fact that Northern Irish parties drew divergent conclusions as to the long-term intentions of the British government was not so much an intentional objective but was, rather, due to inability of Westminster policy-makers to decide on a single initiative that would not make the situation worse. The second theme of this chapter is that the ambiguity of British policy direction actively facilitated further polarisation and entrenchment within Northern Ireland.

This analysis is based on the available primary evidence and continues to raise serious difficulties for the conventional explanation that the Northern Ireland conflict, and its seemingly intractable persistence, was simply a product of the existence of two irreconcilable ethnic blocs.[1] From this assumption, several political scientists have reasonably argued that since the best way to manage or 'regulate' ethnic division is through power-sharing, Westminster must have pursued consociational objectives. They go on to explain that the Troubles continued as a result of a faulty application of consociational logic – unionists were not sufficiently 'coerced' into sharing power;[2] nationalists were not dissuaded from abandoning the 'Irish dimension';[3] or a stronger Anglo-Irish relationship was not developed.[4] As regards the last argument, this chapter specifically highlights the inadequacies in the claim that the British and Irish governments gradually learned how to 'manage' the conflict and eventually establish the conditions for dialogue between the two warring tribes.[5]

There are several problems with the ethnic conflict narrative, especially with regard to British policy direction during the period covered here. First, as pointed out in the introduction, the idea that the Northern Ireland conflict was fundamentally the product of ethnic division is not only simplistic but misleading. State intervention played a central, but unintended role in facilitating the emergence of divergent perceptions of threats and opportunities and the conflict was created and sustained by a series of historical decisions and omissions. In other words, it was not simply a matter of recognising the 'logic' of consociational power-sharing and starting afresh: history mattered. Linked with this is the fact that the ethnic conflict approach is profoundly ahistorical – it begins from assumptions concerning the management of plural societies and looks to the past for evidence to back up its theories. This goes beyond a hypothesis-testing approach and amounts to a teleological reading back into history of what should have happened. In so doing, reveals an unabashed academic elitism. Thus, Michael Kerr claims that, in part, a 'solution' was not possible in the 1970s because 'an advanced understanding of the complexities of the conflict *was not reached* by either administration'.[6] The implication is that had governmental policy-makers been a little more perceptive or taken a broader perspective – such as that claimed by ethnic conflict academics – years of contention would have been avoided.

The ethnic conflict approach is based on normative assumptions about divided societies, but these are not just theoretical abstractions, for the model claims validity for its prescriptions based on its depiction of the past, yet, unfortunately, when it comes to representing the past, the model amounts to poor history.[7] On the one hand, it completely ignores or misrepresents the empirical record, preferring post-hoc elite interviews to archival documents. It fails to specify the constraints under which governmental and political actors operated, instead positing vague and unsubstantiated notions of ethnic 'motivation'.[8] On the other hand, the ethnic conflict approach fails to test its assumptions against what would have happened had its prescriptions been enacted. Indeed, the historical record suggests that had Britain pursued a more fully-fledged intergovernmental joint authority-style approach with the Irish Republic in the 1970s, the situation would have been even worse. Governmental intervention affected the perceptions of local parties as to what was possible, but the two governments were severely constrained in what they could achieve by what the parties would actually agree to. An over-zealous governmental approach was simply not feasible.

Westminster elites themselves speculated on radical initiatives, from granting Northern Ireland 'dominion status' to what Wilson referred to as his 'nuclear' option – the complete withdrawal of the army and the repudiation of all financial and administrative responsibilities. Wilson's senior policy adviser, the historian Bernard Donoughue, *had* pushed for measures along the lines similar to those expressed by Michael Kerr and Brendan O'Duffy – who, incidentally, imply that such proposals were beyond the imaginative capacity of civil service officials.[9] While his advice counteracted Wilson's inclination to withdraw and the Northern Ireland Office's favouring majority rule, his own preferences of greater Dublin involvement and 'dominion status' were, in turn, resisted by his colleagues as equally unfeasible.[10]

Although earlier chapters have argued that a process of 'policy entrenchment' occurred between the main unionist and nationalist groupings during the 1970s, this chapter emphatically rejects what could be viewed as an underlying implication – namely that, *pace* O'Leary and Tannam, Westminster somehow learned to cope with and mitigate the effects of that entrenchment. First, political environments are often too complex to facilitate what could be termed successful or comprehensive learning.[11] Historians also suggest that even if 'learning' does occur, it is often incomplete and highly contingent; the lessons of history are often filtered through a highly personalised and experiential process.[12] The competing conclusions of Wilson, Rees, Thatcher, Donoughue and the NIO – to name but a few – demonstrate the validity of these insights. Indeed, contrary to the depiction of the British government 'brokering' or 'arbitrating' between two ethnic blocs, state intervention facilitated continued political division between the local political parties. In turn, that local division stymied the efforts of the governmental elites to create what the ethnic conflict school anachronistically depict as a gradual process of political rapprochement. Although the idea of arbitration suggests a lack of strategic interests – indeed, there is no evidence in the official papers to suggest any desire for offering overt support to either nationalism or unionism – the ethnic conflict school obscures that basic insight by claiming that Britain pursued a consociationalist, power-sharing strategy.[13] As Donoughue's example demonstrates, British policy-making had no single discernible objective. Furthermore, even if Britain had possessed a coherent, long-term policy, it would have been frustrated by the divergent agendas of the local elites.

The aftermath of Sunningdale

The period following the Ulster Workers' Council strike therefore witnessed the UUUC and the SDLP continuing with radical policies. Both groups continued to pursue divergent goals with little serious appreciation afforded to their potential cross-communal affect. While this process of entrenchment stemmed in part from the prior initiatives of both the British and Irish governments, it is difficult to envisage what Westminster could have done to begin to reverse a process in which the two Northern factions had invested so much political capital. Perhaps understandably, therefore, the attempt to foster political dialogue in the form of the Constitutional Convention was half-hearted and even disingenuous. Certainly, there is little evidence to suggest that Westminster was gradually learning how to manage or 'arbitrate' the communal polarisation through consociational initiatives.[14] Rather, as Donoughue later pointed out, the British priority was to avoid becoming even more involved in the Northern morass:

> Our policy became one of consolidation, trying to contain terrorism and just get through from year to year. The Irish situation regularly appeared on the agenda of the Cabinet Committee on Ireland, but it

was mainly a question of reporting information rather than debating issues, and rarely was anything taken higher to cabinet.[15]

Although many politicians and civil servants subsequently expressed doubts over the Labour government's affinity with the Sunningdale initiative, Westminster officials were perhaps understandably anxious to abandon the (unratified) December agreement following the May strike. At the beginning of June, for example, the Permanent Under-Secretary, Frank Cooper, was advised that 'The strategy devised by the previous administration ... has now run its course'.[16] Picking up on calls by the unionist leadership for a new assembly, and by Rees's 'detection' of an emergent 'Ulster nationalism', officials claimed that 'the concept that the people of Ulster might themselves try to work out some new political arrangements seems to be the most useful idea ... It is clear that the old system of power-sharing is no longer possible.'[17] The idea of 'power-sharing in a new form' would allow the government to isolate the issue and relegate it to the forum of the Constitutional Convention.[18]

In what was perhaps the widest-ranging and most serious critique, Kenneth Bloomfield identified several weaknesses at the heart of the power-sharing executive.[19] For instance, Bloomfield highlighted what he perceived to be a key failing of Whitelaw's approach – the exclusion of dissenting voices from the executive and Sunningdale talks. Although this was effectively 'self-exclusion' on the part of Paisley, Craig and West through their rejection of the Northern Ireland Constitution Act, Bloomfield points out that this had the knock-on effect of 'bringing the SDLP into the executive in greater strength than would otherwise have been the case'. As such, 'To the public mind, the executive from the start was dominated by the SDLP'. For Bloomfield, the prominence of the SDLP undermined Faulkner's efforts to 'sell' the package to the unionist community – particularly in light of the party's frequent visits to Dublin and its 'special relationship' with the Department of Foreign Affairs. In addition to criticising the unwieldy and superficial division of government departments – including the creation of 'non-job' ministries – Bloomfield concluded that the cross-communal executive faced two further 'great weaknesses'. First, the resignation of any one prominent member would seriously damage its credibility and, given the fragile and constructed nature of executive collective responsibility, could result in further resignations and total collapse. Second, Faulkner lacked the authority typically possessed by chief executives: 'Particular individuals were able on occasions to behave in ways which would have led any Prime Minister ... to sack them.'[20]

In a memorandum prepared for Bloomfield (but which went as far as Cooper and Rees), Maurice Hayes argued that Catholics were extremely 'gloomy ... disillusioned [and] frightened' about the future.[21] While the strike had a 'cathartic effect' in that 'Protestant machismo has probably been sufficiently asserted by [its] success', Hayes claimed that Catholics felt 'bitter' about the collapse of the executive, about the extent to which 'employment in heavy industries [the main force behind the strike] was dominated by Protestants' and about the 'reluctance of the British army to face the situation'. He warned that the lack of trust in the British government coupled with the 'severe psychological blow by the apparent withdrawal of Dublin support' could produce 'total alienation' within the Catholic community; leading to the desertion of the SDLP for either 'abstention or Sinn Féin'. Cooper's response was decidedly unsympathetic. He dismissed Hayes' comments as illustrating 'the disillusionment at present felt by middle-class Catholics, most of whom are non-doers anyway'.[22] As regards the SDLP, he concluded that while 'they have had to contend with a difficult situation ... we have no evidence that their electoral support will wither away'.

The White Paper of July 1974 afforded the SDLP some respite, having as it did a degree of continuity with the Sunningdale initiative: it claimed that both power-sharing and the Irish dimension were still on the (official) political agenda, and elections would be held to discuss Northern Ireland's constitutional future.[23] Behind the scenes, however, the government considered other options, given the 'risk of HMG's interests being seriously challenged during the inevitable period of vacuum'.[24] These included the encouragement of political dialogue through security initiatives such as 'community' policing and the withdrawal of the army to barracks.[25] Ruled out was significant movement on either detention or the Irish dimension since 'No delivery of significance by the South seems possible'.[26] Officials also urged a pragmatic caution in the government's approach to the IRA: 'While the search for a disengagement formula could carry severe risks vis-à-vis Protestant, British Parliamentary v. Irish public opinion, any action which guaranteed the complete end to violence should be given thought'. The overriding priority at this time was, however, the need to avoid another strike and the assuaging of unionist fears. Indeed, official briefings give the impression not of ethnic arbitration but of merely managing the 'backlash':

> The province is now moving ineluctably to demands for a Protestant administration based on majority rule. HMG can restrain the Protestant majority but cannot coerce it beyond a certain point.[27]

Again, in this view, little could be offered to the SDLP:

> The question is therefore no longer what can be done to satisfy the minority, but what the minority ... are prepared to do to strengthen the hand of HMG in consolidating the political gains won for the minority since 1968.

By maintaining what the government saw as 'Utopian aims', both the SDLP and the Irish government were, in fact, strengthening the hand of the UUUC and increasing the possibility of leaving Northern nationalists in a 'posture of permanent and impotent opposition'. This 'crisis management' in the face of continued entrenchment found additional expression in the government's reluctance to use the phrase 'power-sharing', preferring 'government by consent', by which it meant 'any form of government which the two communities in Northern Ireland are prepared voluntarily to operate'.[28] This wording began to appear in government statements from the end of 1974. While at the public level the government was committed to power-sharing, behind the scenes officials continued to urge a retreat from Sunningdale. Thus, one eight-page briefing paper of October 1974 concluded:

> we shall have confrontation with the majority (which we shall lose) unless HMG in effect changes its policy towards the Constitutional Convention by watering down the requirement of power-sharing and the Irish dimension to accommodate Protestant views about how these requirements should be met.[29]

In effect, this meant that government 'objectives in relation to the Catholics must be redefined'. The implicit rationale of such backtracking was defence of Catholics. This meant that

> seeking to give [Catholics] parity in political terms is (a) no longer possible (b) produced no response from them when we tried it; (c) in the present climate is positively harmful to their interests.

The resultant constitutional uncertainty and the ongoing violence coloured the attitudes and tactics of both the SDLP and the UUUC in the aftermath of the strike. The 'truce' by the Provisional IRA and the subsequent commencement – and public awareness – of 'secret' talks with the government did little to temper the policy-making of either grouping during late 1974 and into 1975.[30] For the SDLP, the executive's collapse created a range of internal and external pressures, including that the withdrawal of Dublin's unilateral support, together with a resurgent IRA, left the party isolated both strategically and ideologically. Internal discontent also emerged over the leadership's apparent willingness to abandon its internment policy and to countenance a step-wise implementation of the Council of Ireland.[31] While the obliteration of Faulkner at successive elections demolished the first of the SDLP's policy goals of power-sharing, the withdrawal of support by the Irish government was, in its eyes, potentially even more damaging. Hume, for example, complained that the government's retreat threatened the key concession by Westminster in recognising the 'fundamental right' of Dublin to have a say in the North's affairs. Fitt, meanwhile, claimed that it 'might not fight elections. As it were [we seem] to be on a "hiding to nothing" '.[32] Fitt reiterated these sentiments to the Assembly Party in August: 'Without the Irish dimension, the SDLP has no basis and no seats'. In response, the SDLP called for a strengthening of Dublin's role to persuade Britain to make a 'clear statement ... that power-sharing and the Irish dimension are not negotiable'.[33] This, it believed, could have two possible outcomes – either the Unionist camp would split or Britain would have to enforce its commitment to those ideals. The party's isolated position in Northern Ireland politics led to a fatalistic assessment of the future and an apparent willingness to raise the stakes. Thus, as Cooper spelt out to the Assembly Party: 'A final settlement will probably have to be enforced by joint military action.'[34]

As with the SDLP, the UUUC did not re-evaluate its policy following the 1974 strike. West, for example, argued that while the British government was anxious to establish a devolved settlement, 'we would "power share" along with certain elements but not others'.[35] In the meantime, the coalition grew increasingly suspicious of the talks between government officials and the IRA. Thus, a meeting between Paisley and Rees quickly ended after Paisley reportedly started by asking whether 'Harold Wilson had returned from holiday to discuss the terms [of withdrawal]'.[36] At a subsequent (and unannounced) meeting, Paisley and West demanded that Rees should break off the talks and confront the SDLP on its support for the police.[37] Despite this, the government decided to press ahead with the idea of a Convention in 1975, though the UUUC maintained their opposition to having the SDLP in executive positions. Thus, in response to a suggestion that the Convention might facilitate a power-sharing agreement, and in the presence of William Craig and Ernest Baird, Vanguard member Glenn Barr told a press correspondent that 'We'll not be sharing power with any b- - - republicans [sic]'.[38] West also spelt out

UUUC policy to NIO officials and the newly appointed Convention chair, Robert Lowry:

> The Convention would only last six weeks. UUUC would use their majority to vote through: (i) return to pre-1968 Stormont; (ii) return of local government to pre-Macrory structure; and (iii) 21 members at Westminster.

He claimed that the coalition would press ahead with this strategy, despite warnings from his colleague Enoch Powell that Westminster would not accept such recommendations.[39] West told Lowry that the Convention should be a routine affair based on common parliamentary procedures of putting motions to the floor at 'Second Reading', before allowing committees to 'unravel some of the finer details' at a later stage.[40]

The Constitutional Convention

The May 1975 Convention elections ratified the process of political entrenchment as the UUUC won 47 of the 78 seats and 54.8 per cent of the first preference votes to the UUUC. Meanwhile, the SDLP also roughly maintained its standing with 23.7 per cent of first preference votes and 17 seats.[41] The Convention, and particularly the controversy of the voluntary coalition proposal, has come to characterise both the futility of the Convention in particular and the ineffectiveness of Northern Ireland's politicians in general.[42] The Craig proposal, which would have brought the SDLP into an emergency cabinet based on the Westminster precedent of wartime coalition, has provoked a wealth of speculation and comment over the reactions and motives of those involved. That speculation has traditionally centred either on possible internal UUUC leadership clashes[43] or on counterfactuals involving possible SDLP responses.[44]

However, in reality speculation and outright dismissal have resulted in a skewed perspective on the Convention itself. Rather than the Convention parties working to achieve accommodation, the primary evidence suggests that in fact they continued to pursue divergent goals – instead of bringing the parties together, the Convention facilitated a process of entrenchment. In other words, it perpetuated the suspicions and fears that divided the two main communal parties, rendering any possible accommodation unlikely. The Craig initiative declines in importance when placed in the context of historical continuities and the entrenchment of party policies. Although the parties entered the Convention with ideas on how to achieve certain strategic targets, the evidence suggests that they gave little thought as to how they could achieve these in concert with their opponents. Historical imperatives overrode any possible strategic manoeuvres and little bargaining or negotiating occurred, either 'tacitly' or overtly. Instead, the parties' earlier choices carried over to the Convention and the communal division proceeded in a path-dependent fashion, with the parties merely adding 'layers' of experience to prior conclusions and claims. In this view, the Convention lasted as long as it did because of, rather than in spite of, such mutual suspicions as both groupings sought to avoid the accusation that they had brought it down. Neither the UUUC nor the SDLP viewed the Convention as a means to achieve a settlement; rather, their main concern was to use it as a platform to present their case to Westminster.

The UUUC's primary goal was to achieve a majoritarian, cabinet-based system of government with provision for opposition input in a second-tier committee system. However, this conscious return to Faulkner's June 1971 committee proposals remained relatively unstructured. For example, West told Lowry at the beginning of July that while 'power-sharing at cabinet level was "out" ... He was hopeful that the Faulkner scheme ... might form the basis of agreement with three of the five committees going to [the] opposition.'[45] Despite having been a cabinet minister in the Faulkner government, West sought the advice of NIO officials who had been involved in the original proposal.[46] In addition, he queried power-sharing practices in other countries – to be told by officials that, in the absence of cross-communal loyalties, the importation of power-sharing structures would prove unfeasible.[47]

The UUUC position paper for the talks contained the nucleus of Craig's voluntary coalition idea. The final paragraph (para. 8) described possible scenarios for the establishment of a 'multi-party government', including a pre-election pact or a post-election coalition. In addition, para. 8(iii) referred to a situation 'Where an emergency or crisis ... exists and parties by agreement come together'.[48] However, it is a mistake to view the UUUC proposals as anything more than a 'Green Paper-type' document, which set out possible areas for discussion as the document itself did not enjoy widespread approval or even detailed knowledge within the coalition. Nevertheless, Craig strenuously advocated the idea of voluntary coalition as a workable solution to restoring devolved government, based on a UUUC–SDLP coalition. Unlike Sunningdale, voluntary coalition enjoyed an historical precedent in the Westminster democratic tradition in the form of the wartime cabinet. As Clifford Smyth points out, it logically 'bypassed' the UUUC's opposition to 'enforced power-sharing', and would have allowed it to instal a 'premier who would retain the power to "hire and fire" his cabinet colleagues'.[49] Regardless of intra-party confusion over the concept, this reiteration of a majoritarian veto places the idea firmly within the process of policy entrenchment. The voluntary coalition concept not only consolidated unionist gains through its rejection of executive power-sharing, but also did not really attempt to deal seriously with the SDLP position.

Despite its majoritarian implications, key UUUC personnel believed that the idea did not deal with the key problem of having 'republicans' in government. Paisley, for instance, discounted it during a meeting with Lowry the day after the UUUC document had been passed to the SDLP – crucially, in the presence of Craig and West, and two weeks prior to Craig's final push at the beginning of September.[50] The three admitted that the eight-paragraph document had an ambiguous status within the party:

> The UUUC leaders confirmed that, while the paper as such had not at that point in time been seen by each and every member of the coalition, it was based on principles that had been outlined to the latter and had received their full consensus.

The uncertainty surrounding the proposals that surfaced during the meeting with Paisley appear at odds with Craig's position. The DUP leader, for instance, 'wondered how anyone of integrity could demand the institutionalised right to be a full part of a cabinet which had diverse and opposing ideologies'. When questioned directly by Lowry about para. 8(iii), he responded that he 'was not inclined to support this on the grounds that after such a system had been in operation for even a limited period the UUUC would be under pressure to accept that as proving that it could work and should become permanent'. In contrast, Craig reported that he 'was more inclined to examine it as a possibility without specifying a time period' and described the concept as a 'sprat to catch a mackerel'. This debate was, however, about more than concerns over the future strategic positioning of the UUUC. Paisley's concerns with power-sharing and the trio's general criticism of Rees's security policy reveal the genuine ideological and rational fissure that undermined UUUC cohesion. For his part, Paisley believed that protection of the Union was incompatible with SDLP participation in government, while Craig believed that a halfway house between full majoritarian democracy and committee positions was possible. In short, neither Paisley nor

Craig advocated fully-fledged power-sharing with the SDLP. Both sought to maximise unionist gains, however, with Paisley preferring the simpler and more straightforward policy of outright majoritarianism in contrast to Craig's augmented system.

On the SDLP side, only Fitt expressed unqualified confidence in the voluntary coalition idea, remarking to Lowry that 'Even a temporary solution would be beneficial'.[51] For his part, Hume, like David Trimble – at the time a member of Vanguard – favoured the importation of a US-style presidential system.[52] For Hume, the relative independence of the US president from his or her party could actually facilitate executive power-sharing. The diminution of executive responsibilities – in comparison with both the Sunningdale and the Westminster cabinets – was of less importance than the symbolic achievement of ministerial office within an overall context of an island-wide settlement. However, when questioned about the SDLP's flexibility, he replied that while he himself 'saw a distinction between ministerial office and power ... [SDLP] electors would not'. In contrast to the conventional wisdom that Hume became a steadfast nationalist during the 1970s,[53] he actually displayed certain a degree of willingness to entertain alternative strategic options during the Convention negotiations. Indeed, the willingness of commentators to overstate the ideological and rhetorical levels of Hume's politics not only obscures the constructed nature of that rhetoric, but also misses the point that previous SDLP policies had raised Catholic expectations and increasingly constrained the types of policies the leadership could credibly espouse. Paddy Devlin, for instance, supported Hume's declared flexibility, but admitted that while the SDLP were 'ready to consider any proposal ... they were not prepared to concede on the principle of power-sharing in the cabinet'.[54] In short, Hume and the SDLP remained willing to entertain various proposals and initiatives, but the party continued to judge their seriousness and worthiness on whether they would facilitate the end-goals of power-sharing and greater Dublin involvement.

The escalation of IRA activity during August 1975 placed pressure on both the SDLP and the UUUC.[55] Conscious of the possibility of being accused of a 'sell-out', the SDLP remained reluctant to place any firm commitments on the negotiating table as regards a willingness to sign up to voluntary coalition. The violence also contributed to the UUUC's reluctance to strike a deal with their nationalist counterparts. The traditional linkage of security and constitutional certainty within unionism added to growing discontent with Rees's policies. This resulted not only in a heightened emphasis on security as distinct from political progress, but also decreased any willingness to accept a compromise with the SDLP in the Convention. In response, Paisley called on Rees to 'tell the truth' regarding the IRA talks and claimed that the 'ceasefire is a colossal confidence trick and is providing a smokescreen behind which the IRA, aided by Mr Rees, are preparing for another offensive'.[56] In addition, the DUP leader produced what he claimed was a leaked army document which stated that the army was observing the IRA chief of staff, Seamus Twomey, without arresting him.[57] He concluded that Rees was a 'liar' and demanded his removal from office. As such, Paisley's ultimatum on 4 September did not occur *de novo*, still less was it a calculated attempt to undermine Craig. The only new element in his statement in fact was a threat to resign from the Convention – an understandable escalation given that Rees remained in office despite his earlier demand. Paisley urged Rees to close the incident centres, end the negotiations with the IRA and secure the border. If this did not happen, Paisley warned, Convention members 'will be forced to consider entire withdrawal ... until such times as law and order are re-established'.[58]

For Powell, the voluntary coalition idea combined with the Provisional campaign to produce a two-pronged threat to the maintenance of the Union. As with Paisley, he believed that enhanced security should take priority over a political arrangement with the SDLP:

> My view is that the continuance of the Convention now is contributing to the bloodshed. It is of the highest interest that the proceedings of the Convention should be brought to a conclusion as speedily as possible, whatever the results should be.[59]

For his part, Paisley reiterated his concerns with power-sharing to the Convention Chair on 6 September.[60] He argued that 'in the UUC there was insuperable opposition to [the] SDLP in cabinet', and stated that neither Craig nor West could hope to 'carry' both the coalition and the electorate in pushing a singular solution. Instead, Paisley complained that the SDLP had not shown 'the necessary attitudes at a very early stage' conducive to agreement. Two days later Paisley's UUUC motion against 'republicans taking part in any future Cabinet in Northern Ireland' was passed 37 votes to one – Craig being the single dissenting voice.[61]

The conclusion of the Irish government was that representatives from Paisley's Free Presbyterian Church had intervened at the last minute to precipitate a Damascene conversion of their leader.[62] The account speculated that Paisley 'saw the opportunity of capitalising on the fear and distrust that was growing up amongst unionist supporters for the secret negotiations that appeared to be going on'. Clifford Smyth, on the other hand, dismisses this possibility, citing the fact that Paisley could not have known that Craig would be so soundly defeated in the UUUC vote.[63] Placed in the context of the long-term unionist concern with constitutional and physical security, the Paisley–Powell positions are not so much pragmatic or opportunistic, as consistent with the effort to achieve movement on what was considered to be essential to achieving security – namely, a majoritarian system.

Again, contrary to the most recent accounts of the SDLP's political development, the party maintained a consistent policy in the aftermath of Sunningdale.[64] Peter McLoughlin, for instance, contends that a close 'analysis of what Hume and his colleagues were saying at this time showed that they were thinking more deeply about their political strategy and how they might persuade the unionist community of both its integrity and its validity'.[65] Yet the favoured party strategy remained irredentist rather than persuasive and the SDLP did not divert in any meaningful way from its declared aims of executive power-sharing and a strong, institutionalised Irish dimension. This point was recognised by Hume in the immediate aftermath of the UUUC meeting, when he remarked that he 'was surprised that [the] UUUC had broken on power-sharing when it would have been much more embarrassing for the SDLP to have to take a stand publicly in relation to the Irish dimension'.[66]

Northern Irish party politics, 1975–85

The Constitutional Convention was eventually brought to an end by the British government in March 1976, having illustrated an utter lack of realistic opportunities for establishing a power-sharing administration and the inability of the local parties' to overcome the political entrenchment that had arisen from the early 1970s. While fears of being 'outbid' by their intra-ethnic rivals inhibited the middle-ground parties (the UUP and the SDLP), neither was ultimately subject to the logic of a 'dual party system'.[67] For example, the development of unionist politics after 1976 was not driven merely by a crude desire for political power and intra-bloc dominance. Rather, historically informed perceptions that unionism was losing ground to nationalism, genuine fears that the PIRA was 'winning the war', embedded suspicions of British intentions and the recognition that a strong and united front was necessary to resist these trends were all factors in shaping internal unionist debates and influencing the subsequent development of unionist policy direction. Again, this development was affected by prior choices on issues such as power-sharing and the Irish dimension and the constant need to maintain and mobilise support.

In a similar fashion, the SDLP's policy options were severely constrained by prior choices and, again, contrary to the emphatic claims by some political theorists,[68] fear of ethnic outbidding was not the main factor behind the accession of the overtly nationalistic leadership of Hume and Mallon and the departure of the more instinctively left-wing founders Fitt and Devlin at the end of the 1970s. As previous chapters have demonstrated, a 'greening' of the SDLP occurred in the early 1970s following the general perception that shifting political opportunities for the first time favoured Northern nationalists. Accordingly, the SDLP mobilised Catholic opinion around the idea that an internal settlement with unionism was not a sufficient reflection of those shifts. This attachment to Dublin involvement and the reluctance to settle for power-sharing continued to inspire SDLP policy direction in the aftermath of the Constitutional Convention and would eventually find institutional expression in the Anglo-Irish Agreement.

These divergent factors unsurprisingly contrived to produce the failure of the SDLP–UUP talks of March–September 1976. The talks, which began in the last days of the Convention, were initially held in secret and centred on the theme of exploring 'constitutional proposals for a mutually acceptable form of devolved government'.[69] Certainly, grass-roots unease within the Unionist Party, coupled with Paisley's condemnation of the talks, constrained the Unionist delegates' room for manoeuvre. However, the discussions finally wound up in September with the Unionist Party's Martin Smyth explaining that 'there was no point in continuing with the talks unless there was a shift of ground by the SDLP or a response from the British government or other parties'.[70] The SDLP favoured some of the ideas contained in the Convention Report, such as the need for a reduction in the power of the Secretary of State and the possibility of creating a 'governor-like figure'. However, it refused to countenance other unionist proposals, including extra Westminster representation or the suggestion that Paisley should be included in any devolved executive. While the SDLP claimed that power-sharing rather than a Council of Ireland was its main priority, it remained wedded to the need for Dublin's involvement and suspicious of any proposals that would strengthen the North's ties to the UK.[71] Again, it pointed out that it 'would not be able to join in any government of which Dr Paisley was a member in view of his declared anti-Catholicism'.[72]

The resulting impasse did not seem to bother the NIO, which was actually reluctant to offer support when the knowledge of the talks became public in May. As the newly appointed Permanent Under-Secretary, Brian Cubbon, explained in June:

> [there is a risk that] the talks between the Official Unionists and the SDLP would develop a euphoria and a momentum which could lead us being asked to recall the Convention in order to discuss and ratify a flimsy scheme agreed between the parties.[73]

For Cubbon, Paisley's opposition rendered the talks essentially pointless, but he warned that the Unionist Party could use the talks as a way of exerting leverage on the government to grant concessions and thereby raise its profile within the unionist community. He claimed that the Unionists could use the talks to ask for a restoration of the Convention 'as a way of dumping on our lap the problem of coping with Paisley'. Cubbon's implication was that, as with the NIO, the Unionist Party most likely considered that Paisley's exclusion rendered the talks pointless, as they were not strong enough to resist the likely condemnation of any deal with the SDLP. He therefore urged that 'our first line of defence is the SDLP, whom we would want to realise that they had a lot to lose in being conned into a superficial agreement'. Given the gulf that existed between the SDLP and the UUP, the NIO opted to pursue a minimalist policy regarding the two parties and the prospects of any internal accommodation.[74] The marginalisation of the North's local parties was therefore circular and self-reinforcing – the policy divisions effectively closed all options for a credible political accommodation and the lack of options in turn militated against the likelihood of any genuine power-sharing proposals emerging from the local or state levels.

The election of Hume as leader of the SDLP in 1979 simply ratified the process of entrenchment which was initiated in July 1971. The traditional account of the party's political development between the Constitutional Convention and the Anglo-Irish Agreement stresses Hume's attempts to 'Europeanise' or 'internationalise' the Northern Ireland problem.[75] While Michael Cunningham has questioned the ideological coherence of Hume's attempt to broaden the definition of the conflict, claiming that it failed to recognise unionist values,[76] in fact SDLP tactics in the late 1970s and 1980s were quite rational and were influenced by the constraining influence of earlier choices. That is to say, the party's maximalism carried through to restrict its later options and the apparent radicalisation and the Humean broadening of the party's tactics were merely 'layers' added to an established policy path. Therefore, the cumulative effect of historical choices rather than simply ideological preferences shaped the SDLP's policy-making after 1976. Likewise, those choices limited the options available to successive Dublin governments. Although successive Southern governments, again, displayed a broader strategic perspective, they too could not move beyond impractical strategies – notably, Garret FitzGerald's desire to 'reach out' to Northern Protestants as part of his 'constitutional crusade' of the early 1980s.[77] In short, critical decisions made in the early 1970s continued to affect the trajectory of Irish nationalism during the 1980s. Both Dublin and the SDLP pursued maximalist policies that were at odds with the sentiments of the unionist community. A layered, cumulative maximalism characterised nationalist strategy at this point. The 'persuasion' of Ulster unionists to the 'correctness' of the nationalist vision[78] was in fact neither practical nor desirable. Instead, once-plausible moderate alternatives had long been ruled out and an inward perspective continued to form the basis of nationalist decision-making.

The early policy direction of the SDLP carried through to influence its decisions throughout the late 1970s and into the 1980s. The critical end-goals of power-sharing and the Irish dimension remained in place as both Northern and Southern nationalism sought to outmanoeuvre unionism by highlighting its apparent 'pathological' unreasonableness.[79] Hume's conception of what McLoughlin terms 'persuasion' amounted to the adoption of a strategy of attempting to expose this unreasonableness in several spheres – including the United States and European Parliament. Taking the European Community as a model of conflict resolution, Hume argued that cooperation depended on the establishment of institutions that accommodate communal rights and identities.[80] His application of this insight to Northern Ireland sought to undercut traditional unionist suspicions by portraying them as vetoes and claimed that unless Britain became a 'persuader' for Irish unity and removed the constitutional guarantee, unionists would never agree to negotiate with nationalists. Only then, he contended, would an 'agreed Ireland' be possible.[81] Hume's apparent recasting of the Northern Ireland problem proved to be influential in the proceedings and conclusions of the New Ireland Forum (1983–4). Convened by Fitzgerald in order to facilitate 'consultations on the manner in which lasting peace and stability could be achieved in a new Ireland … and to report on possible new structures and processes through which this objective might be achieved',[82] it also provided a mechanism to bolster the SDLP against resurgent republicanism.[83] The Forum's conclusions chimed with traditional nationalist thinking – any solution must occur in an all-Ireland context – all but ignoring unionist difficulties with sharing power with a party dedicated to overturning the Union and with a settlement that ensured a Dublin role in running Northern Ireland.

In a very real sense, therefore, 1973–6 set parameters on what the local Northern Irish parties were willing to concede and, hence, on the shape of any future political initiative. Whereas, for the SDLP, the priorities remained an executive role and Dublin involvement, Ulster unionism divided between at least three policy options: devolution, integration and independence. While the independence received at best desultory support, the other two options threatened to split the Unionist Party itself. Devolutionists within the party promoted the idea of an executive consisting of supporters of the Northern Ireland state, while integrationists, among them James Molyneaux, who assumed leadership of the party in 1979, favoured a continuation of direct rule – albeit with an enhanced local administration – and stronger links to British politics. Having effectively ruled out the type of 'Irish dimension' favoured by the SDLP, the British government was understandably unwilling to set up any strong initiative on either of the first two options creating an unmistakable dynamic that perpetuated direct rule. Coupled with these policy debates, the ongoing paramilitary campaign by the IRA continued to exert a decisive influence on unionist politics in the late 1970s and into the 1980s. Thus, in May 1977 – and in a conscious echo of 1974 – Paisley and the rump of the Vanguard Party were instrumental in initiating a general strike in order to demonstrate unease at the government's response to IRA violence and to indicate the level of support for a majority rule administration.[84] Unlike 1974, the May 1977 strike was strongly opposed by both the Unionist Party and the Orange Order. In fact, grass-roots disquiet over this opposition led the Order to reconsider its initial position. The process of political reflection, however, concluded that the Paisley and Baird's warnings that Britain was on the verge of withdrawing were mistaken. Instead, the Order reiterated its original line and urged cooperation with the security forces.[85] The lack of support from the Unionist Party, the Orange Order and crucially, the power workers meant that a repeat of the earlier strike was unlikely and its failure precipitated the final dissolution of the UUUC in November 1977.

Power-sharing and Irish dimension suspicions continued to shape the DUP's attitude to political initiatives in the aftermath of the Constitutional Convention. Although it expressed a willingness to enter talks with the SDLP in 1979, the latter's refusal to concede its views on the necessity of institutionalised Dublin involvement precipitated a DUP walkout in early 1980.[86] As Alvin Jackson points out, given the breadth of division between nationalist and unionist parties – indeed, the Unionist Party boycotted the talks on the basis that it believed they would not wield an acceptable form of devolution – there was little opportunity to achieve any substantial measure of agreement at this time.[87] Nevertheless, the DUP continued to maintain that there could be what its deputy leader, Peter Robinson, called a possibility of 'giving the SDLP a role in Northern Ireland ... and of normalising relations with the Republic and working together on common problems providing the union was recognised'. Commenting on these developments, the journalist Ed Moloney claimed that the British government was unsure about how to react to what it perceived as a new 'liberal' side to the DUP.[88] In fact, if Moloney's assessment of British uncertainty is correct, it points to the government failing to 'learn' the lesson that it was the lack of appropriate security and constitutional guarantees that had, in large part, precipitated the collapse of the Convention discussions in the summer of 1975. Indeed, the DUP offered some support to Secretary of State James Prior's idea of 'rolling devolution' through which powers would eventually be restored through a Northern assembly. Facing what he later referred to as the 'disturbing' prospect that direct rule 'was coming to be seen as permanent', Prior also believed that a locally oriented political initiative was necessary to counteract the 'flood of support for more extreme attitudes' following the 1981 hunger strikes.[89] However, according to his memoirs, his emphasis on the 'Irish dimension' was excised from the final draft of the 1982 White Paper, *Northern Ireland: A Framework for Devolution* (Cmnd. 8541), by Prime Minister Thatcher.[90] The resultant assembly was boycotted by the SDLP due to its perceived weaknesses on power-sharing and the Irish dimension. However, as several commentators have pointed out, its anodyne nature and unionist orientation may in fact have distracted unionist leaders from the intermittent governmental negotiations which had begun in 1980 and had culminated in the signing of the Anglo-Irish Agreement at Hillsborough in November 1985.[91]

The subsequent impotence of Ulster unionism in the face of the Anglo-Irish Agreement has been often noted;[92] furthermore, commentators have suggested that the DUP's 'intransigence' formed 'part of the reason for the imposition of the accord'.[93] Certainly, British devolution proposals provoked strong reactions within Ulster unionism generally, but the idea that unionism struggled in the face of a new power 'asymmetry' is but one level of analysis.[94] Despite apparent and perceived powerlessness, at the level of policy implementation, unionist resistance and security concerns in fact definitively shaped the agenda of debate – the Anglo-Irish Agreement remained in place, but a policy 'drift' occurred in its operation. In other words, despite the Anglo-Irish Agreement's institutionalisation of the Irish dimension, continued unionist resistance to the notion of increased Dublin involvement – through the deployment of agenda-setting rhetoric – served to modify the Agreement's implementation at ground level. The process to restore power-sharing to the North between 1998 and 2007 was made against the backdrop of constitutional and security guarantees that would satisfy unionist sentiments. In this regard, the idea that the Anglo-Irish Agreement was a precursor to the 1998 Good Friday Agreement is not wholly accurate. Unionist resistance to the Anglo-Irish Agreement served to nullify the idea that the Irish dimension could be 'reduced' if power-sharing structures were established. In other words, even if governmental elites believed that what O'Leary and McGarry refer to as 'coercive consociationalism' was possible, the very fact that both Irish nationalist groupings and the British government went some way towards meeting basic unionist demands in 1998 and 2007 suggests otherwise.[95] Indeed, the contrary argument could be made that at the level of agenda-setting, or what political scientists term the 'hidden face of power',[96] unionist opposition to the terms and operation of the Anglo-Irish Agreement had a decisive effect on future political developments in the North, in the process rendering those terms and their implementation redundant.

Arbitration, distancing and security – British state responses to entrenchment

The fact that there was no overarching strategy does not mean that there was a complete absence of a long-term vision within Westminster in the late 1970s and early 1980s. Arguably, the problem was that there were too many grand schemes. Wilson, for instance, had made numerous references to reunification and greater Dublin involvement during his time in Opposition in the 1960s and early 1970s. Following te collapse of the power-sharing executive in May 1974 he held discussions with his senior policy team, including Robert Armstrong, John Hunt, Joe Haines and Bernard Donoughue, about the possibility of carrying out something Donoughue described as 'unmentionable' – Dominion status or complete withdrawal.[97] Wilson returned to the theme in what he himself called an 'apocalyptic note' in January 1976.[98] In the memorandum, Wilson alerted his advisers to the possibility of terrorist escalation or major industrial unrest and claimed that

In either circumstance HMG would be unable to exercise control of law and order and to ensure peaceful, democratic, civil government. The only solution therefore would be one or other variety of withdrawal and the abnegation of responsibilities for the interior affairs of Northern Ireland in the wider international community. It would mean clear legal, constitutional separation.

Wilson believed that the easiest way to ensure separation would be to grant the North Dominion status – in effect, making it, he said, an independent republic outside the Commonwealth. Despite the inevitable communal bloodbath and negative international reaction, he believed that the 'purblind fanaticism' of sections of the North's population had brought matters to a head and that the government had to ensure that the worst-case scenario 'does not happen in the circumstances we may shortly be facing'. In response, Wilson's officials emphasised that while the 'situation is likely to come to a crunch in the next few months … the prospect of [it] becoming ungovernable … now seems rather less likely than it did at the time when you dictated your minute'.[99] The officials recognised that 'At the end of the day no solution is possible unless the Loyalists are prepared to accept it'. They continued to believe that accommodation was possible and that it could take the form of an optimistically named 'Ministry of all the Talents', which would be elected on a proportional basis and operate according to the principles of voluntary coalition. The officials urged Wilson not to take precipitate action but to consider his options carefully before bringing the possibility of withdrawal before his colleagues. The memorandum concluded with the suggestion that if he thought it 'would be helpful', the cabinet secretary and head of the civil service, John Hunt, and head of the Northern Ireland civil service, Frank Cooper, could come 'to have a word' about those options.

The existence of competing viewpoints, coupled with the polarisation of the Northern Ireland political elites, meant that power-sharing was not a priority for Westminster following the collapse of the Sunningdale executive. Indeed, even before the convening of the Convention, Westminster officials had begun planning for what they perceived as the likely contingency that it would fail to leave aside 'the majority divisive issues' and agree 'on individual' ones.[100] Arguably, however, bureaucratic and procedural concerns were at the heart of the officials' disquiet. Thus, the briefing papers call for an overhaul in the direct rule set-up following the end of the Convention, pointing to administrative friction between the Belfast and London offices of the NIO, and policy discontinuities as examples of 'inefficiencies' in the 'existing arrangements'. The February 1975 briefing set the template for the later ambiguities that can be detected in the government's attitude to the administration of the North: 'If we are faced with long-term direct rule there is much to be said for making it clear that we are embarking on a semi-permanent arrangement rather than a purely temporary one.' Although the officials had begun to sketch ideas about the future shape of direct rule – including a Governor-type office for a 'Minister-Resident' and enhanced local government powers – there is no evidence of an overarching vision of ethnic arbitration. Instead, officials warned that government options were severely limited and that while there were 'formidable' arguments for reform of existing structures, 'the scope for change is, however, not all that great'. In other words, the problem was not that Westminster did not recognise that changes could be made; rather, it was that no 'solutions' existed that would not possibly make the situation worse.

In the late spring and early summer of 1975, NIO briefings were still stressing the government's inability to 'impose a solution'.[101] Thus, officials warned that

> It may ... prove to be the case that we shall have to abandon any hope of devolution in the short term and that this will involve continuing direct rule in one form or another. It may also mean that we shall have to consider a more fundamental change of policy which, in effect, will mean either moving towards some form of integration or deliberately 'distancing' Northern Ireland from Great Britain.

The idea of 'distancing' quickly gained currency among some NIO officials, who believed that while the 'essential characteristics' of direct rule would remain in place – that is, legislation would still be enacted from Westminster and the province headed by UK ministers – the 'execution of policy would be placed on a more local footing'.[102] In other words,

> By 'distancing' is meant the reduction of our commitments in Northern Ireland in constitutional, military, and economic terms – and the relegation of the Northern Ireland problem to a place of lesser importance than it currently occupies on the British political scene.

Officials believed that the machinery of government could be incrementally altered 'to build up the powers of distancing over a period of time' and include the possibility of appointing local people to head the civil service departments, granting enhanced powers to local government authorities, appointing a commission to oversee the transfer of reserved matters and the establishment of a Minister-Resident. Furthermore, the NIO believed that the 'democratic deficit' created by the so-called 'Macrory Gap' – namely, the diminution of powers and the subsequent lack of accountability at local government level and political participation more generally – could be tackled through a 'reduction in the government's involvement' and the strengthening of local administrative structures.[103] Although officials were concerned to 'present it as a positive process' that could facilitate local involvement in politics, dialogue and cooperation, this should not be equated with the notion of a long-term Westminster project to arbitrate between ethnic communities. In the first instance, the objective was to set 'a limit to the period of direct rule'.[104] However, the NIO categorically rejected the institutionalisation or prioritisation of power-sharing. Thus, the chair of the Northern Ireland Committee, Sir John Hunt, pointed out that although 'distancing' would assist in avoiding an open-ended commitment to direct rule, the government should also avoid committing itself to any one option and that, as such:

> Majority rule could best be presented not as an alternative to distancing based on direct rule but as an option which might be considered in the longer term if the majority should themselves in our judgment be prepared to act in a responsible fashion and to respect entrenched safeguards which the minority regarded as satisfactory.

Given the pre-Convention manifesto pledges and the fall-out from the voluntary coalition proposal in September 1975, it is understandable that government officials did not rule out the possibility of countenancing some form of majoritarian devolution. Among the obstacles to this, however, was the fact that 'the government is widely perceived as having nailed its colours to the mast of joint rule between Protestants and Catholics'.[105] In addition, pressure from the Irish government before the United Nations and the likely possibility that the SDLP would complain of Westminster 'knowingly abandoning the minority to their fate' militated against an easy acquiescence in the UUUC's majoritarian preferences. Despite this, officials argued that sanctions could be brought to bear to 'ensure that minority safeguards were not ignored or jettisoned' in any new devolved government – including financial penalties and the threat of a return to direct rule or 'severance of the UK link'. Although these plans were contingent on the Convention Report and therefore not fleshed out in detail, they nevertheless serve as evidence of a strand of thinking within Westminster that power-sharing was not a *sine qua non* of government policy and that majoritarian devolution was a real possibility. Thus, the briefing concluded that 'The re-establishment of majority rule could be defended as a not unreasonable settlement in a democracy. The Convention Report will present us with an opportunity for taking this course.'

Frank Cooper alluded to the lack of a definitive agenda during a meeting of senior officials at the beginning of October 1975.[106] While he emphasised that there was no pressure within the government for withdrawal and that 'Repartition and integration were equally non-starters', beyond the need to 'reconsider' the direct rule machinery of government, Cooper left open the possibility of a range of initiatives. These included a referendum on continued direct rule or an internal 'accommodation' and the vaguely expressed sentiment that 'Perhaps it was ... necessary to replace the current politicians [who] had mostly been in the game too long'. As regards the idea of 'arbitration', the minutes note that one official did broach the topic, but only in making the 'suggestion ... that a skilled mediator might help'. Finally, Cooper alluded to the need to keep 'in touch with the South', which, although it could offer no positive intervention given the risk of raising loyalist suspicions, could nevertheless cause the government acute international embarrassment.[107]

Despite the openness of certain sections of the NIO to a range of possibilities and the interest shown in majoritarian devolution and a 'distanced' approach, other officials were more reticent over the question of a major policy initiative, warning that

> unless one can be sure that what one is leaving behind is an inherently stable form of government, any withdrawal of the British presence which removes the restraint on Protestant domination is likely to lead to a scale of disturbances which would cause much trouble for Great Britain ...[108]

Indeed, Donoughue was most exercised about the trend of thinking within the NIO. In a September memorandum to the prime minister, he claimed that the officials' advice on future policy options was 'totally inadequate' – specifically, the policy they recommended, 'a mixture of majority rule and "distancing", could be disastrous'.[109] Furthermore, he pointed out, the officials did not give sufficient attention to Wilson's preference for a joint Anglo-Irish approach and that they 'show their hand' in espousing majority rule. Donoughue rejected the coupling of distancing and majority rule since the government would find it virtually impossible to exert any influence over the projected 'Protestant regime' and guarantee minority safeguards. Elaborating on this, Donoughue pointed out that:

> Officials admit that there is a 'risk' that more of the Catholic population might be driven actively to sympathise with the IRA; it is not a risk but a bloody certainty, since under permanent majority rule they would have absolutely no other outlet for their legitimate aspirations. It is pie in the sky that the Catholics "would participate in security" in this kind of situation.

As such, he warned that the North would be no more geographically 'distant' but a great deal closer to a civil war, which would have inevitable repercussions in Britain. He rejected the idea that 'the Irish dimension' would disappear with 'distancing'; on the contrary, 'The return to majority Protestants rule and "distancing" by the United Kingdom will certainly produce a reappearance of the Irish dimension'. Given these arguments, it is unsurprising that Donoughue's assessment of the 'distancing' proposal was unequivocal: 'It is a formula for continued disaster and violence in the North.' Donoughue later pointed out that while he had held 'little sympathy towards the dour Orangemen', he had subsequently moderated his pro-nationalist beliefs.[110] At the time he was convinced that 'the Northern Ireland question could never be resolved when confined within the historic and parochial context of the United Kingdom ... I was particularly concerned to involve the Republic of Ireland ...' While he favoured what he called 'radical long-term thinking', such as making Northern Ireland a Dominion on a par with Canada, it is far from certain how helpful such proposals would have proved.

The multilayered and often contradictory processes that shaped British policy-making in the constitutional arena were also in evidence as regards security issues. Indeed, the very fact that state policy-making was context-specific and singularly lacking in any long-term, overarching vision of ethnic arbitration suggests that the tendency to separate 'politics' from 'security' obscures and misrepresents the historical record. For example, having assumed that governmental elites targeted consociational power-sharing as the most reasonable way to broker a settlement, McGarry and O'Leary claim that 'under [Merlyn] Rees' successor, Roy Mason, wide-ranging political initiatives were shunned lest they heighten expectations and create instability'. Instead, they argue, British policy-makers 'partitioned' security and political proposals, and concentrated on the former, decisively turning away from the latter.[111] As the primary evidence reveals, however, 'much of the new arrangements were in place before Mason assumed office' in September 1976.[112]

It is therefore anachronistic and inaccurate to portray British policy-making as following a long-term agenda. A more historically sensitive approach – one that, unsurprisingly, chimes with the primary material – points out that policy decisions were made to deal with historically unfolding events. Emphatically, this is not to suggest that it is impossible to identify cross-time trends in British policy-making, it is only to point out that it is unreasonable to assume that British state intervention could have possibly followed a lucid vision of how best to manage or arbitrate an ethnic conflict when that conflict itself was constantly changing. Indeed, the government's response to the Provisional IRA ceasefire during 1975 points to a calculated effort to marginalise the republican movement rather than accommodate it. Although Rees offered a cautious appraisal of the relative success of this strategy in November 1975, he also warned Wilson that it could well provoke an intense 'suicidal' counter-response by the Provisionals, including an extensive bombing campaign in Britain.[113] Indeed, rather than presenting a coherent vision of managing the conflict, Rees frankly admitted that 'what they [the IRA] might do next is difficult to predict'. Although he reported that 1,122 people had been charged with terrorist offences that year, he advised against 'going back to "hard" security policies, which have not worked in the past' or 'giving the Provisionals what they want, which would set the Protestants at our throats'.

Rees's assessment was based on secret talks with a republican 'contact', who had been accompanied on one occasion by what the report refers to as a 'notorious "provisional priest" ', 'to bear witness [to the leadership] that he had put the party line faithfully to us'. According to Rees, there had been no recent direct contact with Sinn Féin because the party had refused to meet the government in the absence of a declaration of intent to withdraw. Nevertheless, he gained the impression from the 'contact' that the leadership was 'aware of the lack of support in urban Catholic areas ... for a return to all-out violence' and that there was an emerging groundswell of discontent with what was perceived as an insufficiently radical leadership. The situation was serious enough for Rees to warn Wilson that the Ruairí Ó'Brádaigh-Dáithí Ó'Conaill faction 'might be overthrown by new leaders' who would be prepared to escalate the armed campaign. In addition, Rees reported that 'discrete contacts' between the paramilitary leaderships were 'currently' being held in The Netherlands, 'ostensibly to discuss their respective cooperative ventures'. Despite these talks, Rees reported that

> the UDA have cold-shouldered an approach from the Provisionals about political terms for the end of their campaign. O'Brady [Ó Brádaigh] would like to try now with the Protestant politicians but does not know how to go about this with any hope of success.[114]

The IRA ceasefire had emerged from secret meetings in Derry at the end of 1974, at the same time as republicans were meeting with Church leaders in Feakle, Co. Clare.[115] In fact, the Provisionals had been in secret contact with James Allan of the NIO and Michael Oatley of the British Secret Intelligence Service since the IRA ceasefire of 1972.[116] Prior to the ceasefire of 1975, the IRA had claimed that 'It is sovereignty rather than political or territorial interests, which is the basic issue'.[117] Furthermore, it demanded that the British government establish a

> Constituent Assembly elected by the people of Ireland through universal adult suffrage and proportional representation ... to draft a new All-Ireland Constitution which would provide for a Provincial Parliament for Ulster (9 Counties) with meaningful powers.

Other demands included a 'public commitment by the British government to withdraw from Ireland within twelve months of the adoption of the new All-Ireland Constitution', a declaration of amnesty for political prisoners and the initiation of tripartite talks with 'Loyalist and British Army Forces to secure their cooperation in the implementation of the ceasefire and the maintenance of community peace'. In effect, the IRA was presenting the British government with terms for surrender. That the government continued to negotiate with the movement and maintain the ceasefire until September 1975 indicates that it had an alternative vision. Indeed, the Church leader's assessment of the republican movement would have offered it encouragement that a more nuanced approach was possible rather than simply rejecting the Provisionals' demands. Thus, the Church leaders told Rees that

> The representatives of the political wing appreciated that although they could continue to wage an armed struggle indefinitely, they could never hope by those means to win [the] struggle [for] men's minds.[118]

British strategy during 1975 appears to have been to reject republican demands for a statement for withdrawal, but at the same time, conveying the message that they needed help to create *'circumstances out of which the structures of disengagement can naturally grow'*.[119] By late summer, it had become apparent to the Provisionals that movement was not going to be forthcoming and they began a 'step-wise' withdrawal from the ceasefire and in order to return to the armed campaign.[120] At this point, Rees himself had come under sustained criticism from Unionist and Conservative MPs over the fact that known republican leaders such as Seamus Twomey had been seen on the streets of Belfast without being arrested. Garret FitzGerald had also complained to Rees following the arrest of Ó Conaill in Dublin, who had been carrying what appeared to be a document setting out terms for a truce between the Provisionals and the British army.[121] By this point, Rees's line that he was not engaged in secret negotiations, while literally true, appeared disingenuous. Despite subsequent claim in his memoirs that the talks had concluded by the end of 1975, recently released material reveals that they had in fact continued well into 1976 – and beyond.[122] Thus, the British government 'contact' reported in February of that year that Ó Brádaigh and Billy McKee said that they 'had both genuinely come to terms with loyalist leaders, but their attempts had been frustrated'.[123] Again, the republican leaders reiterated that 'nothing short of a British government statement of long-term intentions (to withdraw from Ireland) would provide conditions to bring the two communities together in a search for peace'. The meeting concluded with an agreement for the further 'exchange of views through the contact'.

Following the collapse of the ceasefire and the Convention, government policy-making continued to respond to a changing political context, as an official memorandum of June 1977 explained:

> The defeat of terrorism, agreement on durable and acceptable constitutional arrangements, and the improvement of the economy are interdependent, and lie at the heart of the government's policy.[124]

The move away from what Rees called 'major initiatives' was therefore a response to the political entrenchment as revealed in the outcome of the Constitutional Convention.[125] As such, he advised the cabinet that

> Direct rule would have to continue ... We would need to avoid any sense of crisis or drama and to make clear that there was no question of our withdrawing from our responsibilities'.[126]

Having begun planning for a reformed machinery of government even before the Convention met, it is unsurprising that Westminster was reluctant to countenance further power-sharing proposals during the late 1970s. The political entrenchment and divergent policies among the North's political parties severely limited the government's scope for manoeuvre. This also affected its capacity for 'insulating' or 'distancing' the North's politics. The reality of the situation for British policy-makers was therefore that:

> In the absence of a devolved political system, it is almost certain that consensus on future arrangements will not emerge from within. Moreover, increasingly we must decide in a United Kingdom, not a Northern Ireland context.[127]

Contradictions, competing voices, ostensible incoherence and ad hoc reactions, rather than a comprehensive overarching vision, continued to characterise British policy-making in Northern Ireland in the aftermath of the Convention and direct rule was viewed as a way of 'essentially buying time before we opted for a long-term solution'.[128]

Towards the Anglo-Irish Agreement

For Margaret Thatcher, the Anglo-Irish Agreement was the immediate outcome of what she had identified as a pressing 'need for greater security'.[129] For the then Taoiseach, Garret FitzGerald, however, the need to tackle nationalist alienation and constrain the rise of Sinn Féin in the aftermath of the hunger strikes provided the original impetus for closer governmental cooperation.[130] Amidst the plethora of academic studies, the 'nationalist alienation' and 'security cooperation' theses find echoes in recent histories by Paul Bew and Henry Patterson.[131] For Patterson, the Thatcherite concern with security was shaped by unionist arguments that the Republic 'was not doing its bit in the struggle against IRA'; while Bew points out that despite the Agreement's declared intention of facilitating cross-communal devolution, it was not possible to 'knock out' its Irish dimension – namely, the consultative Inter-Governmental Conference. In Eamonn O'Kane's recent analysis, on the other hand, the New Ireland Forum is evidence of the recognition by Southern elites of the 'need to move away from stressing the traditional belief in the inevitability of Irish unity, to looking at how the situation within the North could be stabilised'.[132] An additional factor in convincing Thatcher to support the Agreement came in the form of behind-the-scenes pressure from the Reagan administration. The change in traditional Washington disinterest originated from the White House's attempt to create what one National Security Council official called a 'lever' against the Speaker, Tip O'Neill's criticism of Reagan's Nicaragua policy. In order to get aid money through to the Nicaraguan 'Contras', the White House dangled a stronger Irish policy as a carrot to entice O'Neill – himself a long-time ally of Hume – to tone down his trenchant attack on the administration's Central American policy.[133]

While these accounts stress contingent events and a gradually unfolding historical development in Anglo-Irish and Northern Irish politics, the ethnic conflict model argues that the Anglo-Irish Agreement was the rational outcome of inter-governmental arbitration. Specifically, the model argues that the Agreement represented a recognition by government policy-makers that the best way to manage the Northern conflict was to offer the warring factions – particularly, the Ulster unionist community – 'selective incentives to induce them to accept power-sharing'.[134] While both the Thatcher and FitzGerald accounts can be reconciled under a rubric of governmental self-interest, they, like the ethnic-conflict approach, underplay the range of historical constraints that affected political developments in the 1980s and that effectively set parameters on what the state policy-makers could actually achieve. As earlier chapters have demonstrated, those constraints emerged early in the Troubles and that, contrary to the ethnic conflict approach, it was the historical choices of the local elites that severely limited what governmental actors could actually hope to achieve.

As O'Kane points out, the ethnic conflict model struggles to accommodate the empirical record in the case of the 1985 Agreement. Thus, the McGarry–O'Leary 'coercive consociationalism' view is undermined by their implicit recognition that the Inter-Governmental Conference was a permanent feature of the new structure and would be, in theory, unaffected by unionist acquiescence in power-sharing.[135] O'Leary and McGarry's metaphor of the 'twin tracks' of devolution and Dublin involvement is, therefore, a closer description of the Agreement's essential architecture than the post-hoc reading that the Agreement was part of an overarching ethno-nationalist arbitration strategy. Indeed, even if McGarry and O'Leary and Etain Tannam are correct in divining governmental intentions, the pertinent fact remains that, barring an anachronistic 'back-reading' of an ethnic perspective, there is no logical reason why those intentions could be separated from the long-term historical processes that shaped the Anglo-Irish negotiating process. In this, McGarry and O'Leary do recognise that a reputed nationalistic bias of the final agreement was a vindication of Hume and the SDLP's long-term policy of establishing an institutional role for Dublin, regardless of unionist opposition.[136] The outstanding and unrecognised methodological question concerns sequencing: the ethnic conflict model projects what is an ostensibly rational approach to conflict management back onto governmental elites with no understanding of the historical processes that shape and constrain governmental thinking. This not only distorts the historical record, but ignores the role of non-state actors in helping to create those constraints and those processes in the first instance.

A second problem surrounds the issues of timing and pace. The disjuncture between ethnic conflict representations and the historical record throws light on this – namely, that the facts do not fit the description of 'ethnic policy learning' or state arbitration. In other words, Tannam's argument that Britain eventually learned how to manage the Northern conflict leaves unanswered a host of questions regarding how where and when that learning took place and why it took so long – at least over a decade – to occur. In this regard, Alvin Jackson's historically informed verdict that the two governments 'cherry picked those lessons from Sunningdale which they felt they could stomach, while leaving other unpalatable truths untouched',[137] although in some ways more provisional than the overarching ethnic conflict thesis, is arguably a more accurate reflection of political realities. Indeed, the available archival sources chime with a more ad hoc reading of government policymaking. For example, the primary material reveals that while British officials were debating whether they could 'encourage the paramilitaries ... to "go political" ' in 1976, the argument for offering incentives to either the paramilitaries or local politicians was rejected following the recognition that

> The extent to which HMG can hope to influence the basic political forces in Northern Ireland by 'education' ... seems small. This strategy has fewer prospects of success than our attempts to shift majority opinion by appealing to the rationality of majority leaders, which have so far failed.[138]

In short, although the British government recognised that the local elites could be offered incentives or disincentives to encourage desired responses, it was also acutely aware that those elites, like itself and the Irish government, were severely constrained by long-term and ongoing historical processes. In short, in the view of the Westminster officials, the local elites faced too many limitations: 'The plain fact is that the present generation of political leaders are finished. Their attitudes are fossilised. They are unable to see the big picture because they are involved with local detail.'[139] The ad hoc or short-term nature of government policy-making is underscored by the fact that the Northern Ireland political local leaders were no more or no less constrained by historical forces than Westminster officials were. This was something that the officials were well aware of: 'Direct rule has now assumed a rather different appearance – that of an enduring system of government during which HMG does not intend to take political initiatives.'[140]

The assertion that a more 'inclusive' process, or one that would have raised the authority of the South, would have had a better effect on community relations and eased the political stalemate, is extremely dubious. As pointed out, it is based on an anachronistic methodology that reads normative assumptions about how to deal with ethnic conflicts back into the historical record with little awareness of the importance of sequencing or context. The lack of knowledge about the empirical record surfaces in the striking absence of the question of what would have happened had Britain increased Southern involvement or negotiated openly with the IRA. Given the continued obduracy of the republican movement and the embedded suspicions of the direction of political developments within unionism, the answer seems relatively straightforward and is one that Westminster was well aware of – such proposals would have made the situation irrevocably worse. Thus, while state intervention encouraged political entrenchment, when faced with the results of that entrenchment, there was little the British state could do to ameliorate it. The dilemma for the British state between 1972 and 1985 was that the absence of political initiatives increased entrenchment and polarisation, but that very absence was itself an unintended by-product of the political stalemate that had developed in Northern Ireland since the early 1970s.

5
The Northern Ireland Peace Process, 1985–97

Change and continuity

Defining what is meant by the term 'peace process' is logically prior to its dating; hence this chapter explores the winding down of the conflict and examines how, despite the move from bombings and shootings, political entrenchment remained untouched and communal polarisation persisted. The reason for this was that the political context in which emerging debates over equality agendas, 'parity of esteem', identity politics and reform and reconciliation were framed by longer-term historical trends. In particular, the basic *structure* of Westminster policy for restoring devolved power carried through with little change since the early 1970s – namely, an institutionalised Dublin involvement and the desirability in principle of devolved power-sharing. While these ideas continued to shape the basic tenets of unionist and nationalist policy-making, decisive changes in policy *direction* nevertheless took place at a lower level. In other words, during the 1990s the operation of state policy took place against a radically different background from that which had existed during the 1970s and 1980s.

Thus, this chapter describes a story of simultaneous change and continuity: the underlying policies of the key actors remained relatively untouched and largely consonant with the decisions made in the early 1970s; however, the practical, ground-level operation of those policies began to take a different perspective. Changes occurred especially in nationalists' and republicans' attitude to constitutional and security issues in which they made crucial concessions to the embedded unionist demands for minimum guarantees for physical and political protection. However, while nationalists accepted, for instance, that cross-border links should operate through consultative mechanisms and that they be answerable to a Northern Assembly, the underlying principle of gradual reunification continued to mobilise Catholic opinion. This chapter argues that the unionist contribution to the peace process cannot be plausibly represented as being reactive to nationalist alternations.[1] While it is certainly the case that unionists never felt 'ownership' of the events in the same way that nationalists did,[2] this chapter points out that unionist resistance to certain proposals was crucial to shaping the eventual Agreement of 1998. By resisting unwelcome ideas unionism's apparent passivity was instrumental in moulding the terms of the debate over what changes would be realistic and possible.

This tension between ground or operational level changes in policy direction and longer-term continuities in the structure of policy-making underpinned not only the dynamics of the peace process, but also belies the idea that there was an inevitable, gradual and cumulative movement towards peace. This mode of interpretation has been favoured by Irish nationalist leaders who emphasise how John Hume's decision to meet Gerry Adams in 1988 and his subsequent cajoling of a reluctant British government to recognise republicans' democratic credentials created the context for an all-inclusive dialogue leading to the Good Friday/Belfast Agreement.[3] The nationalist narrative finds echoes in some journalistic and academic accounts of the peace process – particularly in the idea that the Agreement was the culmination of the work and thinking of Hume.[4] Ed Moloney and Kevin Bean have substantially revised that narrative. Moloney, for example, argues that the republican movement towards constitutionalism began as early as 1982 with the power struggle that saw Adams assume leadership of Sinn Féin.[5] Bean, on the other hand, describes how a key effect of the community regeneration initiatives pursued by the Thatcher government was to bring republicans within the broad auspices of the state:

> Community organisations and political structures that had started out as agencies of revolutionary mobilisation became gatekeepers between the state and the nationalist community, as well as acting as transmission belts for the provisional movement. The result was that by the early 1990s the Provisional movement's position within the nationalist community had some of the characteristics of a state power.[6]

Regardless of this revisionist literature and of the fact that the talks process was not in fact all-inclusive given the decision by the DUP and Robert McCartney's UK Unionist Party to leave in July 1997[7] – a growing 'peace process industry' has been founded on the moral that it is essential to 'talk to terrorists'.[8] The self-serving goal of the attempts to read lessons back into history is encapsulated by the consociational narrative, which describes how Britain and Ireland eventually learned to manage the two warring ethnic communities and gradually convinced these belligerents of the benefits of consociational logic.[9] Although the teleological approach has been criticised by historians, it nevertheless threatens to become the dominant narrative of the peace process.[10] Not only does it utterly misrepresent the historical record of these years, it is also profoundly political – smuggling in assumptions about conflict resolution under the guise of informed, objective analysis.[11]

The identification of long-term historical trajectories or paths chimes with the general approach of Joseph Ruane and Jennifer Todd.[12] However, the presence of ground-level changes, coupled with the persistence of embedded and long-term policy goals, suggests a different picture from the 'settlement' processes mapped in their work. Those resilient policy goals, coupled with the widespread and deeply rooted polarisation – inspired principally by the Drumcree stand-off, but also apparent in other contests over ethnic symbols, and in particular the reform of the RUC, and commemorative practices[13] – is taken as evidence of patterns of continued disjuncture and inter-communal disconnect. While Ruane and Todd link Protestant disenchantment with the Good Friday Agreement to the politics of ambiguity or 'deception', this chapter points out that unionist disquiet with post-1985 politics was profound and widespread. The period between the Anglo-Irish and Belfast/Good Friday agreements was thus marked by two main historical trends. First, polarisation, division and entrenchment occurred at both the elite and popular level in Northern Ireland. Despite the paramilitaries' ceasefires, radicalisation of the two communal blocs proved to be resilient as embedded goals, perceptions and expectations of what the future might bring continued to affect and constrain political developments. Second, at a less obvious level, the effects of this polarisation were offset by the residual presence of moderate opinion within both unionism and nationalism. Although the SDLP, for example, sought to represent nationalist anger during the worst of the Drumcree-related violence, it also served as an antidote for republican calls for street protests. Within unionism a moderate discourse was established by Church leaders in particular, whose views the *Newsletter* (and the *Belfast Telegraph*) endorsed.

The Anglo-Irish Agreement and northern nationalism

The institutionalisation of a consultative role for Dublin in the Anglo-Irish Agreement effectively ratified the SDLP's long-term policy priority. As such, it represented a crucial concession by the British government and one that, in Hume's mind, would force unionists to negotiate with nationalists on their own terms.[14] Hume's prediction quickly proved to be erroneous since unionists embraced a mass campaign of protest while the leadership of the UUP and DUP pledged not to enter talks while the Agreement was in operation. On the other hand, although Sinn Féin's electoral surge had stalled prior to the signing of the Agreement,[15] the SDLP failed to reverse republican electoral gains as its share of the vote settled at around 11 per cent (one in every three Catholic votes).[16]

The Anglo-Irish Agreement set the context for an emerging pan-nationalist approach to the Northern Ireland conflict. Having secured the concession of a role for Dublin in Northern Ireland, the SDLP were reluctant to endanger or reduce that with the prospect of talks aimed at setting up a devolved administration. The nationalist trajectory underpinning the party's policy-making since the early 1970s continued to push the party away from an 'internalist' accommodation. The Anglo-Irish Agreement served as a mechanism for maintaining this momentum, and while constitutional nationalists quickly realised that it would not precipitate radical constitutional changes, it nevertheless encouraged small, incremental changes in the politics of the North:

> in the absence of a settlement or assembly, the Agreement *was* the political system, assisted by a raft of quangos. There was not a hospital closure, fisheries initiative or cultural programme that the Irish government didn't have a 'view' on.[17]

For Irish nationalists, therefore, the implication of the Anglo-Irish Agreement was closer North-South relations rather than the possibility of restoring power to Belfast. The decision by Hume to forgo the opportunity of re-engaging seriously with unionism and instead trying to lure republicans away from violence occurred within this context. Critics of Hume's approach – particularly, those dependent on Protestant votes, such as Eddie McGrady in the South Down constituency or Joe Hendron in West Belfast[18] – claimed that what Hume was actually doing was giving the republicans a legitimacy that the Provisionals' armed campaign was otherwise frustrating.[19] Again, Currie, for example, argued that the Anglo-Irish Agreement should provide a spur to entering into devolution talks with the unionists as it provided a default position in the event of a failure to reach agreement. Currie, however, balanced that argument against the idea of bringing republicans into the political arena:

> The clincher was that if we were successful in convincing Sinn Féin that our policies were right and a political alternative to violence could be built for the republican movement, then that could lead to the ending of violence.[20]

Hume's decision ratified the logic of the 1985 Agreement and served as a 'pivotal' intervention in political developments.[21] Its effect was to switch the dynamics of Northern Irish politics decisively from the promotion of accommodation and the building-up of a moderate centre around the SDLP-UUP axis towards the possibility of meeting the demands of the extremes. This changed dynamic was also recognised by elements of the British policy-making apparatus. As John Chilcott, the head of the NIO between 1990 and 1997, remarked:

> all-party talks minus Sinn Féin would present a hell of a problem if they succeeded ... to get Sinn Féin in subsequently would be far too difficult. You'd have to renegotiate the whole thing.[22]

The Hume-Adams talks began in 1988, following preliminary mediation by the West Belfast priest and Adams' confidant, Father Alex Reid. The talks were aimed at exploring 'whether there could be agreement on an overall nationalist political strategy for justice and peace', and concentrated on identifying a common nationalist strategy on reunification.[23] The talks provided Sinn Féin with a way of ending its political marginality. The Hume-Adams talks were framed by three events: the interception of the *Eksund*, a freighter loaded with matériel, by the French authorities *en route* to Ireland; the Enniskillen Memorial Day bombing, in which eleven people were killed and 63 injured; and the publication by the party of the policy paper 'A Scenario for Peace'. While the Enniskillen bombing and the capture of the *Eksund* undermined the republicans' propaganda campaign which went hand-in-hand with the IRA's armed struggle, the 'Scenario for Peace' document represented the first tentative steps by Sinn Féin to develop a political strategy since the early 1970s.[24] The paper spelled an end to a federalist vision of reunification and acknowledged that dialogue rather than military victory represented an alternative means of securing republican objectives. However, the extent of this movement should not be overestimated:

> The resolution of the conflict would free unionists from their historic laager mentality and would grant them real security instead of tenure based on repression and triumphalism. We do not intend to turn back the pages of history ... and foolishly attempt to reverse the Plantation. We offer them a settlement based on their throwing their lot in with the rest of the Irish people ... We offer them peace. We offer them equality. It is only through the process of decolonisation and dialogue that a peaceful, stable Ireland will emerge.[25]

In fact, this assessment of Ulster unionism proved to be one of the two major sticking points of the Hume-Adams talks. Sinn Féin argued that reunification was primarily about territory: 'to concede a veto on the exercise of national rights to a national minority ... would flout the basic principles of democracy'.[26] Hume, on the other hand, pushed the argument that the unification of Ireland must precede British withdrawal – reunification was primarily about people. Thus, he contended that 'whether or not the unionists may or may not have a *right* to a veto on Irish unity, they in reality possess such a veto ... they have it as a matter of fact, based on numbers, geography and history'.[27] The second major point of division was Sinn Féin's rejection of Hume's characterisation of the IRA campaign as counterproductive since it alienated unionists from the reunification project. Instead, Sinn Féin claimed that responsibility for the violence lay with the British state, which was also the obstacle to peace. Republicans also argued that Northern Ireland represented a major strategic interest for the UK and – despite the then £1.6 billion annual subvention – they claimed that British involvement in Ireland benefited the capitalist West. Sinn Féin argued that British strategy in Northern Ireland was based on undermining unionism through the Anglo-Irish Agreement so that a new pragmatic leadership would cut a deal with the SDLP and freeze out republicans. It claimed that republicans would resist such a strategy and any moves to re-establish devolution:

> Sinn Féin is totally opposed to a power-sharing Stormont assembly and states that there cannot be a partitionist solution. Stormont is not a stepping-stone to Irish unity. We believe that the SDLP's gradualist theory is therefore invalid and seriously flawed.

However, despite these points of division, the two parties found common ground around the idea that Britain should become a 'persuader' for Irish unity. What this meant was that the British government would give up its policy of upholding the principle of consent and instead adopt a position of persuading Ulster unionists of the benefits of Irish unification. How realistic an assessment this objective was in terms of unionist identity or British state policy is open to serious questioning. Indeed, its inherent impracticality and illogicality can only be explained by looking at the wider context and previous policy paths that informed SDLP and Sinn Féin thinking at this time.[28]

Following the break-up of the talks in September 1988, Hume and Adams continued to hold secret communications until the early 1990s. As part of this rapprochement, both parties began to explore the idea of a pan-nationalist alliance, recruiting the Irish American lobby and the Dublin government to this end.[29] The target of this post-Anglo-Irish Agreement activity was, as Hume later pointed out, joint authority. An internal power-sharing settlement was therefore effectively ruled out and the October 1988 inter-party talks with Alliance, the DUP and the UUP in Duisburg were effectively stillborn.[30]

Although the SDLP's rapprochement with Sinn Féin reflected its entrenched nationalistic policy trajectory, the relationship was far from unproblematic, particularly while the IRA continued its armed campaign. Hume, for example, consistently protested about republican terrorism during the latter half of the 1980s, arguing that

> it isn't just the unionist people who are their victims. Leaders of Sinn Féin have been saying recently that the nationalist nightmare has not ended. They are dead right because they and their military wing are the major part of that nightmare. In the last twenty years republicans have killed more than twice as many Catholics as the security forces and in the last ten have killed more than the loyalists.[31]

The killings also prevented Hume from welcoming republicans to possible all-party talks:

> every party [should sit] down on the same terms bringing nothing to the table but their own beliefs and powers of persuasion. There should be no right at this table for any party if it is either using force or reserving the right to use force if they do not get their way.[32]

At the SDLP's annual conference in 1989, Hume gave a detailed breakdown of republican killings and questioned how Sinn Féin could claim to be 'public representatives in the pursuit of justice ... the injustice of [IRA] methods ... can never be corrected in any way. Their victims cannot come out of their graves.'[33] Again, in 1990, Hume claimed that the IRA campaign had belied the 'hope generated by the civil rights movement' and that republicans believed that 'change was worthless and unpatriotic unless it was steeped in blood. Their basic view of Ireland is as a piece of territory. Its people are expendable'.[34] By 1993, however, his stance had mellowed: 'The provisional republican movement has been repeatedly dismissed as mindless, as criminals and gangsters. I wish they were because if they were they could be easily dealt with.' Referring to his 'dialogue' with Adams, he claimed that

> the flexibility that they have shown in the language of that debate and in our direct dialogue has convinced me that they are serious about lasting peace and a total cessation of violence. Leaving aside my total disagreement with their methods it has been my case that while their reasons were historically correct and correct in the past when the heart of the British-Irish conflict was a conflict of sovereignty ... these reasons are out of date, their legacy remains, the legacy is a deeply divided people in the island of Ireland.[35]

While several academics and journalists have remarked on how during the 1990s Sinn Féin appropriated the language of the SDLP – particularly with regard to the 'equality discourse', the desirability of a 'new and agreed' Ireland, and the need to achieve parity of expression for unionist and nationalist identities in Northern Ireland[36] – the key factor explaining nationalist-republican convergence lies in the fact that essentially the SDLP and Sinn Féin had a common understanding of the Northern Ireland problem and a similar preference for its solution. That understanding stressed the primordial nature of the Northern Ireland conflict – regardless of whether the ultimate responsibility lay with the British state, contention was inevitable given the deep ethnic divisions within the North. Contrary to the transformationalist deconstructions of Sinn Féin and SDLP rhetoric, this narrative is consonant with traditional nationalist thinking on the Northern 'problem'.[37] The 'solutions' likewise mirror traditional nationalist ideas in which equality concerns and institutional change are part and parcel of a much broader project of constitutional reform.[38]

The SDLP's submission to the inter-party talks convened by Secretary of State Peter Brooke, in 1991 illustrates these points, claiming, as it does, that the party's analysis and proposals for the 'Northern Ireland problem' stem from 'its historical origins'. These origins, the party claimed, lay in the

> wider historical relationship between the two islands ... For centuries this was a relationship characterised by conflict and instability ... The Northern Ireland conflict is the last negative legacy of the ancient quarrel between the peoples of Ireland and Britain. It is clear that the ultimate resolution of that conflict can only come about within the context and framework of the Anglo-Irish process.[39]

The paper concluded that any solution had to be based on a consensus that recognised those relationships. The logic of this recognition, it argued was the need to award equality for the 'two traditions'. While the document speaks of 'changes in Europe' and 'human rights realities' – including policing reform – the assumption that the conflict arose from 'ancient quarrels' allowed it to elide unionist opposition to reunification and the republican armed campaign. Thus, while a 'major factor [in the quarrel] has been unionist distrust of the rest of the people of the island'; this is linked to the 'failures' of Home Rule, Sunningdale and the Anglo-Irish Agreement. The 'human costs' of the violence, on the other hand, warrant just one paragraph out of 56 which studiously avoids any temptation to apportion blame for what the party calls 'the longest running and most serious civil disturbance in Western Europe since the end of the Second World War'.

Although it emphatically pointed a finger of blame – namely, at British interference in Ireland – Sinn Féin employed a similar explanatory narrative to the SDLP. Thus, Adams argued that '[t]here are two problems: Firstly, there is the problem of decolonising Ireland. Further, there is the problem of uniting the Irish people and building a just society.'[40] Senior Sinn Féin strategists argued that a prerequisite for this unification was the unification of the 'wider nationalist community', which, they pointed out, had broadly rejected republican violence. At a republican conference in 1988, Tom Hartley, for instance, noted that republicans' 'own shortcomings (poor organisation and lack of discipline and varied levels of politicisation)' did not help.[41] He argued, however, that the SDLP's 'green wing' was vulnerable to the national democratic demands and suggested that

> every effort should be made by republicans to get the SDLP to take on board correct political demands. Correct political demands do not

necessarily have to be republican political demands, though it would be left to Sinn Féin to formulate such demands. Each time the SDLP move into a position of accepting as its policy one of these demands Sinn Féin should proceed to up the ante by bringing forward new demands.[42]

At the same conference in which Hartley offered this critical appraisal, the Belfast City councillor Martin Ó Muilleor pointed out the opportunities offered in the constitutional arena, arguing that if Sinn Féin tackled 'mainstream' political issues such as NHS cutbacks,

> we will be seen as having an intelligent and vigorous response to the political issue which affects our people and our hospitals ... The possibilities are endless, but [taking the initiative] will undoubtedly help boost our credibility, strengthen our base and entrench us in the political mainstream.[43]

While Ó Muilleor admitted that there were 'contradictions between the armed struggle and our political work' – namely, that IRA bombs blew up the workplaces and shops that their voters depended on – he also counselled that republicans should 'not beat ourselves up about them ... At the very least let's be mature enough to discuss the contradictions.' However, even in the midst of its attempts at outflanking the SDLP, Sinn Féin was itself being increasingly brought into the Northern state apparatus. This occurred primarily under the auspices of the Conservative government's sponsorship of community regeneration schemes in the republican heartlands of West and North Belfast. This process has been extensively documented by Kevin Bean, who also points out that it is wrong to see it as all one-way: although republicans were responsible for implementing and overseeing community initiatives, the funding also contributed to growing Catholic cultural self-confidence.[44] A knock-on effect of this was that in certain symbolically salient areas – such as the parading controversy – these processes helped to reproduce the entrenched political and cultural division.

The peace process – the politics of resistance and transformation

The story of the Northern Ireland peace process is often rendered as entailing radical transformations by constitutional and, especially, physical force nationalists and a growing sense of disillusionment among

Ulster unionists and loyalists. Variations on that basic narrative emphasise different aspects of British state policy-making. On the one hand, journalistic accounts (together with elite nationalist memoirs) claim that a reluctant and suspicious British government had to be consistently persuaded of the benefits of peace.[45] On the other hand, a second mode of interpretation of the British government stresses its duplicity, or, in more positive terms, its pragmatism at encouraging republicans to give up the armed struggle and concludes that this acquiescence drained the confidence of unionist voters, in particular, in the democratic process.[46]

Although the more enthusiastic accounts of the peace process being a story of nationalist transformation[47] are simply not plausible when the primary evidence is taken into account, that is not to say that the peace process was not nationalist-driven or that unionist alienation can be discounted. In fact, a key dynamic of the peace process *was* unionist discontent, but it was emphatically not something that was simply passive or something that had to be surmounted. Rather, unionist discontent with the broad thrust of political change – particularly, since the Anglo-Irish Agreement – was instrumental in shaping the development and outcome of the peace process. Unlike much of nationalist politics, this dynamic occurred at a 'hidden' level in which unionism's persistent resistance to Westminster's devolution policies and nationalist constitutional proposals prevented their effective operation. In particular, unionism's reiteration of the security issue – in terms of requiring both physical and constitutional guarantees – meant that any proposals could only operate within certain parameters. In other words, the parameters of unionist discomfort and comfort delimited the process of change.

While the effect of the Anglo-Irish Agreement on unionist politics was profound, the resistance, blocking and agenda-setting activities of unionist groups also continued to influence the terms of debate and reshaped the policy background against which ideas about power-sharing or cross-border institutions would be introduced. Certainly, Ulster unionism was intensely shaken by the Anglo-Irish Agreement, which seemed to provide a dramatic illustration of unionism's marginality within Westminster's priorities, all of which partly contributed to the feelings of alienation that anti-Belfast Agreement unionist discourse articulated.[48] However, unionist marginalisation was not the entire story. While unionists had to confront a 'new reality' in the aftermath of the Anglo-Irish Agreement,[49] their resistance to government proposals also served to transform the context in which they would be enacted. Without being powerful enough to directly influence policy reform, the consistent opposition by unionists to what were perceived as unfavourable proposals slowly transformed the direction of political progress.

This framework suggests that the so-called 'Trimble project' of proactive unionism can be seen as a reaction to the repeated demands by nationalists – echoed in Westminster initiatives such as the Anglo-Irish Agreement – for 'meaningful' power-sharing and a strong Irish dimension. The framework, however, also suggests an important counterfactual: that but for those repeated demands, Ulster unionist politics may have offered a less maximalist resistance and that an alternative to entrenchment might have been possible. The crucial point about unionist resistance is, therefore, that it was part and parcel of the long-term trends of polarisation and entrenchment within Northern Ireland. At the same time, that resistance was consistently tempered by what was an essentially conservative strain within the unionist community – while unfavourable demands were to be repudiated, the preferred form of protest was through constitutional means. Thus, despite the occasional intervention of radical voices such as Joel Patton and the Spirit of Drumcree group, the actions by loyalist terrorists such as Billy Wright and Johnny Adair and the extremist Loyalist Volunteer Force (LVF), or the destabilising threats from loyalist spokespersons such as David Ervine, an undercurrent of moderation shaped unionist responses and served to restrain the extremes throughout the period between the Anglo-Irish Agreement and the Good Friday Agreement.

The Anglo-Irish Agreement transformed the political landscape in Northern Ireland. Although it fell short of the kind of joint authority Hume and the SDLP desired, it afforded Dublin an institutionalised consultative role in the affairs of the North. The logic of this guarantee meant that the Agreement also served to provide a disincentive for the SDLP to enter into dialogue with Ulster unionists for an 'internal', devolutionary settlement that would be dependent on the maintenance of good relations.[50] Whereas for the SDLP the Anglo-Irish Agreement represented a 'bankable' concession, for Ulster unionists the Agreement was a devastating setback. Not only were unionist leaders excluded from the negotiations leading up to the Agreement, but the fact that Dublin was now entitled to a place in the running of Northern Ireland was perceived as irrefutable evidence that unionists were 'losing the argument' for maintaining the constitutional link. As such, it served to symbolise the embedded perception that their British identity was becoming increasingly attenuated.[51] The ongoing paramilitary campaigns served to underline these political divisions: the 1985 low of 59 deaths rose to 66 in 1986, 106 and 1987 and 105 in1988.[52] In short, in the post-Agreement landscape, the prospects for inter-communal rapprochement looked decidedly threadbare.

The immediate unionist reaction to the Anglo-Irish Agreement was outrage and anger, expressed in a campaign of mass mobilisation that saw the UUP and DUP Westminster MPs resign and a protest rally, attended by over 100,000 in Belfast city centre. However, unlike 1974, the Anglo-Irish Agreement was designed to operate at an inter-governmental level and did not require democratic approval by Ulster unionists; furthermore, the establishment of a cross-party task force in 1987 signified an 'implicit admission that the protest campaign had run out of steam'.[53] The Task Force was set up specifically to assess the campaign against the Agreement and to suggest alternatives to it. It began by describing how the political context looked to the unionist community:

> The catalogue of injury and insult is endless. The net effect is a community increasingly confused as to what is and what is not acceptable in a democratic society; a community torn between loyalty to the law and established order, and the compelling conclusion that violence and anarchy are the likeliest route to political reward.[54]

Although the Report acknowledged that one effect of this estrangement were calls for 'negotiated independence', it rejected this option, along with the idea of a return to 'majority rule devolution'. Again, while it remarked that the idea of 'total integration continues to attract substantial support in the unionist community', it also pointed out that Westminster strongly opposed this option and thus that 'devolution is a more attainable objective'. However, the Report's authors avoided specifying what form devolution would take, and their suggestion that the two unionist leaders, James Molyneaux and Ian Paisley, give further consideration to the idea to a large extent belied the underlying theme of the Report, which suggested disquiet, in particular over Molyneaux's intensely conservative and softly-softly leadership style.

The key problem that both Molyneaux and the authors of the Report faced was that it was far from certain whether any of the unionist alternatives to the Anglo-Irish Agreement would meet with success, or, as such, whether any realistic alternatives actually existed. As pointed out, the logic of the Anglo-Irish Agreement pointed towards Dublin involvement and away from internal power-sharing – as the Report's authors acknowledged, the Agreement could not be 'devolved away' since there was no incentive for nationalists to share power at the expense of losing Dublin influence. Coupled with this was the fact that, on the whole, nationalist politics had been progressively radicalised since the 'irruption' of Sinn Féin into electoral politics in 1982.[55] The Report's analysis, therefore, contained a great deal more common sense than the loyalist position paper of the same year.[56] Although one sociologist has praised the Ulster Political Research Group's paper as 'an unusually even-handed interpretation of how Northern Ireland had got into its present parlous state', placed in the context of the political impasse that assessment appears injudiciously generous and even extremely puzzling.[57] The loyalist paper, in fact, studiously avoids all reference to the killing of Catholics – let alone the vast majority of people in the North who refused to take up arms. Instead, it asserts that 'we are all part of the problem', a claim justified by way of analogy with the inevitability of conflict and stalemate in every country that experiences 'serious ethnic, religious or class divisions in society'. Again, although the paper claims that its 'proposals do not in any way deny any section of the community its aspirations', quite why the SDLP would assent to its prescription – a stolid internalist settlement, based on a majoritarian reading of power-sharing – is never answered.

The British government was also disappointed with the outworkings of the Anglo-Irish Agreement. Thatcher, for example, later expressed her 'disappointment' that '[o]ur concessions alienated the unionists without gaining the level of security cooperation we had a right to expect'.[58] In January 1990, Brooke initiated a series of informal inter-party talks. As a way of inducing unionist participation, Brooke suggested that the Anglo-Irish Agreement could be suspended if the talks progressed to a more formal level. In November that year, and in what would come to be regarded as a landmark speech, Brooke stated that 'the heart and core of the British presence is ... the reality of nearly a million people living in a part of the island of Ireland who are, and who certainly regard themselves as, British'. He claimed that the British government's presence was not related to national self-interest. Rather, 'The British government has no selfish strategic or economic interest in Northern Ireland, our role is to help, enable, and encourage.'[59]

The initial republican response was tepid: they claimed that the default position of Westminster was still pro-Union; in addition, they hoped that the forthcoming general election would bring an end to the Thatcher premiership and the accession of a government that would be more congenial to republican aspirations.[60] Despite this, the British continued with the backchannel discussions which had been going on with the Provisionals since October 1990. The record of these talks was later published by Sinn Féin and reveal that the British continually rejected the idea that they should become 'persuaders' for Irish unity.[61] The talks coincided with the collapse of the Soviet Union and the ending of the Cold War, which effectively eliminated the Provisionals' long-standing claim that Northern Ireland provided a crucial strategic base for the UK and NATO. In addition, these global shifts helped to remove the traditional US reticence about commenting on Northern Ireland because it might be interpreted as interfering in the internal affairs of the UK. As Jonathan Tonge points out, although Adams' project of an 'Irish peace process' pre-dated these international developments, the ending of the Cold War was important insofar as it

> provided a convenient framework to develop the process and allowed the ditching of ideological baggage. Britain could begin to refute the charge of it being a colonial aggressor; republicans could tacitly, though not publicly, accept this; and the US could act as an honest broker.[62]

In addition, the election of Bill Clinton in 1992 as US president coincided with a renewed American interest in the North and, in the absence of substantial movement on republican demands, provided Adams with a 'compensatory mechanism' for accommodating to a more minimal agenda than he or Hume had envisaged.[63]

During 1991 and 1992 the British government continued to press ahead with the inter-party talks, concentrating on what Brooke called

> the three main relationships: those within Northern Ireland, including the relationship between any new institutions there and the Westminster Parliament; among the people of the island of Ireland; and between the two governments.[64]

This conceptualisation echoed the SDLP's submission to the talks; however, Britain rejected the SDLP's insistence that such a conceptualisation demanded joint authority, which it claimed could be implemented with the North being run by six commissioners: three elected in Northern Ireland and three appointed by London, Dublin and the EU. Unionists complained that that insistence really represented a reluctance to engage in any substantive manner on the issue of a devolved assembly and that Hume, in particular, was 'always willing to speak to "those well known democrats in the Army Council" while refusing to engage with unionists …'.[65] For his part, Hume believed that the inter-party talks were 'designed to exclude a large body of nationalist opinion without whom peace would be impossible'.⁶⁶ Hume's belief that a 'larger settlement was possible' was shared with segments of the Irish policy-making apparatus, with one official echoing the sentiment expressed by John Chilcott to the effect that 'the Provos would have to be "stitched into [any] settlement"'.⁶⁷

Hume's faith in Adams underpinned their continued dialogue and represented something of a high-water mark of nationalist consensus.⁶⁸ The final draft of their discussion papers were circulated to the British and Irish governments in 1993 and again called on Westminster to state that it had no 'selfish, strategic, political, or economic interest in Northern Ireland' and that it would use its 'influence and energy to win the consent of a majority in Northern Ireland' to endorse self-determination.⁶⁹ What this meant was that Britain would not interfere in the right of political parties on the island of Ireland to enter into talks and it would encourage a 'process of national reconciliation'.⁷⁰

In late 1993 a series of leaks regarding the intergovernmental response to Hume and Adams and the backchannel discussions threatened to destabilise the gradual process of winding down the IRA campaign.⁷¹ In response, the two governments jointly published the Downing Street Declaration in December. This confirmed the Republic's commitment to the consent principle and the British declaration of having no 'selfish or economic interest'. While it was pitched in the 'green language' of the Hume-Adams discussions,⁷² its substance was fundamentally different from the nationalist documents. Thus, Britain would 'facilitate' an agreement rather than act as a 'persuader' for reunification and the 'agreed Ireland' would be premised on unionist consent rather than governmental encouragement. In other words, the import behind the language was a stabilised North, not a reunified island:

> The British government agree that it is for the people of the island of Ireland alone, by agreement between the two parts respectively, to exercise the right of self-determination on the basis of consent, freely and concurrently given, North and South, to bring about a united Ireland, if that is their wish.⁷³

Although this reaffirmation of the principle of consent represented a setback for the Hume-Adams project, it was in fact taken as something akin to an opening gambit by the nationalist and republican leadership. Adams, for example, refused to recognise the logic of the Declaration and called for 'clarification'.⁷⁴ For both groups the target remained eventual reunification, and while policy-making was still directed towards that end, republicans in particular recalibrated their strategy. The persistence of a steady policy direction was evidenced in the Sinn Féin Ard Fheis (party conference) of 1994. The senior party strategist, Mitchell McLaughlin, for example, employed rhetoric that would not have seemed out of place at the SDLP annual conference: 'The unity of the Irish people will be achieved by a process of national reconciliation, never by force.'[75]

Although unionists were no longer to be 'forcibly reconciled' (i.e. at gunpoint), McLaughlin's reasoning and vision for what that process meant were also not a million miles away from Hume's notions of 'persuasion':

> There are man problems to be overcome before we can enjoy a lasting peace in Ireland. Not least of these are the problems of convincing the unionist community that they have a legitimate and essential roles as part of, and within an agreed Irish democracy ... Surely it is so obvious as to be beyond dispute, that it is the British government which can bring a constructive influence to bear on the considerations of the unionist community?[76]

This vision, in fact, largely harmonised with the traditional nationalist and republican understanding of consent, which was outlined by Adams in his address to the Ard Fheis:

> The unionists must be told plainly that, contrary to their illogical belief, the Six-County area does not belong to them. It belongs to all our people equally, irrespective of falsely created majorities and minorities.[77]

The idea that the reunification project is about ends not means lay behind the Provisionals' decision to call a ceasefire on 31 August 1994. While critics of the IRA have seen the ceasefire was an admission of defeat in that the change of tactic represents an implicit acknowledgement that there was something wrong with the first plan, the cessation was 'sold' to volunteers as a new alternative to physical force: the new political front would create a pan-nationalist alliance comprising Sinn Féin, the SDLP, Dublin and Irish-America and 'advance the struggle' by the promotion of 'basic republican principles'. British withdrawal would be a gradual process, but would inevitably arise due to the momentum of this new phase of the struggle: 'another front has opened up and we should have the confidence and put in the effort to succeed on that front'.[78]

The response of the *Newsletter* highlighted these ambiguities:

> Sinn Féin leaders have certainly not been mealy-mouthed about their real intentions for the future of this Province. Realistically though, one would not have expected Sinn Féin to change its political standpoint as a result of the ceasefire ...[79]

Likewise, the *Belfast Telegraph* emphasised that clarification on the IRA's intentions was essential: 'Everyone must know where they stand on such an important matter as whether violence has or has not been abandoned for good as a political weapon, when they come to sit around a conference table.'[80] One of its columnists questioned Hume's idea that a line should be drawn under the past:

> As you listened to [the news reports] ... your thoughts were not with the warmongers on either side, but with their victims ... It is hard to imagine quite how 3,168 families will ever draw a line under their past.[81]

Amidst the republican euphoria over the ceasefire, the *Irish Times* acknowledged that unionist and British concerns over its permanency required clarification, although it drew back from calling for concrete actions by the Provisionals:

> The conviction runs deep that only a secret deal could have brought about yesterday's declaration ... But the overall tenor of the announcement – and its interpretation by political leaders including John Bruton, John Hume and Seamus Mallon – would seem to make its intention clear enough. The IRA intends to shoot and bomb no more.[82]

Given the polarisation of political opinion in and about Northern Ireland, it was inevitable that the ceasefire would divide opinion so radically. This was compounded by the decision of the then Taoiseach, Albert Reynolds, to meet Hume and Adams a few days after the ceasefire. The *Irish News*, for instance, concentrated on the theme of Adams' speech – 'We threaten you [unionists] only with democracy' – to emphasise that unionists must respond positively: 'The unionist people must have the confidence in their arguments and in their ability to engage with nationalism in a debate about the future relationships within these islands.'[83] The *Newsletter*, on the other hand, claimed that the Dublin summit was destabilising and 'certainly did not help to reassure unionists that they faced absolutely no threat from these quarters'.[84]

Throughout the end of 1994 the British government, in particular, continued to pressure republicans for an act of decommissioning as a gesture of their goodwill. In fact, the government had indicated that decommissioning was expected of the IRA at least as early as January 1994.[85] A BBC TV *Panorama* special on the IRA ceasefire in January 1995 revealed something of the extent to which republicans captivated the imaginations of certain governmental officials and ministers, and points to at least one reason why influential figures in London and Dublin acquiesced to Sinn Féin's demands for so long. Reynolds, for example, spoke of Adams' 'vision' and remarked on how he had congratulated him on his 'courage' at what he called their 'historic' meeting the previous September. The Dublin mandarin Michael Lillis likewise stressed the significance of the ceasefire and claimed that Sinn Féin's leadership actually played down its importance in their public statements. Brooke was even more effusive in his praise for Adams' 'courage': 'He had a leadership role. He performed it. And I think the whole of Ireland and the whole of these islands, and I think arguably the whole of the world, is grateful for him for having done it.'[86] These assessments were not limited to former statesmen, however. The reaction by the *Irish News* to the Framework Documents of February 1995 claimed them as a vindication of the 'nationalist dream' and the 'culmination of twenty-five years of work by John Hume'. It went on to point out that

> Mr Hume could not have done it without the skill and patience of Sinn Féin President Gerry Adams, who has shown statesmanlike potential in his courageous attempts to lead the republican movement away from the gun.[87]

Although the consultation Document has been seen as being a 'carrot' for republicans to encourage them to maintain their ceasefire,[88] the published version also revealed signs of having been significantly watered down in recognition of the unionist position. For example, the final Document significantly reduced the remit of the cross-border bodies from the proposals contained in a leaked version that had been published in January.[89] Likewise, these institutions would be made answerable to a Northern assembly and were a far cry from the 'dynamic, enabling progressive extensions' envisaged in the early draft.[90] However, despite this apparent setback, nationalists recognised the Document as a major concession on the part of the British.[91] While the *Newsletter* also pointed out that it had 'unionist segments laced with the usual sugary phrases', it also warned that 'large parts ... have a distinctive nationalist agenda ... Permanent peace, we are assured is the objective of the whole exercise, but on whose terms?'[92]

While the *Irish News* claimed that the Document had not been assimilated by Sinn Féin, which held its Ard Fheis a few days later, it also pointed out that uncertainty over republican intentions was becoming extremely destabilising: 'Mr Adams ... will have to find some way of making progress over the decommissioning of republican arms.'[93] The republican response was to place the onus on Britain. Thus, as the former hunger striker Pat McGeown told the Ard Fheis:

> The British as part of the process of building peace and reconciliation must be as prepared as they demand others to be to admit their part in the horrors and terrors of war that have engulfed this community.

Furthermore, he pointed out, that process required that the 'outstanding issue of those imprisoned ... must be dealt with positively and speedily'.[94] Importantly, for republicans, decommissioning was only part of a broader agenda – while the British and unionists insisted on it as a precondition for entering talks, Sinn Féin's rank-and-file were effectively being told that certain concessions from Britain were a precondition to their participation in the peace process.

This was the context for the Secretary of State for Northern Ireland, Patrick Mayhew's three preconditions of March 1995: a willingness to disarm progressively; an understanding of what decommissioning would entail; and the actual destruction of arms at the start of any talks. While John Major's later assessment that these preconditions represented a 'reasonable proposition ... [and] a softening of the government's position',[95] they also symbolised an exceedingly narrow view of the republican policy direction. In other words, although the government had banked on the lure of peace being strong enough as to assuage nagging doubts, the problem was that while its ambiguous relationship with Sinn Féin was a product of the conflict and distrust existed between the two sets of actors.

Parading and agreement – between moderation and extremism

Dominic Bryan has alluded to a tendency to separate Northern Irish politics during the 1990s into two separate spheres:[96] on the one hand, there is the story of elite accommodation, epochal transformations and history and hope rhyming; on the other, the controversy, contention and killings over parading disputes conjured up images of Winston Churchill's 'dreary steeples' and ancient antagonisms. Although the parading disputes were essentially about political power,[97] this section highlights a relatively unremarked aspect of that power struggle – namely, the hidden, covert influence of moderate opinion. This was particularly the case within the unionist community, in which influential opinion was not only instrumental in repudiating loyalist violence but had effectively shaped the terms of the debate over what was and what was not acceptable protest during the years leading up to the Belfast/Good Friday Agreement. In other words, although the confrontation with state forces – in particular, the RUC – was a significant factor in splitting the 'weak coalition of interests' that was represented annually at Drumcree (see below),[98] the *sotte voce* presence of moderate opinion acted as a restraining influence. As the final section of this chapter points out, despite growing Protestant alienation with the direction of the peace process, it was this moderate constituency that was critical in Trimble's slender victory in the referendum of May 1998.

Importantly, however, the direction of this moderation was intra- rather than cross-communal. In other words, while an elite agreement was signed between the main representatives of nationalism and unionism in April 1998, in terms of policy direction and broader communal sentiment, division remained as wide and as salient as ever. This seemingly paradoxical or two-way dynamic is dramatically illustrated in the nationalist response to the unfolding events. Thus, while republicans gradually came into the constitutional realm, they and the SDLP agreed to a watered-down version of Sunningdale, this was painted as a British concession and as a necessary stepping stone towards the target of reunification – in other words, just as nationalists were being brought into the state, they were simultaneously withdrawing from it at both the elite and popular levels. The parading crisis of the mid-1990s acted as a prism for this process of 'transcending' the state.

As Eric Kaufmann has pointed out, in simple terms, during much of the 1990s, disputes over parading came down to force of numbers and threat: 'both sides in the conflict have an incentive to cause as much trouble as possible so as to influence the police cost-benefit calculus over whether to halt or permit a march'. In other words, if Orangemen could credibly present a greater threat than local residents, then they would most likely get to parade; however, if residents could threaten greater disorder, then the planned march would be re-routed. However, as Kaufmann goes on to describe, marches are never simply disputed at a local level, and several of these local disputes became 'proxies' for the broader Northern Irish power struggle.[99] Two disputes in particular came to symbolise that wider stand-off: the first involving the Upper Ormeau Road Ballynafeigh Lodge march along the nationalist enclave of the Lower Ormeau Road, and the second involving the Portadown District Lodge march from their service in Drumcree Church back to Portadown town centre along the Garvaghy Road (the 'lower end' of which was a nationalist estate).

The Garvaghy Road-Drumcree dispute arose from a number of factors: diminishing Orange influence within the Northern state, the emergence of a blatantly sectarian strain of 'kick-the-Pope' loyalist marching bands, growing cultural self-confidence among Northern Catholics, and demographic changes within the Portadown area due to Catholic in-migration. While the first three factors relate to broader structural changes, they nevertheless combined with the fourth to initiate a modern-day dispute, which can be dated to nationalist protests over marching in 1985.[100] By 1995 that stand-off and those trends combined with the deepening Protestant suspicion over the peace process together with the emergence of Sinn Féin as an articulate force within the media.[101] The immediate cause of the Ormeau dispute was a 'five-fingered salute' which one marching band gave while passing the Sean Graham bookmaker shop in July 1992 – a provocative reference to the five Catholics who had been murdered there by loyalist gunmen the previous February. In 1995, however, the leader of the Lower Ormeau Concerned Community Group, Gerard Rice, linked the Ormeau parade directly to the Drumcree dispute following the presence of the Ballynafeigh Lodge at the Portadown stand-off. According to one journalist who was present at that residents' meeting, although a substantial minority favoured a low-key approach to their own issue, no vote was taken, nor was the floor opened to discussion. Instead, a combination of moral and social force determined that the local community would confront the RUC and Orangemen.[102]

The idea that republicans were actively orchestrating the residents' protests as part of a post-ceasefire strategy was widely held among many Orangemen and this perception in itself helped to increase the stakes. The underlying suspicion was that the growth in residents' protests was a product of the republicans' 'Tactical Use of the Armed Struggle' – street tensions would be heightened and local nationalists would be targeted by Orange reprisals and physical force on the part of the police.[103] Orangemen and unionist leaders pointed to the presence of convicted republicans as the residents' leaders – Gerard Rice on the Ormeau Road and Brendan MacCionnaith on the Garvaghy Road had both served time for terrorist-related offences – as evidence of this manipulation. A statement by Adams that 'three years of work went in to creating that situation [Drumcree], and fair play to those who put the work in' seemed to point to a dedicated strategy.[104] However, as Malachi O'Doherty has pointed out, Adams' statement was made to a republican audience, members of which had grown sceptical of his management of the Sinn Féin peace strategy.[105] In reality, then, the strategy was much more complex than straightforward manipulation. It did, however, enable republicans to claim vindication of their narrative of 'RUC brutality' and the impossibility of reforming the Northern state. The parades disputes could, therefore, fit easily within traditional republican ideas about Catholic victimhood and be used to mobilise younger generations who remembered little about the actual conflict – in other words, the parades dispute could dramatise the story that Orange forces continued to repress Catholics in the 1990s just as they did in the 1980s and 1970s and earlier.

At the beginning of July 1995, the *Newsletter* referred to these concerns and claimed that republicans' strategy was to use the decommissioning stalemate and the parades protests in order to increase the pressure on Westminster yielding to their demands:

> The sinister twin-track approach of IRA-Sinn Féin is working overtime, not in attempting to heal the wounds opened by the past twenty-five years of murder and mayhem, but in seeking to create further instability in this society with confrontational protests against the unionist community and the security forces and brutal 'punishment' attacks on vulnerable individuals within the nationalist community.[106]

The release from imprisonment of Private Lee Clegg on 3 July radically heightened tensions. Clegg had been given a life sentence four years previously for shooting dead two teenage joy-riders who had driven through an army checkpoint in West Belfast, and the news of his early release sparked two nights of rioting in nationalist areas across the North.[107] In the wake of the release, both loyalists and republicans threatened to end their ceasefire unless there was 'consequent reciprocal benefit for paramilitary prisoners'.[108] By 8 July, it was estimated that these riots, plus the clashes over parades on the Lower Ormeau Road and in Bellaghy, had cost the state around £10 million. This figure was to soar following the onset of the stand-off between police and Orangemen, which began in Portadown on 9 July.[109] The Orangemen refused to negotiate directly with the residents' group, claiming that it was a front for republicans, and, despite the intervention of the local MP, David Trimble, and the DUP leader, Ian Paisley, tensions on the Orange side escalated into riots against the police. Although the *Newsletter* condemned these attacks, it suggested that the riots were not an unforeseen consequence of the ethnic power struggle:

> The RUC, through its re-routing of the [Garvaghy march] has once again allowed itself to be blackmailed by the most undemocratic elements in our society and those who would diligently uphold the law have been pushed into a cul-de-sac.[110]

Although the Orange Order attempted to calm the tensions by calling on its members to stay away from the Ormeau Road,[111] a further radicalising factor in the 'Siege of Drumcree' was the fact that 1995 marked the 200th anniversary of the founding of the Orange Order. Paisley captured something of the millenarian sentiments involved in his hyperbolic speech to the protesters: 'If we don't win this battle, all is lost; it is a matter of life or death, Ulster or the Irish Republic, freedom or slavery, light or darkness.'[112]

The *Newsletter* echoed these sentiments and justified protest. However, it also condemned the 'thuggery' which had 'tarnished' the 'vast majority of law-abiding members' of the Orange Order: 'Those who gathered on Sunday for their traditional parade to and from a church believed they were underpinning their sense of identity and exercising their civil rights.'[113] The newspaper argued that although Drumcree was a 'tinder box', it was only with the onset of violence against the police that the possibility for accommodation was lost and it placed the blame for the collapse on 'an element bent on violence'. The newspaper had previously called for 'cool heads' and 'common sense' among local leaders and echoed the pleas of the Church of Ireland Primate, Robin Eames, who appealed 'to the good sense and proven responsibility of community leaders in both traditions there to do all they can to reduce the tension'.[114]

An eventual resolution was reached when residents agreed to a limited number of Orangemen passing down the road without any bands. However, the confrontational approach of Trimble to the police during the protest and his 'triumphalist' speech at the culmination of the march was roundly condemned by the nationalist press. His 'victory jig' when he joined Paisley to march the final few yards of the parade route poisoned his future relations with the nationalist community. At the time, the *Irish News* not only criticised unionism's use of 'mob rule' and 'brute force to get its way'; it also claimed that

> Mr Trimble did his cause no good with a 'victory speech' in which he danced over the feelings of his Garvaghy Road constituents who had allowed the march to pass, and in which he threatened them with more of the same in the future. Those who believe that republican intransigence is the sole cause of Northern Ireland's problems will have to think again.[115]

And the *Irish Times* dismissed Trimble's speech as 'cant' and warned that he was 'playing with fire':

> within a few months ... Mr Molyneaux is likely to retire, and Mr Trimble has a fighting chance of succeeding him. Time and again in the troubled history of the North, narrow political ambitions have ridden wild horse of hatred and sectarianism to achieve their aims. Mr Trimble knows better, but he chooses not to know.[116]

One of the immediate effects of the Drumcree dispute was a coalescing of nationalist opinion around the idea that all-party talks were a necessity. Thus, Hume and Adams met the Taoiseach John Bruton and the Tanaiste (deputy prime minister) Dick Spring in Dublin a couple of days after the Twelfth (the annual Protestant celebration of the 12 July 1690 Battle of the Boyne). The current impasse, they said, in a joint statement, 'must be overcome. Accordingly, we are seeking a commencement as soon as possible of the inclusive all-party talks to the achievement or our objective.'[117] The following day, the *Irish News* editorial remarked that Britain's 'stalling verges on criminality':

> The magnanimity which was promised is lacking, and a willingness to make the tough decisions necessary to broker a lasting peace is nowhere to be seen ... [The British government] cannot afford, any longer, to alienate those within both paramilitary blocks who have made a significant down-payment on democracy.[118]

Although the idea that Trimble deliberately sought to manipulate the Drumcree dispute to raise his political profile is doubtful – not least because he could not have known how it would have turned out.[119] Nevertheless, the *Irish Times* was correct in saying that Molyneaux's leadership of the Ulster Unionist Party was on its last legs. In fact, his hold on the leadership had been increasingly tenuous since the publications of the Frameworks Documents in February, and in March a 21-year-old student had mounted a leadership challenge, winning an 'audacious' 15 per cent of the votes.[120] Trimble's victory in the September 1995 leadership election was, however, greeted with some shock and dismay by nationalists North and South of the border.[121] Dick Grogan, the Northern editor of The *Irish Times*, for example, made the gloomy prediction that

> At a time when mainstream unionism might have seemed ready to re-examine its narrow ideological base and make adjustments aimed at mellowing its sectarian image and attracting support across the religious divide, Mr Trimble's form would seem to rule out such a prospect.[122]

The editorial of the *Irish News* was much more restrained and claimed that Trimble started with a 'clean sheet'.[123] It also sought to accentuate the positive: as a hard-liner Trimble might be able to sell a deal to the unionist right in a way that moderates such as John Taylor would have struggled to do. The *Irish Times*, however, also noted that Dublin political elites were 'stunned' at Trimble's victory, and reported that it 'was seen by the government here as another blow to the peace process':

> While Dublin had little time for Mr Trimble and his extremist positions even before his triumphalist strutting in Portadown with the DUP leader, Rev Ian Paisley, that performance shocked ministers and politicians as showing an even more fanatical streak in the law lecturer...[124]

The *Newsletter*, on the other hand, welcomed the fact that Trimble won an outright majority, arguing that this 'strength should allow [him] to present the unionist case to our government'.[125] However, the paper did warn that while Trimble would be encouraged to talk with the SDLP, 'there can be no all-embracing talks with the political representatives of the IRA or the fringe loyalist groupings until both sides abandon for good their illegal murder weaponry and announce their organisations as redundant'. In fact, this was Trimble's viewpoint: 'Unionists cannot be asked to accept the IRA ceasefire as permanent as an act of faith, as John Bruton this week said he has done. There must be a demonstration of their intentions.'[126] Trimble also challenged the Irish government to set out its intentions regarding the Irish dimension. Although, he pointed out, he would not support 'any all-Ireland institutions with governmental powers', he would agree to 'genuine cooperation'.[127] However, he claimed that 'the Irish government has never actually put forward any arguments for [such] projects on the basis of their merits. It's always been for an institution which has political and constitutional significance'.[128]

At the end of September Trimble urged Westminster 'not [to] allow itself to be bullied' on the decommissioning issue.[129] 'The government has been flexible', he stated, 'but it has reacted a point where this requirement cannot be watered down any further'. However, by the start of November the government had actually moved further towards fudging the issue. Thus, an NIO paper suggested the idea of decommissioning occurring alongside 'preparatory' talks, with all-party negotiations following 'constructive' progress.[130] The details of how this would work in practice were only filled in at the eleventh hour prior to a visit by Clinton at the end of the month: all the parties would be invited to the preparatory talks, while an 'international body', chaired by US Senator, George Mitchell, would report on decommissioning.[131] Clinton's visit in itself made little tangible or material impact on the development of the peace process. What it did do, according to the *Irish News*, was that it 'lifted spirits, concentrated minds and [gave] an entirely new lease of life to a peace process which has been experiencing potentially fatal problems'.[132] Unfortunately, while Clinton's powers of resuscitation may have worked for his own career in the US, they were rather more limited in Northern Ireland. In fact, the *Newsletter* warned its readers not to get carried away with the international attention:

> There is a danger that after the morale-boosting visit of the American president expectations for an early breakthrough on the political front may 2be pitched too high. The grim reality is that not one terrorist gun, one bullet, or one ounce of Semtex explosive have been voluntarily surrendered since the IRA and loyalist paramilitary ceasefires commenced. The large caches of illegal weaponry are still in place, for use at any time which the terrorist godfathers may decide.[133]

The Mitchell Commission on decommissioning reported to John Major at the end of January 1996. Among its recommendations (what came to be known as the 'Mitchell principles') were that all parties involved in discussions should affirm their commitment to exclusively peaceful methods and the total disarmament of paramilitary organisations; and that they renounce the use of force or the threat of force; that they agree to abide by the terms of any settlement.[134] Although Hume reacted bitterly to the suggestion that elections must precede talks, which he believed was only made to placate Trimble, the evidence suggests a certain flexibility on the part of unionists towards republicans at this point.[135] The Ulster Unionist Party MP, Ken Maginnis, in particular, indicated a willingness to engage with republicans while decommissioning was ongoing,[136] while John Taylor, also UUP, suggested to his constituency party the idea that unionists enter into negotiations to try to water down the Frameworks proposals.[137]

At the beginning of February Mitchell and Sir Hugh Annesley, the RUC chief constable, warned that his sources indicated that the IRA was in danger of splitting over the republican peace strategy, while Annesley stated that the organisation was keeping its 'terror machine in Great Britain "well-oiled" '. In fact, the immediate context for these warnings was an attack on the home of an RUC officer in which 57 shots were fired. Although the IRA denied involvement, the police claimed that one of its 'favoured weapons', an AK47, was used.[138] A few days later, on the evening of Friday, 9 February, the ceasefire definitively ended with a massive explosion at Canary Wharf in the City of London in which two people were killed and over 100 injured. Although Dublin broke off ministerial contact with Sinn Féin, it nevertheless maintained links through governmental officials.[139] More importantly, nationalists, North and South of the border, emphasised that it was Britain's reluctance to capitalise on the ceasefire by insisting on decommissioning before talks that was the underlying explanation for its breakdown. For example, although the Dublin government was reported as having felt that 'the republican movement had broken faith with it', it maintained its belief in the necessity of a 'proximity multilateral conference', following another ceasefire.[140] The *Irish News*, furthermore, contended that:

> From the very first hour of the IRA ceasefire, the isolation of republicans was a central part of British policy. The unseemly row over the permanence or otherwise of the ceasefires was followed by the precondition on decommissioning ... Sinn Féin has been willing to talk to anyone and everyone without preconditions; unionists have not.[141]

Although the *Irish Times* claimed that Adams demonstrated a 'lack of political realism' when he claimed that 'dialogue works' ('what kind of dialogue does he imagine is possible with the perpetrators of the deaths, injuries and destruction at Canary Wharf?'), it also argued that 'there is an urgent need not to allow politics to flag'.[142] As Malachi O'Doherty pointed out, the nationalist narrative of British reluctance effectively made it 'easier for the IRA to sell this return to bombing than was anticipated'.[143] In fact, the IRA's decision to return to war was taken in the early autumn of 1995 and thus pre-dated the manoeuvring of the Major administration around the issue of decommissioning in late 1995 and early 1996.[144] At the end of the month, however, the British and Irish governments launched a new package with the aim of restoring the peace process: dates were set for elections and all-party talks, to which Sinn Féin would be admitted following a renewed IRA ceasefire.[145]

The IRA campaign inevitably hardened opinion within unionism, particularly on decommissioning, David Ervine warning that the loyalist ceasefire was itself at breaking point.[146] In fact, the actions of the paramilitaries over the summer months suggested a desire to heighten tension and provoke the 'other side' into a return to all-out hostilities. For example, in June republicans shot a Detective-Garda, Jerry McCabe, during a mail van robbery in County Limerick, exploded a massive bomb in Manchester city centre injuring 200 people and fired two mortars at a British army base in Osnabrück, Germany. On 14 July a breakaway dissident group, the Continuity IRA, bombed the Killyhevlin Hotel in Enniskillen. Loyalists also added to the troubled atmosphere: a Catholic taxi driver, Michael McGoldrick, was shot dead by Portadown members of the Ulster Volunteer Force (UVF) near Lurgan, and Ervine warned: 'I think we have the potential to go to hell and back and that's the reality of life in Northern Ireland … someone, somewhere on the nationalist side is not ready for peace.'[147]

The inter-party talks, which had begun in June under the chairmanship of George Mitchell, did little to ease the tensions prior to the Twelfth holidays; and, when the RUC banned the Drumcree march on 7 July, a re-run of the previous year's stand-off quickly developed. The Orange Order blamed the decision on interference from the Dublin government and republican militants,[148] and the Portadown District Orange master, Harold Gracey, described the situation as being akin to the Alamo.[149] Although Trimble assured journalists that 'There will be no violence in Drumcree. The Orange Order will ensure that its members behave responsibly', the Order's leader, Martin Smyth, said that 'If the security services can block the roads, so can we' and commented that if loyalists were breaking the law, 'the people had no other way'.[150] As the impasse continued, Taylor warned that the police could be faced with as many as 100,000 Orangemen should the march still be prohibited on the Twelfth.[151] Meanwhile, Smyth claimed that it was 'tragic to think in the same week in which the slaughter on the Somme was remembered, the Army was being deployed to stop Orangemen coming home from a church service'.

A common thread in Orangemen's complaints was that the RUC decision was a victory for republicans: 'it is bowing to an element who have orchestrated this protest for the last two years'.[152] David Burnside, the UUP MP for South Antrim, claimed that a domino effect was discernible in the republican agenda:

> [Ballycastle] has a large population ... But what happens if Sinn Féin decides that Ballycastle is a Catholic town? Do ten protestors stop us in North Antrim going to Ballycastle? It is ludicrous. This is their way of splitting up Northern Ireland as a political entity.

Burnside's fundamental point, however, was to return to a majoritarian logic that took no heed of local sentiments: 'No area of Northern Ireland is nationalist ... irrespective of how people vote. Northern Ireland is British, every inch of it.'[153] A similar disingenuousness was apparent in the attempt by some in the Orange leadership to disassociate the Order from the loyalist violence. Jeffrey Donaldson, the UUP MP for Lagan Valley, for example, claimed that the Orange Order tried to steward its protests and simply ignored the problems and responsibilities inherent in bringing large emotionally charged crowds onto the streets: 'We regret violence when it occurs ... [but the] overwhelming majority of our protests have passed off peacefully. There has been violence, but not exclusively on one side'.[154]

Despite the spiralling riots and the atmosphere of threat and tension associated with the construction of road blocks across the North, the *Newsletter* urged restraint:

> We have over the past few days been highly critical of the RUC decision to block [the Drumcree parade] ... However, we have no hesitation in fully supporting the RUC in taking resolute action to deal with the unruly loutish elements responsible for the wave of destruction in our cities and towns over the past 24 hours.[155]

The paper suggested that one way to break the impasse was for the Garvaghy Road residents to sideline Brendan MacCionnaith and reach a compromise with the Orangemen themselves.[156] In fact, the paper's line was a direct echo of that taken by Protestant church leaders. The Presbyterian Moderator, Dr Harry Allen, for example, pointed out that while protest was justified, it should be restrained and dignified: that '[t]hreats should never be grounds on which serious decisions are reached'.[157] The Archbishop of All Ireland, Robin Eames, reiterated these ideas and again appealed for 'reasonableness':

> Protest on either side will be utterly diluted by the sort of behaviour we've seen trying to bring this province to its knees again by violence and by burnings and by evictions. We have got to find a way out of this impasse.[158]

The nationalist press also pointed to the need for reasonableness and referred to the language of human rights. However, it drew different conclusions as regards whose human rights were being infringed, and claimed that the onus was on the Orangemen and the unionist leadership. The *Irish Times*, for example, condemned what it perceived as Trimble's sectarian stance: 'Mr Trimble owes his current position in large measure to his perceived "victory" in Portadown one year ago ... The pity is that he still feels obliged to support some elemental forces and dubious traditions in his own community.'[159] The *Irish News* also referred to the previous year's events and claimed that nationalist alienation was understandable:

> We hope a resolution can be found. But when they come to consider any deal this year, the nationalist people of Portadown will not forget the ease with which Mr Trimble, and his partner the Rev Ian Paisley, danced over 1995's compromise. A deal is not impossible, but the events over the past few days indicate that David Trimble has an enormous distance to move if he is to address the real concerns of the people whose area he wants to march through.[160]

This wave of destruction convinced the chief constable to overturn his original decision and force the Drumcree march down the Garvaghy Road by forcibly removing the nationalist protesters on 11 July. Immediately, unionist anger was taken up by nationalists – Derry city, for example witnessed the worst rioting 'ever seen', with 900 petrol bombs being thrown at the police, and three policemen being shot in gun attacks in Belfast.[161] The *Irish News* referred to the nationalist anger claiming that:

> If yesterday's shameful events in Portadown prove anything, it is that nationalists are living in Northern Ireland under sufferance. The state has abandoned them to the whim of unionist politicians, the Orange

Order, and loyalist bully boys ... There is no security, there is just the rule of the mob.[162]

Although Trimble claimed that the Province would have 'lurched into anarchy' if the Orangemen had not exercise restraint,[163] his decision to meet with loyalist leaders was roundly condemned by both nationalists and unionists.[164] Although he criticised politicians who supported democracy and non-violence on an '*à la carte* basis', John Bruton reserved much of his anger for the British government: 'If governments are seen to yield to that sort of pressure, then governments will not be taken seriously in the future ... A state cannot afford to yield to force.'[165] The former Taoiseach, Garret FitzGerald, echoed a general disbelief regarding unionist motivation:

> Do they [unionists] realise that when our politicians, backed overwhelmingly by public opinion, now join with the British government in putting forward proposals like those in the Framework Document, they do so with a view to stabilising Northern Ireland in the interests of peace on this island – and not with the devious purpose of taking the North over by stealth?[166]

In the North, nationalist anger was vented in a series of rallies in which, according to the *Irish News*, tens of thousands participated. At the West Belfast rally, Adams drew his own lesson from the crisis: 'If anyone ever wanted a reason why the IRA said it will not surrender its weapons, then look back on what happened this week.'[167]

The stalemate over decommissioning continued throughout the second half of 1996 and the last months of Major's premiership in 1997. During this period, the SDLP maintained its position that decommissioning should not be a prerequisite for talks. For example, Hume told his party conference in November that the demand was counterproductive for securing a new ceasefire and that 'Turning objectives into preconditions is not good politics'.[168] Although republicans anticipated that a Labour government would be more sympathetic to their concerns than it would to those of unionists, Tony Blair's first major policy speech on Northern Ireland after becoming prime minister was a straightforward reaffirmation of the principle of consent:

> none of us in this hall today, even the youngest, is likely to see Northern Ireland as anything but a part of the UK. That is the reality, because the consent principle is now almost universally accepted ... A political

settlement is not a slippery slope to a united Ireland. The government will not be persuaders for unity.[169]

However, both Blair and his Secretary of State for Northern Ireland, Mo Mowlam, indicated some willingness to entertain Sinn Féin's arguments regarding decommissioning – the priority, the government said, was a new ceasefire; decommissioning would not be a 'stumbling block'.[170]

On 27 June, Mowlam held 'proximity talks' with the Orange Order and the Garvaghy Road residents, but these failed to breach the impasse. A few days later, on 1 July, the new Fianna Fáil Taoiseach, Bertie Ahern, visited the Garvaghy Road and stated that he would not support the Secretary of State were she to decide to force the march along the road.[171] Despite this warning, the chief constable, Ronnie Flanagan, pushed the march through on Sunday, 6 July. Whereas the *Irish Times* hinted at one of the reasons behind the decision was to secure the Trimble leadership,[172] the *Irish News* highlighted the symbolic aspects of the action:

> One of the most striking images from yesterday was not the phalanx of Orangemen marching down the Garvaghy Road, it was the open air mass celebrated in the shadow of soldiers and police. Nothing underlines the enormity of what happened yesterday more than the realisation that Catholics were prevented from worshipping in their own church because Orangemen, who normally worship elsewhere, wanted to attend a service at Drumcree.[173]

Nevertheless, the *Newsletter* urged restraint: 'The only way of overturning the Orange state in which we live is through political engagement leading to a settlement which respects the rights of all, not just those who put on a sash.' Again, the paper's response to the escalating crisis drew from the moderate discourse expounded by Church leaders. On this occasion Eames' condemnation of fringe elements chimed with the paper's explanation of the rioting in 1995 and 1996:

> Dr Eames quite properly highlights the risks of trouble from elements on the fringes of the unionist and nationalist society and he calls on the voices of the 'silent majority' in the two communities to make their voices [heard] and recognised.[174]

While Adams called for 'republicans to get involved' in protests against the Garvaghy decision and McGuinness demanded 'confrontation' on the streets, Hume also urged restraint: 'I would certainly hope that, given the current situation and given the very deep anger that is now widespread in the [nationalist] community, people will remain calm ...'[175] Another call for moderation was made by the *Newsletter*, which claimed that 'Law-abiding people, Protestants and Roman Catholics, will not get solutions to their problems from the likes of Gerry Adams and Martin McGuinness provocatively posturing at war-cry rallies'.[176]

Mowlam's credibility in the eyes of nationalists plummeted the following day after a secret memorandum on the Drumcree dispute was leaked to the press.[177] This was dated 20 June – that is, prior to Mowlam's 'proximity talks' – and appeared to have been drafted in response to a query from the Secretary of State asking for a 'game plan' for pushing the Orange parade down the Garvaghy Road. The 'game plan' itself was to be premised on the idea that 'a controlled parade on the Garvaghy Road is the least-worst option'. The document went on to recommend various strategies for achieving that end, including the government refusing to avoid an 'early fixed position' and claiming that the 'chief constable has genuinely not made a decision'. Although both the *Irish Times* and the *Irish News* pointed out that the document lacked context, the Northern paper was particularly angered at the apparent duplicity:

> The credibility of the NIO was completely undermined [by the document] which reveals that its attempts to reach a settlement of the Drumcree situation were a cynical exercise in manipulation and entrapment.[178]

The paper went on to claim that the '[w]illingness by unionists to play the "Orange Card" remains the single biggest impediment to peace in Northern Ireland'. The revelation of two letters written by the Garvaghy residents to Trimble during the IRA ceasefire exacerbated nationalist sentiment still further. The *Irish News* pointed out that Trimble had failed to answer the letters, despite being willing to talk to a convicted loyalist terrorist in the shape of Billy Wright:

> The UUP leader's refusal to defuse the Drumcree crisis has already brought his judgement into question. These latest revelations make his position as leader of a major constitutional party increasingly untenable.[179]

Although the *Irish News* correctly highlighted Trimble's doublestandards, it failed to differentiate between what was a valid attempt to deal with the ringleaders of the violence and the hand-wringing abdication of other Orange leaders who denied all responsibility for their supporters' actions. In part, this condemnation must be linked to the nationalist distrust and dislike of the UUP leader, which again may account for some of the unwillingness of constitutional nationalists to empathise with his loss of unionist confidence in the post-Good Friday period.

Conclusion

As a careful reading of the events between 1985 and 1997 reveals, unionist resistance and opposition meant that political dynamics eventually leaned towards conforming to their bottom line: Britain would not be a persuader for Irish unity; the principle of consent was agreed to by Irish nationalists; and cross-border bodies would not be evolutionary or represent an 'embryonic' all-Ireland parliament, but would be answerable to a unionist veto in a devolved Northern Assembly.[180] This occurred despite deepening Protestant suspicion over political developments – and, in particular, over Sinn Féin's emergence as a media-savvy modern party – one of the key reasons for these developments was repeated unionist resistance to what they perceived as unfavourable terms. The decommissioning debate, however, revealed not only the limits to unionism's 'soft' power; it also demonstrated how an informal convergence occurred within Irish nationalism. As with unionism, this was characterised by an inward-focused conservatism: republicans came further into the political arena, but the end-goal of gradual reunification remained untouched and served as the lens through which strategic change was viewed. The gulf between nationalism and unionism was not only perpetuated at the level of policy-making, as the Drumcree crises demonstrated, deep-seated fear and distrust remained a central dynamic of Northern Irish politics even as the armed campaigns began to wind down. The next chapter explores how these trends influenced the Belfast/Good Friday Agreement and carried over to shape the political developments in the post-1998 period.

6
The Politics of the Past, 1998–2008

Acquiescing peace

This chapter looks at the politics of the 1998 Belfast/Good Friday Agreement and argues that the faltering attempts to establish devolution in Northern Ireland were a product of the ways in which contemporary political developments are saturated with the politics of the past. This chapter explores how the legacies of the conflict continued to influence post-Agreement politics in the North. The underlying question is the extent to which it is possible to speak of peace and transition in a society that is still characterised by sectarian division at the social and geographic levels and political entrenchment and polarisation at the level of elite politics. The chapter examines the episodic attempts to establish a power-sharing government at Stormont and the similarly sporadic attempts by the Northern Ireland Office and the Northern Ireland Assembly to establish mechanisms for dealing with the legacies of the Troubles. Although these mechanisms have created financial and medical assistance for victims, the debate over the meaning of the conflict reveals an underlying trend concerning the ability of the past to influence the present. Thus, while governmental initiatives may appear to deal with the past in a piecemeal fashion, in fact, the divisions over power-sharing and the meaning of the Troubles simply reflect the fact that the contributory causes of the conflict – namely, antagonistic policy objectives and different, communally-based experiences of the violence – continue to shape contemporary politics.

The policy direction of the main nationalist and unionist parties effectively shaped their responses to the 1998 Agreement. The Ulster Unionist Party, for its part, claimed that the Agreement ratified its interpretation of the conflict in that it secured nationalist acceptance of the constitutional position and delegitimised the republican rationale for violence.[1] On the other hand, anti-Agreement unionists, such as Ian Paisley's DUP and Robert McCartney's UK Unionist Party (UKUP), argued that it represented the latest attempt by Britain and the Republic to impose a settlement on Northern Ireland against the wishes of the majority of the unionist electorate.[2] As regards the nationalist community, the SDLP claimed that the Agreement vindicated its long-term approach to the conflict: the 'three strands' of the Agreement were premised on the party's description of three relationships – those within Northern Ireland; those between the North and the South; and those between the island of Ireland and Britain – and that it provided for the legitimate expression of nationalist identity and culture in Northern Ireland.[3] Republicans argued that the Agreement represented a stepping-stone or a transitional point in the struggle for bringing partition to an end.[4]

In effect, the Good Friday institutions reified these divisions. Contrary to the hopes of those who believed that the best way of proceeding was to divide political power and apportion it to the leaders of the communal blocs,[5] the institutions established in 1998 failed to tackle the escalating sectarianism and division that characterise everyday life across Northern Ireland.[6] As Paul Dixon has pointed out, the ambiguity, manipulation and deception involved in setting up the institutions fed growing disillusionment, particularly in the unionist community, and contributed to the eclipsing of the moderate UUP and SDLP by the DUP and Sinn Féin, respectively.[7] However, the Agreement and its outworking were also a product of the saturation of contemporary politics in the North with the legacies of the past. Although peace came to Northern Ireland, as the Assembly's political culture demonstrates, it is a peace based on an uneasy calm regarding the constitutional and communal divide. Such quiescence is largely based on the legacy of the conflict, which continues to inform people's views about the present and expectations about the future. This two-way dynamic and somewhat paradoxical relationship – the experiences of the past influencing contemporary perceptions and contemporary perceptions shaping about the past – has ensured that the history of the Troubles has become a major site of political confrontation. Indeed, as this chapter points out, post-1998 developments in Northern Ireland revealed deep continuities with the past in that historical choices and interventions continued to constrain political reactions and colour perceptions of change.

Negotiating the Agreement

The immediate aftermath of Drumcree 1997 saw Blair deciding to bring Sinn Féin into the political talks. The decommissioning precondition was dropped in favour of a renewed ceasefire and a commitment to the Mitchell principles. Although this climb-down utterly undermined Trimble's position,[8] it also presented him with the dilemma that, if he rejected it, then 'unionists [would be] cast as the enemies of peace'.[9] His response was based on two ideas. First, he said, abstentionism was self-defeating:

> [London and Dublin are] more than capable of imposing so-called solutions against our will. Is the best way to defend and promote the cause of the Union to abandon the playing field and leave our goals wide open for our opponents to score time after time and win the game?[10]

Second, Trimble alluded to his determination to safeguard the principle of consent: 'If there are going to be talks they will be on the basis that the consent of the people of Northern Ireland will be paramount in determining their destiny.'[11] Sinn Féin's participation at talks quickly followed the renewed ceasefire and began on 9 September. The governments clarified their position on 15 September in a joint statement in which they said that decommissioning should occur as part of the 'process of negotiation'. Although the governments still talked about a 'resolution' to the issue, in fact decommissioning had become a 'process' in itself, one that would be overseen by a newly appointed International Commission on Decommissioning headed by General John de Chastelain.[12]

The narrative of the negotiations leading up to the Belfast/Good Friday Agreement of April 1998 and the details of the Agreement have been the subject of several academic studies.[13] As the previous chapter suggested, the broad outlines of a settlement – power-sharing and cross-border bodies – were clear from at least the Brooke-Mayhew talks of the early 1990s,[14] and were outlined in the January 1998 Heads of Agreement document, which the governments circulated to the parties. In many ways, therefore, the peace process was about filling in the gaps. In this regard, Richard English pointed out that the talks were 'as likely to be a symptom of [the] conflict as they are to be a cause'.[15] While the events of the 1990s – in particular, the parading disputes – reproduced the communal division, O'Leary and McGarry's suggestion that the 'governments could outline the parameters of what they regard as a reasonable settlement' to see if the parties agreed was a facile view of political realities.[16] First, such a scenario would have proved counterproductive in that it would have destabilised unionist politics and led to an imposed arrangement. There is little evidence that either Britain or the Republic was inclined to see through what would have amounted to joint authority.[17] Second, the idea that ready-made, consociational solutions were always present is not only a glib and morally questionable representation of the conflict which left almost 4,000 people dead, it obscures much of the historical record and ignores the dynamics involved in the negotiating process.[18] While there was no inevitability about the 1998 Agreement, as Arthur Aughey points out, the decision by the major parties to engage on serious terms meant that some sort of agreement was 'more likely' than on previous occasions.[19]

The Agreement itself provided for political institutions along the three strands agreed at the Brooke-Mayhew talks of 1991–2.[20] Strand 1 was concerned with democratic institutions in Northern Ireland and called for a 108-member Assembly, which would be elected by proportional representation (single transferable vote) and would have responsibility for the range of areas administered by the Northern Irish civil service (reserved matters such as policing and criminal justice remained under the auspices of the office of the Secretary of State). The Assembly would be headed by an executive seats in which would be proportionally selected on the basis of party size (in other words, by using the highest averages or, d'Hondt, method). Strand 2 established the cross-border North/South Ministerial Council, whose remit would cover a range of socio-economic areas such as tourism, agriculture and the environment, and whose decisions would be reached by 'agreement between the two sides'. Finally, strand 3 provided for a British-Irish Council, which would 'promote the harmonious and mutually beneficial development of the totality of relationships among the peoples of these islands'. In addition, the Agreement provided for the introduction of a range of human rights reforms, the establishment of a commission on police reform, the early release of paramilitary prisoners and a requirement that all parties 'use any influence they may have, to achieve the decommissioning of all paramilitary arms within two years'.

Selling the Agreement

The SDLP's response to the Belfast Agreement reflected its understanding of historical continuities. Hume, for example, castigated those who disagreed with his policy of including Sinn Féin in talks, claiming that his approach profoundly challenged and transformed republican politics: 'Gerry Adams, Martin McGuiness and their colleagues deserve our commendation for their on-going leadership and management of that complex and intense process [of change].'[21] Although he admitted that the Drumcree dispute and the Omagh bombing of August 1998 – in which 28 people, among them a woman pregnant with twins, were killed by a Real IRA car bomb – meant that 'putting the genie of violence back in the bottle is no easy task', he also claimed that '[w]e have decommissioned the reality of violence. We have decommissioned in a profound way the prospect of conflict leading to more victims'. Importantly, Hume placed the Good Friday Agreement within the nationalist narrative of ancient antagonisms:

> In 'Towards a New Ireland', in 1972, we said, speaking of our outdated quarrel, that 'We in this island cannot remain in the seventeenth century'. We in the SDLP ... have been at the forefront in seeking a resolution to our long conflict. We have never been closer to success than we now are.[22]

As with the SDLP, Sinn Féin's presentation of the Agreement stemmed from its interpretation of the past. Within this understanding, the peace process and the Agreement were part of a longer campaign of reunification. The idea, then, that republicans radically transformed their politics is superficially plausible – certainly, the IRA had stopped killing scores of people each year – but it also profoundly misrepresents the primary evidence and decontextualises the broad thrust of republican policy direction. For example, Roger MacGinty claims that '[r]epublican gains in two non-constitutional areas, notably in relation to security grievances and self-esteem', overshadowed its failure to change the constitutional status quo.[23] However, republicans did not see the issues in these simplistic terms; rather, equality reforms and institutional innovation were part of their longer-term project for gradual constitutional change.[24] The Agreement *did* transform republican politics. However, it was transformational not in a progressive, accommodative sense; rather, it institutionalised an airbrushed historical narrative and a revisionist approach to the past that sought to legitimate republican violence and reinforce their peace process strategy.[25] Thus, in the republican story, the peace process is

> one of a number of international examples of situations where a long war between entrenched colonial or settler interests and various oppressed groups has been brought to an end through

negotiations between former combatants which address the issues of discrimination and structural inequality that generated the original conflict.[26]

For Sinn Féin, post-1998 politics is a matter of ends rather than means – an interpretation that allows Adams to maintain that the armed struggle was 'worth it'.[27] Rather than being locked in to a partitionist conclusion, republicans saw the Agreement as another significant concession by the British government:

> while the Agreement is not a settlement, it is the basis for advancement. It heralds a change in the status quo. And it could become a transitional stage towards reunification but only if all those who express an interest in that objective, especially the powerful and influential, move beyond rhetoric to build a real dynamic for national democratic change.[28]

Shrugging off responsibility for the majority of deaths and the adoption of a concession-gaining approach imply a forward-moving political trajectory and a confrontational, destabilising stance rather than the consensus-building called for by Adams in 1998. An essential part of this project is what Henry McDonald has referred to as the intensification of commemoration on an 'industrial scale'.[29] Contrary to the 'transformational' representation of Catholic politics by Claire Mitchell, republicans have gone to great lengths to perpetuate nationalist narratives of 'victimhood'.[30] The language of rights and equality, enshrined in the Good Friday Agreement, underpins this project. Thus, as Tom Hartley argued in a Belfast City Council debate on how the First World War should be remembered:

> We cannot escape from history, we can deny it but we can't wipe it away. History is not one-dimensional Today we find ourselves in a new political epoch [where] we are challenged to create a political equilibrium between the unionist and nationalist communities. From this, I believe, will come points of common interest, of new ways of sharing, a common memory and the potential to create new forms of common remembrance.[31]

Admirable as these sentiments are, their application to republican remembrance would seriously jeopardise the self-perpetuating momentum of Sinn Féin's mobilisation strategies. Thus, Hartley's remembrance of the Troubles conforms to the parameters of the republican narrative:

> In their efforts to subdue us and to silence our demand for equality and independence, the British sought out our children and our mothers as their targets. Systematic brutality and injustice were the instruments of British domination. English government in Ireland has always sought to drown out our cry for freedom in the despair of our pain.[32]

As Sara McDowell points out, however, this particularistic form of remembering the past is not limited to republican (and loyalist) history-making. In fact, the creation of self-justifying narratives has occurred with the active encouragement of the state in the form of council funding for civil society heritage initiatives such as the 'Troubles tours' in North and West Belfast.[33] In short, while republicans have been brought into the state, the persistence of long-term policies and their justification and explanation in traditional nationalist narratives have been a central feature of post-1998 politics. The paradox at the heart of the consociational structures is that by empowering an ethnicised understanding of the conflict, the Good Friday Agreement, in effect, introduced a destabilising dynamic and a policy trajectory that seeks to transcend the constitutional limitations of the 1998 Agreement.

The debate within Ulster unionism over the Agreement also largely occurred within pre-existing parameters. While uncertainty and profound reservations, particularly over the release of paramilitary prisoners, overshadowed unionist responses, again, an underlying and residual conservative tendency or strain of thought proved instrumental in securing sufficient backing for the May 1998 referendum on the Agreement. This conservatism is distinct from the public relations assault by the two governments – Blair in particular – and largely belies the idea that unionists were tricked by media arch-manipulators and New Labour spin-doctors into voting 'Yes' to the Agreement. What this underlying conservatism or moderation meant was that although there was considered debate within unionist politics, there is no doubt that it occurred in terms favourable to Trimble and the 'Yes' camp.

The key to the debate was the need for unionist unity in what was undoubtedly a crucial moment in modern Northern Irish history. This served as the touchstone for the *Newsletter*'s position:

> UUP leader David Trimble should move swiftly to bring to book the dissenters within his own parliamentary party. If they are out of step

with the ruling council, out of step with their own constituencies, is it not time they were invited to step outside the [realms] of the party on whose platform they were elected? There is only one future for the Ulster Unionist Party, and that is to stand resolutely [behind] their leader who has [fashioned] success out of failure, and an opportunity out of what could so easily have been an unmitigated disaster.[34]

The release of the PIRA's 'Balcombe Street Gang' to appear at a special Sinn Féin Ard Fheis at the beginning of May encapsulated what the *Newsletter* called 'one of the most difficult aspects of the peace process'.[35] However, the paper counselled against the potential for over-reaction. Rather, it pointed to the benefits that the process was going to bring: 'Gordon Brown [Chancellor of the Exchequer] has raised morale with a £315 million aid package while Sir Kenneth Bloomfield's [Northern Ireland Victims Commissioner] diligent and sensitive report on the victims of violence has helped to demonstrate the government's commitment to those on both sides who have suffered most from 30 years of conflict.'[36] The paper went on to discount a poll conducted by the *Irish Times* which revealed the 'Yes' vote would be under 60 per cent, pointing out that the data related to the immediate aftermath of the Balcombe Street Gang's appearance:

> Ordinary people on both sides have a right to vent their disgust over such sickening events but nothing that happens within the confines of a militant republican or loyalist environment should be allowed to dissuade decent people from delivering the vote that will give us all a chance to build a better future for ourselves and for coming generations.[37]

Blair and Trimble did not share the paper's faith in there being sufficient numbers of 'decent' people to carry the vote. Blair, for example, warned the Orange Order that the Agreement represented 'the best opportunity we have had to secure a stable and peace future for Northern Ireland within the United Kingdom'.[38] He also promised that

> There will not be people taking their seats in the Northern Ireland executive, nor will there be the accelerated prisoner release programme unless violence is given up for good. I cannot make it clearer than that ... People cannot pick and choose in this Agreement. All parts of the Agreement, including the elements on decommissioning, the elements on non-violent democratic means, are all there and they

are all matters that come to affect both prisoner release and people taking their seats in the Northern Ireland Assembly.³⁹

For his part, Trimble claimed that a 'critical point' had been reached and warned:

> Those who have sought to united Ireland by violence have failed. While we do not believe that voting 'Yes' will of itself guarantee a long and lasting peace, voting 'No' will guarantee a return to violence ... Over the next few weeks, people in Northern Ireland and in the Irish Republic can choose to live in the future – one not haunted by the past.⁴⁰

Bill Clinton was also recruited to push the case for a 'Yes' vote. Echoing Blair, he claimed that there was 'no plan B' in the event of a majority 'No' vote, and promised that a 'successful outcome' would increase investment in Northern Ireland.⁴¹

Together with these thinly veiled threats, moral pressure was exerted in the form of what was then an emerging victims' lobby. On 12 May, for example, the Northern Ireland Security Minister, Adam Ingram, was appointed as the first 'Minister for Victims'. The Church of Ireland Primate for All Ireland, Robin Eames, also praised the government's decision to award £4 million to the victims of the conflict: 'No one can be compensated for the loss of a loved one. But at least this recent move can be welcomed as recognition of a genuine need.' Although he avoided making a categorical statement on how people should vote, Eames claimed that the 'Agreement is a vital point in the Irish pilgrimage of peace'.⁴² These ideas were echoed by the Methodist Minster Rev. Harold Good, who had been involved in secret talks with the Provisionals during the conflict. Addressing the prisoner-release issue, Good sought to concentrate on what he saw as its underlying theological significance:

> In a very real way, we are all asking for release – release from conflict and uncertainty, release from a troubled and violent society. I believe that prisoners, like any party to this appalling conflict, must be included in this chance for a new beginning.⁴³

Underscoring these ideas, the *Newsletter* interviewed the relatives of people who had died at the hands of republicans, including Alan McBride, whose wife was killed in the Shankill bombing: 'I am voting Yes in the referendum because I believe it will create a better world for my child and her children ... we victims are being asked to accept the most with this deal, but I am still voting in favour of it.'⁴⁴

Although the Orange Order resisted directing its members on how to vote, it nevertheless roundly rejected Blair's overtures: 'We had hoped that [the Agreement] would offer such a real prospect of peace that we could positively endorse it. Sadly, that has not been the case.'[45] The Ulster Unionists suspected Paisley of playing to the galleries during the referendum campaign and of targeting a summer of discontent as a way of mobilising anti-Agreement opinion. For instance, when Paisley withdrew from two Northern Irish political television programmes, Trimble refused his request for a debate in the Ulster Hall:

> Obviously he wants to have a huge mob there to change the nature of the debate. Instead of trying to inform people and laying out the issues to people, he wishes to engage in a bit of theatre and get his supporters to shout down opposition.[46]

That Paisley was playing a long-term game and was prepared to lose the referendum was further evidenced in an interview he gave shortly before it was held:

> I am personally opposed to power-sharing with nationalists because nationalists are only power-sharing to destroy Northern Ireland and you don't put people into a government to destroy a country ... I would like to win the referendum. It is only a shadow Assembly that we are elected to ... And it can't be a real assembly except everything is working [sic], including the cross-border bodies with executive powers, and we will not work those bodies at all. We will not have anything to do with them. We will enter the Assembly to destroy the attempt to put us into a united Ireland.[47]

Nevertheless, around 53 per cent of the unionist electorate voted in favour of the Agreement,[48] with a total 'Yes' vote of 71.1 per cent. Despite the slender unionist margin, the *Newsletter* claimed that its stance had been vindicated: 'Unionists whose hearts a week earlier had been set against the agreement because of the manifestation of the prisoners issue at Sinn Féin and loyalist rallies, put their anger aside and, looking a the bigger picture, liked what they saw.'[49] Following the referendum result the debate within unionism became more fractious, leading the paper to warn that 'Unionism's real challenge has only just begun'. Returning to the idea of unionist unity, the paper claimed that

> Petty party bickering, both internal and external, has blunted the dynamic thrust of the pro-Union message and unless unionist politicians begin to sing of the same hymn sheet for the positive

advancement of life in Northern Ireland, they will continue to fall short of their maximum targets.[50]

Trimble failed to win an outright unionist majority in the Assembly election. Although his party won 28 seats, this was matched by the combined forces of anti-Agreement unionism: the DUP won 20, the UKUP five and independents three. Despite massive media hype, the small loyalist parties failed to perform, with the Progressive Unionist Party winning just two seats. The election results, however, signalled an even greater sea-change within nationalist politics: while the SDLP won 24 seats to Sinn Féin's 18, republicans had closed the gap in Catholic voting from a 70:30 ratio in 1992 to 55:45 in 1998. A contributory factor in Sinn Féin's rise was the party's emphasis on a growing Catholic electorate in the North, which in the May 1997 general election had reached a high point of 40.2 per cent.[51]

Following the appointment of Trimble and Mallon as First and Deputy First Ministers on 1 July, the Province was facing a summer of intense political uncertainty. On 22 June the chief constable of the RUC, Ronnie Flanagan, had apparently stated that, were the threat of violence judged to be too great, the police would force the Orange march along the Garvaghy Road, even if the recently formed Parades Commission ruled in favour of a ban. Flanagan later claimed his remarks were taken out of context and that he would enforce the Commission's decision.[52] The Commission announced its decision to reroute the march away from the Garvaghy Road on 29 June owing to the Order's refusal to negotiate with the residents' group. In response the Order pledged to remain at Drumcree as long as it would take to complete its march down the road. In response to the developments, loyalists carried out arson attacks on ten Catholic churches on 2 July and, amidst continued rioting, fired shots at RUC patrols in Belfast. A week later, on 10 July, four republicans were arrested in London suspected of planning a fire-bomb attack. As in previous years, an underlying discourse of moderation and restraint was promoted by Protestant church leaders and echoed by some unionist leaders and the *Newsletter*. Trimble, for example, visited the destroyed Catholic churches and blamed the Loyalist Volunteer Force. A spokesman for the County Armagh Orange Order also condemned the attacks, and, like Trimble, called on 'all right-thinking people in the Protestant and loyalist community to isolate those who would engage in such sacrilege and wanton destruction'.[53]

The killing of three Catholic children by a loyalist mob in an arson attack in Ballymoney on 12 July represented something of a tipping point in the escalating series of events. Their deaths undermined the extremist campaign and gave moderates an opportunity to make their voices heard.[54] Rev. William Bingham, the chaplain of the County Armagh Orange Order, tapped into the feeling of moral outrage among many unionists and called for an immediate end to that year's Drumcree stand-off, saying that 'no road is worth a life'. Trimble again attacked the loyalist intensification and asked the Order to call off its protest:

> I know that they have tried to conduct their protest peacefully, but those responsible for these murders and other violence have used this protest as an excuse for an appalling act of barbarity and I must say to the Portadown brethren that the only way in which they can clearly distance themselves from these murders and show the world that they repudiate those who murder young children, the only way to repudiate that is to come down off the hill.[55]

Insulation and devolution

The intermittent periods of direct rule between 1998 and 2007 gave indications of the differing priorities of the various actors involved in its implementation. The evidence suggests that, although London and Dublin occasionally disagreed over specific actions and often perceived and interpreted events differently, they nevertheless shared a common interest in using the Agreement as a means of insulating Westminster and Dáil politics from the Northern Ireland question. Likewise, the broad thrust of the evidence points to a republican preference for institutional and cultural reform rather than devolution *per se*. The failure to accommodate Trimble's difficulties in terms of a haemorrhaging of unionist confidence undoubtedly reflected the residual nationalist wariness of the unionist leader. However, the republican delay in decommissioning until 2005 was also a product of its use of the latent IRA threat to leverage further concessions from the British government on a range of issues, such as police reform, troop reduction, disbanding of the Royal Irish Regiment, prisoner releases and the institution of restorative justice schemes. Although the post-Good Friday debate came to focus on the question of decommissioning, each of these issues was emotionally salient to both the republican/nationalist and unionist communities. Thus, while Trimble may have secured what he termed 'accountable government' for Northern Ireland, and was probably correct in his assessment that the debate over police reform had been lost with the publication of the Patten Report in September 1999,[56] these judgements did not reflect Protestant disquiet. Although unionist conservatism continued to underpin the Trimble project, support for the Agreement remained tenuous given the fact that not only were unionists effectively being asked to acquiesce – for the 'sake of peace' and the 'new dispensation' – in the republican attack on the security apparatus, but that they were also being asked by Trimble to share power with them.

Trimble's position was compromised by the fact that the issues on the republican agenda were the responsibility of the British government. As such, much of the debate and the crucial decisions took place between Blair and Sinn Féin. Blair's willingness to entertain republican fears of an IRA split over decommissioning gave the impression of being 'exceptionally keen to placate republicans in such a way as to greatly intensify fears of a mafia state'.[57] Nor was Trimble's case helped by the fact that the Provisionals not only retained their organisation intact, but that they demonstrated a willingness to embark on strategic actions such as that which led to the arrest of republicans in the FARC-controlled area of Colombia in August 2001, the raid on the Castlereagh security headquarters in March 2002 or the revelation of the spy ring at Stormont in October that year. Furthermore, although Trimble's repeated survival of the leadership battles within the UUC illustrated a residual moderate constituency, these victories could not mask the fact that if his intra-party opponents were added to the anti-Agreement DUP voters a unionist majority against the Agreement could be constructed. The continued high-profile battles with UUP MPs encapsulated this widespread unease and served to represent the party's inability to provide a coherent direction.[58] The drift in support was captured by a BBC poll in October 2002:

Table 6.1 Declining unionist support for the Belfast/Good Friday Agreement[59]

If the [1998] referendum was held again today, how would you vote?

	Yes (%)	No (%)
1998 May (Referendum)	55.0	45.0
1999 March	45.6	54.4
2000 May	42.8	57.2
2001 September	42.3	57.7
2002 October	32.9	67.1

The publication of the Patten Report on policing, which took place on 9 September 1999, served to crystallise and perpetuate the growing polarisation: while 69 per cent of Catholics were in favour of the recommendations, 65 per cent of Protestants disapproved.[60] Chris Patten (a former NIO minister in the Thatcher administration and Governor of Hong Kong) recommended that the RUC be stripped of all paraphernalia that could be considered biased in favour of one section of the community – in effect, this meant neutralising the unionist and British symbolism of the force. Among the 175 specific proposals, Patten recommended that the name would be changed to the Police Service of Northern Ireland (PSNI); its badge would be redesigned; the Union flag would not be flown from police stations; and recruits would be drawn on a 50/50 basis from the Protestant and Catholic communities. The new Secretary of State in Blair's administration, Peter Mandelson, announced in January 2000 that almost all of the recommendations were being accepted.[61] The disbandment of the RUC was a key republican demand insofar as it encapsulated its narrative understanding of the conflict being about, in the first instance, British state and loyalist violence. Unionists, on the other hand, pointed to the fact that the IRA had killed 1,771 people, in comparison to the RUC's responsibility for 52 Troubles-related killings, and that the police sustained 303 deaths to the Provisionals' 293.[62] The report's fundamental political impact was to undermine Trimble's suggestion that the Agreement represented a victory for unionism and the unionist interpretation of the Northern Ireland question; as such, it seriously destabilised the political atmosphere in the North and thereby inhibited the chances of fostering accommodation through devolved power-sharing.[63] This was because Patten not only sought to 'obliterate' symbols that held great significance to unionists,[64] it also implied a fundamental rewriting of their own understanding of the Troubles as one of republican aggression against the forces of law and order.

The uncertainty over IRA decommissioning delayed the formal transfer of powers to the Assembly until the end of 1999. For its part, Sinn Féin claimed that the decommissioning was the responsibility of all parties to the Agreement and that it could only be achieved in the context of a final settlement and a demilitarised North. Again, republican justifications conformed to its master-narrative: the IRA was an undefeated army whose struggle had been justified, asking it to decommission was tantamount to 'humiliation'.[65] Again, the narrative is notable for its lacunae – asking the IRA to decommission was not simply about humiliation; it involved recognition of the fact that the armed struggle had fundamentally divided the North.[66] As Eamonn O'Kane points out, the logic of this refusal demanded that the governments exert pressure elsewhere.[67]

George Mitchell was once again drafted in and a review process began which placed the emphasis on the Northern parties reaching agreement. The result of this review was an orchestrated process in which Trimble announced in November that he would enter into power-sharing with Sinn Féin, Sinn Féin agreed that decommissioning was essential and the IRA pledged its commitment to 'freedom, justice and peace in Ireland'.[68] Trimble, however, still had to win the approval of the UUC, which he achieved by writing a post-dated letter of resignation that would come into effect in February 2000 in the absence of movement on decommissioning.

The first period of devolution lasted from 2 December 1999 until 11 February when the British government pushed the Northern Ireland Act through parliament, which suspended the Assembly while preserving Trimble as First Minister and, in the process, obviating the need for another Assembly election. The Dublin government and Northern nationalists claimed, with some justification, that this was an abuse of British power; however, the alternative was that a seriously weakened Trimble would be returned in any election, which would risk the sustainability of the devolution project.[69] This makeshift manoeuvre did not, however, address the underlying problem of decommissioning. Having prioritised Northern Irish devolution, Trimble continued to be susceptible to the general drift of governmental thinking – namely, that the best way to convince the IRA to decommission was to have a sustained period of power-sharing. Trimble secured a victory in a leadership context, by 57 per cent to his challenger Martin Smyth's 43 per cent, and agreed to re-enter the power-sharing executive in May 2000. Again, however, the restoration of devolution was accompanied by a series of political manoeuvres: the British government agreed to further demilitarisation and the IRA pledged to put its arms 'completely and verifiably ... beyond use' in the context of the 'full implementation' of the Agreement.[70]

Distrust and power politics continued to characterise elite relations in the second period of post-1998 devolution. Nationalists and republicans denounced Trimble's decision to ban Sinn Féin ministers from attending North-South Ministerial Council meetings, and argued that London was stalling on implementing Patten's proposals and reducing the army's presence.[71] Furthermore, the IRA broke off contacts with the decommissioning body, while loyalist paramilitaries initiated an internecine feud along with a sectarian picket of a Catholic primary school in North Belfast.[72] In response to growing disquiet over power-sharing with Sinn Féin within his party and the threat of a wipe-out at the hands of the DUP in the forthcoming general election, on 23 May 2001 Trimble wrote another post-dated letter promising to resign on 1 July if decommissioning had not begun. Although the UUP subsequently lost two seats to Sinn Féin and three to the DUP, its core vote had actually held up since the 1998 Assembly election: in fact, its share of the vote had increased from 21.3 per cent in 1998 to 26.8 per cent in 2001. Revealingly, the DUP had itself moderated its discourse from 'smashing' the Assembly to 'renegotiating' the Agreement, and had taken up its allotted seats in the executive.[73]

The IRA's decision to begin decommissioning in October 2001 despite loyalist attacks on Catholic houses belied its earlier stance that it needed its weapons for defensive purposes. While its decision followed from the adverse publicity of the arrests in Colombia and the changed international climate following 9/11, these events may only have accelerated the process.[74] Not only had the IRA always resisted international pressure, but its decision to disarm in October should also be placed in the context of the government's position paper of August in which London reaffirmed its commitment to the implementation of wide-ranging policing reforms; a substantial programme of demilitarisation; a criminal justice review; and inquiries into cases of suspected collusion.[75] In this context, the act of limited decommissioning was a *quid pro quo* – a demonstration of good faith that would lead to further concessions in the future.

The third period of devolution lasted slightly under a year, from November 2001 to October 2002. Again, the political debate centred on the long-term intentions of the IRA, which again effectively undermined Trimble's standing within unionism and contributed to a serious destabilisation of the peace through a series of 'adventurist' activities – notably, the raid on Castlereagh barracks and the Stormont spy-ring.[76] In response, Blair delivered his most trenchant speech on 17 October 2002:

> The fork in the road has finally come ... we cannot carry on with the IRA half in, half out of this process. Not just because it isn't right any more. It won't work anymore ... Remove the threat of violence and the peace process is on an unstoppable path. That threat, no matter how damped down, is no longer reinforcing the political, it is actually destroying it ... There cannot be two police forces. As the changes in criminal justice take effect, how can there seriously be calls on the one hand for human rights and on the other, the savage beatings of people without any trial or due process, without any rights, human or otherwise?[77]

Despite this rhetoric, Blair continued to bank on Adams and McGuinness delivering the IRA. This faith stemmed from the considerable personal interest he had invested in the Northern Irish peace process – at this period, it was estimated that it took up 40 per cent of Blair's time. Although the files will most likely not be available for a considerable period of time, it is reasonable to assume that Blair's faith was also based on intelligence reports that the Provisionals were committed to winding the war down completely – certainly, the series of leaks regarding high-profile informants suggested that the British security forces had thoroughly infiltrated the Provisionals by the 1990s.[78]

The emphasis on republicans was not, however, balanced by concern for Trimble's unionists, and Blair called for fresh elections in November 2003 without requiring further movement from the IRA.[79] Again, this decision was based on the idea that devolution would provide the best context for decommissioning and saving the Unionist Party. As Eamonn O'Kane points out, the reasoning involved in this idea was based on ignoring the plight of the SDLP, whose 2001 slump to being the second largest nationalist party behind Sinn Féin was confirmed with its return of 18 Assembly seats to Sinn Féin's 24 in November 2003.[80] The election also confirmed the DUP's ascendancy within unionism, gaining 30 seats to the UUP's 27. Despite the fact that the DUP's victory had been at the expense of the anti-Agreement independents rather than the UUP's core constituency (the UUP's share was slightly up from the 1998 Assembly election to 22.7 per cent), the election results precipitated a change in government thinking that now looked to a possible agreement between Sinn Féin and the DUP as the best way of proceeding.

As with previous efforts to bring republicans more firmly into the constitutional sphere, the gradual movement towards a Sinn Féin-DUP détente was a hostage to the IRA's continued activities – in particular, the Northern Bank robbery of December 2004 and the killing of Robert McCartney in a Belfast bar and its subsequent cover-up in early 2005. The 'final act' of decommissioning in September 2005 occurred in the context of the dissolution of the pan-nationalist project.[81] Fianna Fáil's condemnation of the McCartney killing in particular threatened Sinn Féin's electoral surge in the South, which had seen it winning five seats in the 2002 general election, and the IRA's continued existence placed a serious question mark over whether Sinn Féin would fulfil its goal of getting into government on both sides of the border.[82] While the October 2006 St Andrew's Agreement promised the DUP the 'fig-leaf' of not having to vote for a Sinn Féin Deputy First Minister,[83] it also required republican acceptance of 'exclusively peaceful means … [and to] uphold the rule of law' by extending the promise of the devolution of policing and criminal justice powers.[84]

The May 2007 accord entrenched Northern Ireland's two main ethnic parties in a power-sharing administration at Stormont. Although the media's coverage was restrained and relatively low-key, there was a general acknowledgement that the pact between the two extremes represented an historic moment. For his part, Trimble legitimately asked why the DUP rejected the Belfast Agreement only to accept 'its identical twin' in St Andrew's,[85] and pointed out that as regards the consultative North-South bodies, '[t]he silence of the DUP ... is eloquent testimony to our success'.[86] Both Mallon and Mandelson asked the pertinent question of whether Blair's policy of sidelining the moderates was 'worth it' morally or politically. Mandelson commented that while there 'was a lot to be said for paying a price to keep the bicycle moving. The issue is whether Tony Blair paid too big a price.' And in a damning indictment of Blair's Northern Irish policy, Mallon claimed that 'Anyone who knows the North of Ireland would not have contemplated actions which sold middle unionism to Paisley, just as the same way in which our party was treated'.[87] Few republicans were willing to reflect on whether the 'price' of almost 4,000 deaths, a generation of polarised communities and a border more entrenched than ever had been worth it. Those who did were either dissidents opposed to the peace process or ostracised individuals such as Brendan Hughes or Anthony McIntyre who had objected to the cynicism of the Adams-McGuinness leadership.[88] Republican apologists and propagandists were by this stage well versed in ignoring ethical questions – for them, the important thing was the symbolic momentum of Sinn Féin's surge:

> The elections last week saw Sinn Féin register its largest vote since partition. The lesson Mandelson and those who nod so approvingly at his interview have to learn is that the party's success is an acknowledgement by voters that the republican leadership drove the peace process, while the British government and unionists have proved ... dilatory in pursuit of a settlement.[89]

A shared future

Arguably, it is not in the interests of either the DUP or Sinn Féin to withdraw from the Northern Ireland Assembly; however, nor is it in their interests to pursue accommodative politics. Although the need to pursue political moderates – the median voters – required that Sinn Féin and the DUP curtail their extremes, this occurred because, and not in spite of, the parties retaining their long-term policy directions. While moderation occurred at a surface level, deeper continuities persisted that helped to perpetuate division at the elite level. For example, in February 2008, Sinn Féin began consultations on a 'roadmap for unity',[90] while the following month Peter Robinson announced that his party preferred a majoritarian 'voluntary coalition' system rather than the mandatory power-sharing of the 1998 Agreement.[91]

These divisions did not occur just at the elite level; rather, deep-seated animosities continued to characterise almost all aspects of Northern Irish society. According to PSNI statistics, between 1996 and 2004, 6,623 sectarian incidents occurred in North Belfast alone; and since 1991 an average of 1,378 people sought rehousing each year due to sectarian attacks. Between 2000 and 2003, over 500 people complained to the Office of Industrial Tribunals and Fair Employment Tribunals of religious discrimination at work. Sites of symbolic importance and communal belonging (churches, Orange Halls, GAA clubs) continue to be easy targets for arson attacks and witnessed almost 600 sectarian attacks between 1994 and 2002.[92] Although overt violence by paramilitaries has steadily declined in the post-1998 period, former terrorists continue to be transformed into peacemakers with the willing help of academics and the NIO in the form of community restorative justice schemes. Police statistics for the year-end 31 March reveal that in the twelve months after the DUP–Sinn Féin pact 42 shootings and 47 bombing incidents occurred; the following year (2008–9) saw 54 shootings and 112 bombing incidents.[93]

The Belfast/Good Friday structures in Northern Ireland have singularly failed to tackle the politics of entrenchment. In fact, the power-sharing institutions have created incentives for the local elites to pursue their long-term goals through democratic channels. This is hardly surprising given that the power-sharing pact simply reflected the ethnicised experiences of 30 years' violence, suspicion and sectarianism. The fact that the conflict ended in a stalemate compounded this situation as it meant that none of the main perpetrators of violence (the IRA, loyalist paramilitaries and the British army) were required to confront their past actions. Historical legacies from the conflict have, therefore, continued to set the parameters and determine the context in which the North has begun to assess the meaning of its past. In other words, although the idea of a sporadic, episodic or 'piecemeal' approach to 'dealing with the past' is a thinly plausible representation of how the NIO in particular has been working,[94] actually the historical continuities from the conflict have profoundly influenced how the past is used and abused in Northern Ireland.

Various institutional mechanisms have been introduced since the late 1990s to deal with these legacies. Invariably, they become subject to the same historical dynamics that perpetuated political conflict and entrenchment for so long. The first attempt to deal with the legacies of the Troubles was the appointment of Sir Kenneth Bloomfield as Victims' Commissioner in October 1997. This move was itself seen as a response to the growing unionist perception that republicans 'owned' the peace process. Although Bloomfield's report recommended a series of measures for dealing with victims' issues, including greater compensation to victims and their support groups; asking the government to give greater priority to trauma and pain treatment; improved employment opportunities for victims; and a series of symbolic ideas for a memorial day and an archive for victims' stories, it was roundly condemned by nationalists, who felt that it ignored the victims of state-sponsored violence.[95] In June 1998, the first Minister for Victims, Adam Ingram, established the Victims Liaison Unit within the NIO to implement Bloomfield's proposals concerning financial assistance. The announcement by the British government in January 1998 of an inquiry into Bloody Sunday served to alleviate nationalists' concerns. Although the Inquiry has yet to report, its effect on British politics has been profound – not least in the fact that its ballooning costs and its open-ended remit and terms of investigation influenced the government's decision to curtail the subsequent Butler and Hutton inquiries into the Iraq war.

In reality, there was no need to leave the issue of the past aside in case it would 'undo the deal' of the 1998 Agreement. In fact, the past was an intrinsic part of the politics of the Agreement. Institutional innovation and reform were part of the attempt by both unionist and nationalist elites to impose their own, highly ethnicised versions of the past on the present. The result was that victims merited just three paragraphs on page 18 of the 30-page document, while a key provision was the 'accelerated release of prisoners' within a two-year time frame. The failure to link prisoner releases to decommissioning and the demonstrable gulf in the treatment of convicted terrorists and their victims angered many people in constitutional nationalist and unionist communities. For unionists in particular it gave rise to the perception that the Agreement was about the valorisation of the republican explanatory narrative and the simultaneous obliteration of their experiences of the conflict out of history.[96]

As pointed out above, the reform of the police was intrinsic to this growing disillusionment. Although the police ombudsman – which was established under the Patten reforms – was instrumental in securing additional funding for injured RUC officers and their widows, it is undeniable that much of the ombudsman's work has been perceived by unionists as perpetuating republican ideas about the corruption of the police and the impossibility of reforming the Northern state. This perception is heightened due to the lack of reciprocation or serious engagement from republicans on the question of their actions – that is, beyond the recourse to history, 'if you had been there, you would have done the same' argument.[97] For example, the ombudsman's 2007 report into collusion between the RUC's special branch and loyalist paramilitaries seemingly confirmed republican narratives about the state being the main instigator of sectarian violence.[98] The main UVF informant at the centre of the investigation, Mark Haddock, had been accused in the Dáil of carrying out at least 21 murders, not only of Catholics but also fellow loyalists and a Protestant minister.[99] The Patten reforms also provided for the establishment of an Historical Enquiries Team to investigate unsolved murders relating to the Troubles. The team's continued value has, however, come under increasing scrutiny. For example, the then Secretary of State, Peter Hain, commented in 2007 that

> Huge amounts of money are involved which cannot be spent on meeting the concerns of today. Recent political progress in Northern Ireland should make us pause and ask whether re-living or even re-fighting the Troubles in the courtroom or the public inquiry or through police investigation is really a healthy way forward.[100]

That Hain was speaking at the launch of the Consultative Group on the Past in Northern Ireland (CPGNI) says something about the mindset of the government to the past and the rationale behind their decision to establish such a venture. In fact, the Group was charged with a particularly instrumental approach to the conflict – its dual task was to find the best way in which Northern Ireland should 'deal with the past' and to make 'recommendations ... on any steps that might be taken to support Northern Ireland society in building a shared future'.[101] That the Group accurately understood its task of making the past subservient to the needs of the present was reflected in its choice of an epigraph: 'To look backward for a while is to refresh the eye, to restore it, and to render it more fit for its prime function of looking forward.'[102] The public relations shambles of its launch also suggested to some more sceptical observers that in fact it recognised its task only too well – the proposed £12,000 award to all victims regardless of whether or not their relatives had been killed on active terrorist duty in the first instance served to distract attention from its other recommendations.

In fact, the Group envisaged a four-stranded process, overseen by a 'Legacy Commission', for dealing with the past. The first strand would involve bringing forward measures to help Northern Ireland move 'towards a shared and reconciled future', by tackling sectarianism, social division and inter-community polarisation. The second strand would review and investigate unresolved killings and would incorporate the PSNI Historical Enquiries Team. The third and fourth strands would deal with cases for which insufficient evidence existed to pursue through that legal review, with information being provided to the families in the case of strand three, and cases with 'thematic' linkages (such as those involving collusion) being dealt with separately in strand four. The Group argued that the Legacy Commission would negate the need for any further public inquiries, while its proposed five-year term would presumably allow the government to draw a line under its official responsibilities for the conflict.[103]

CPGNI's proposals avoid the crucial question of how sectarianism and social division can be managed when it is institutionalised in the communal carve-up of political power at the elite level of Stormont. Furthermore, while the Legacy Commission will have the power to compel the release of suppressed governmental inquiries into shoot-to-kill and collusion policies (the Stalker and the Stevens Reports); there is no indication that the Group gave much thought as to how the Commission is it gain access to documents or submissions from the paramilitaries. The Group has suggested that 'moral' pressure will elicit compliance; however, if republican and loyalist communities could not stop almost 4,000 deaths, there is little to suggest that they will be able to convince terrorists to place themselves before a judicial process.[104]

The Group's recommendations reveal not only a lack of common sense; they are saturated with extremely problematic political and moral assumptions. What CPGNI proposes, in short, is that the vast majority of people who did not join terrorist organisations should and must be reconciled to the murderous actions of others. If the Group's proposals are adopted, Northern Ireland's 'shared future' – for the next five years at least – will consist in being forced to listen to the self-serving, post-hoc justifications that have already served as the basis for countless terrorist speeches, autobiographies and other writings.[105]

The work of the four-person Commission for Victims and Survivors, which was appointed by Paisley and McGuinness in July 2008, largely duplicates that of the NIO's Victims' Unit. This was understandable given the Commission's origins as a sticking plaster to cover the widening rift in the executive over Hain's appointment of Bertha McDougal as interim Victims' Commissioner in 2006–7.[106] The fact that McDougal was the DUP's favoured candidate only upped the political stakes. If the subsequent appointment of two Catholics and two Protestants (and two men and two women) suggested a political fudge, the list of questions asked by the *Belfast Telegraph* gave the impression of a sad ethnic farce: How would the commissioners' decisions 'carry the same weight' as a single individual? How would the commissioners engage with other groups? Would the commissioners develop expertise along communal lines?[107] The Commission began holding public consultations on victims' issues in the summer of 2008; at the time of writing it is still to issue a report.

These attempts by the British state and the Northern Ireland Assembly to tackle the legacies of the Troubles have been guided by an inescapable presentist narrative of what the conflict was about and where the peace should be going. Essentially, this is a rerun of the traditional nationalistic approach to the past – namely, that history should be made to serve the present in 'progressive' ways. The NIO paper of March 2005 crystallises this approach in its call for

> The establishment over time of a normal, civic society, in which all individuals are considered as equals, where differences are resolved through dialogue in the public sphere, and where all people are treated impartially. A society where there is equity, respect for diversity and a recognition of our inter-dependence.[108]

As with Tom Hartley's programme for commemoration, this polished rhetoric not only avoids the problem of the practical implications of institutionalised sectarian divisions at Stormont, it is also permeated with implicit political assumptions and moral values about what Northern Irish society should look like and what is required of individuals to make it so. Thus, the pragmatism of using former terrorists to police social misdemeanours and enforce 'community restorative justice' simply covers the self-serving and platitudinous morality of forgiving and forgetting or drawing a line under the past.[109] In short, blind faith takes precedence over pragmatism as the shared future vision does not deal with the question of why either nationalists or unionists would wish for the current status quo existing in perpetuity.[110] Again, the idea that ethnic entrepreneurs should be empowered because of their apparent permanence in society is another expression of the *force majeur* morality contained in Blair's reputed analysis of the SDLP's 'problem' being that it didn't have guns.[111] The resort to pragmatism is underscored by the argument put forward by elite politicians, consociational political scientists or transitional justice theorists that they don't have any panaceas, but that their prognoses are better than the alternatives.[112] The moral malaise at the heart of this common approach is made all the more egregious by the fact that it often involves ignoring the events and the crimes of the past in favour of a valorised shared future, and the blithe disregard of the reproduction of terrorist narratives through pragmatic acquiescence.

Conclusion

Contemporary politics in Northern Ireland is inextricably tied to competing histories and ways of forgetting. Nowhere is this more apparent than in the response of the three main groups of perpetrators of death and destruction – particularly, in the construction by republicans and loyalists of what Marie Breen-Smyth has called 'cultures of victimhood'.[113] For republicans, this has meant emphasising state-sponsored violence and the sectarian killings of the 'loyalist death-squads'; while for loyalists, it has involved highlighting republican terror. Both sets of narratives serve to create common grievances and portray the paramilitaries as the defenders of embattled, unprotected minorities – since victims are, by definition, vulnerable, the paramilitaries' narratives incorporate the moral of justified aggression, which restored the balance of power. The politics of this culture of victimhood has therefore removed the need to admit responsibility. Loyalists, for example, argue that the past should be buried for the safety of individual former combatants and because '[c]hildren today will probably find it difficult to imagine the threats and fears that inspired their fathers to take up arms'.[114] Contemporary political considerations also inform republicans' views on how the past should be dealt with and represented. For example, although Sinn Féin favours a 'truth recovery process',[115] it has argued that it would be unacceptable if any such mechanism were run under the auspices of the British government: 'The British government was the major protagonist in the conflict in Ireland. They therefore cannot be the objective facilitator of any truth recovery process.'[116] For its part, the British government has been demonstrably reticent about establishing any such process. The interim report of the House of Commons Northern Ireland Affairs Committee, for instance, pointed to the lack of political consensus about the past and the absence of any agreement about what form a truth recovery process should take.[117] Indeed, some commentators have expressed scepticism about whether the British security apparatus really wants to entertain a truth recovery process.[118] Among the supporting evidence for this view, sceptics cite the suppression of the Stevens and Stalker inquiries into collusion and the shoot-to-kill controversy and the passing of the Inquiries Act 2005 – seen as designed specifically to hinder investigations into the killing of the defence lawyer Patrick Finucane.

The reluctance of the British state and the paramilitaries to engage openly in the debate about the past does not necessarily mean that victims' concerns and their experiences of the past are doomed to being permanently marginalised, overlooked, or even written out of the historical record. The proliferation of victims' groups has brought the debate over the meaning of the past more firmly into the wider public discourse. However, the critical questions on which that debate rests relate to how the debate itself is presented and represented and what meaning and interpretation are given to the past. Victims' groups, of course, can foster new meanings about the past and give rise to alternative explanations and promote alternative experiences of what the Troubles were about. On the other hand, there exists the very real possibility that the narratives produced by victims' groups may simply reproduce dominant understandings at a more local and more particularised level.[119] Indeed, this seems to be the logical implication of the 'storytelling' movement promoted by the NIO-sponsored Healing Through Remembering organisation in which primary and supporting evidence, context and historical patterns are eschewed in favour of psychotherapeutic catharsis.[120] The historical ignorance and political naivety of such initiatives point to unquestioned and ethically vacuous assumptions about contemporary Northern Irish politics. On the other hand, this chapter has sought to highlight how those contemporary politics are saturated with the legacies of the past. In contrast to the dominant conflict management and transformation approaches – which analyse the Northern Irish conflict and its legacies and attempt to 'deal with the past' by rendering it subservient to morally, politically, and historically compromised futures – this chapter has suggested that, in fact, the past may not be quite as malleable. In other words, the endurance of historical legacies and the existence of empirical facts belie facile attempts to wish the Northern Irish past out of existence, and the troubling persistence of those facts indicate that the past itself may actually only be 'worked with' rather than 'dealt with'.[121]

Conclusion

> ... at that moment, for the first time, I had the deceptive intuition that the past is not a stable place but changeable, permanently altered by the future, and that therefore none of what had already happened was irreversible.[1]

Northern Ireland and the politics of entrenchment

As the narrator of Javier Cercas' novel, cited above, points out, changing circumstances in the present affect our ideas about the past. However, he also recognises that the notion that the past is malleable can be misleading; and in fact, the past impinges on the present – often in a constraining and highly restrictive fashion. This study has claimed that the release of new archival material allows us to explore in greater depth than was previously possible the various ways in which the early years of the Northern Ireland conflict affected later events. In particular, it argued that the Northern Ireland conflict did not occur simply because of the presence of two distinct communities; although ethno-national differences were a distinctive characteristic of the Troubles, they did not in themselves perpetuate the conflict. Instead, political conflict in Northern Ireland emerged due to specific historical decisions and omissions, and the persistence of policy goals and exclusivist communal sentiments drove that conflict forward. In other words, the Northern Irish troubles occurred and lasted so long not because perennial ethnic sentiments caused a breakdown of rationality or because it took too long for the relevant elites to work out how to cooperate; rather, the conflict persisted simply because a long-term process of political entrenchment worked too well.

This book has described how that process operated, in particular, how the decisions of the SDLP and Brian Faulkner in 1971 established the basic framework for later political relationships within and between Irish nationalism and Ulster unionism. In particular, it argued that the SDLP's decision to withdraw from Stormont in July 1971 reversed the party's early reformism and instituted a more nationalistic agenda based on power-sharing and an Irish dimension. Internal party papers reveal that from September of that year these ideas would be but interim measures for establishing a context in which reunification would be a seamless and logical progression. This perspective carried through and was reinforced by subsequent events such as the fall of Stormont and the recognition of an Irish dimension by the British government in 1973. Thus the party did not simply react to the threat of republican 'outbidding', nor was it merely responding pragmatically to British intervention. Instead, the SDLP sought to manage Catholic radicalism and mould it into a coherent political programme based on the gradual accumulation of gains. This agenda resonated with the objectives of successive Dublin governments and led to an emphasis being placed on the Irish dimension above that of power-sharing.

The primary evidence reveals that Faulkner agreed to countenance some form of cross-border body to deal with terrorism and security at the Chequers meeting in September 1971. His decision carried through because of pressure from his intra-bloc rivals and the British government. The gradual mobilisation of the unionist right from 1972 is often largely overlooked as it mostly happened 'off-screen', coming into view most forcefully in May 1974. Although deeply suspicious and jealous of each other, Faulkner's unionist rivals – Ian Paisley, William Craig and Harry West – had a common objective of frustrating executive power-sharing, and their stance compelled Faulkner along an alternative trajectory in which he sought to balance pressure from Westminster for change with the need to maintain a unionist veto. It is important to remember that Faulkner only agreed to share power with the SDLP as long as he had the larger share – a promise that won him the support of the Ulster Unionist Council in November 1973. Faulkner's historical trajectory mirrored that of his rivals in the sense that he largely advocated alternative policies and witnessed his levels of support move in the opposite direction. While divided over issues such as unilateral independence, dominion status, the restoration of Stormont or full integration with the United Kingdom, his rivals agreed on the undesirability of executive power-sharing and the need for strong security measures. While it is true that their constitutional alternatives were unrealistic,[2] the essential point is that the catalyst behind unionist politics was fear of the perceived direction of change and the ongoing IRA campaign. In this respect, Faulkner's balancing act meant little to the repeated claims of the *Newsletter* that

> There are those who, for their own ends and to cover their own deplorable deficiencies, would put it abroad that the establishment of a new, artificial form of government is the answer to the ghastly problem of violence.[3]

What this means is that the fate of the Sunningdale experiment was effectively determined much earlier than 1974. From 1971 onwards political divisions in Northern Ireland became progressively more entrenched. The paradox of Faulkner and the SDLP's early choices was that while they exerted a moderating force within their own political blocs – the SDLP's agenda undercutting republican radicalism and Faulkner's forestalling the emergence of the unionist right – they also militated against inter-communal dialogue. As such, prospects for accommodation succeeding at either Sunningdale or the Constitutional Convention were slight. The underlying story of the Convention is one of growing political entrenchment, meaning that what actually came to attract most attention – Craig's voluntary coalition proposal – was merely a subplot. In fact, political entrenchment persisted beyond the Convention and influenced later decisions by the SDLP and the Ulster Unionists not to resist dialogue. In the post-Convention period this reluctance was viewed favourably by the Northern Ireland Office, who feared potential destabilising effects. While both parties sought to maintain their positions as the dominant parties in their communal blocs, concepts such as 'outbidding', 'reaction' and 'pragmatism' do not do justice to the complexity of the historical record. Instead, the idea of political entrenchment also stresses how the SDLP and the UUP sought to mobilise support by articulating a coherent programme and a consistent strategy across time. Those programmes were largely determined by each grouping's response to the constitutional uncertainty that reigned in the early 1970s.

The final chapters describe how the Anglo-Irish Agreement exacerbated inter-communal division and encouraged a gradual coalescing of nationalist policy-making and policy direction – as in earlier years, the core element of this agenda was a conservative and traditionalist vision of gradual reunification. Despite the sectarian excesses surrounding the Drumcree dispute in the 1990s, unionist politics was also shaped by conservative and traditionalist voices. Again, as was the case with Irish nationalism, this occurred in an insulated and self-referential discourse.

In short, the ending of the paramilitary campaigns occurred alongside the persistence of political entrenchment. Despite the apparent 'transformationist' nuances of the rhetoric of political elites – for example, Trimble's 'articulate unionism' or the Adams-McGuinness 'peace strategy' – the Northern Irish peace process witnessed the reproduction of deep-seated continuities at the level of policy-making and the continuation of division and suspicion at the popular level.

The primary evidence, therefore, points to a need to reappraise certain accepted narratives relating to unionist and nationalist politics during the early years of the Troubles. Thus, from as early as the summer of 1971, the SDLP began to target maximal goals and prioritised a strong Irish dimension – even at the expense of power-sharing. The conventional narrative describes how a 'greening' of the SDLP occurred definitively at the end of the 1970s in response to unionist 'obduracy' and republican 'outbidding'. However, the present study points to a distinct nationalistic emphasis within the party during its formative years and points to more continuity between the SDLP and traditional, pre-Troubles Irish nationalist thinking. In this, while the idea of consent introduced a new element to nationalist discourse, at the level of policy direction, the traditional end-goal of gradual reunification remained constant.

The book has also pointed towards new ways of conceptualising Ulster unionist politics. In addition to locating the fracturing of unionism to before the 1972–4 – again, stressing the importance of the year 1971 – it has also highlighted the importance of long-term continuities and gradual transformative processes. While the book chimes with a key strand in the literature regarding the structural weakness of unionist politics vis-à-vis the British state and Irish nationalism,[4] it also points out that the politics of resistance and opposition may be transformative forces in their own right. Thus, while unionist politics lacked the power to exert 'overt' changes on governmental or Irish nationalist policy-making, the long-term effect of opposition to security and constitutional proposals transformed the context in which those proposals were suggested. In other words, while devolved power-sharing remained a key pillar of governmental policy-making, its implementation was continually frustrated by unionist dissatisfaction over the terms on offer. The two general conclusions of the book as regards nationalism and unionism are therefore: (a) that traditionalism and conservatism are important features in the trajectory of Northern nationalism; and (b) that it is at a ground or implementation level that Ulster unionist political capacity is to be found.

The release of state papers also allows a reappraisal of British state policy-making. The evidence suggests that the Westminster policy apparatus was a multi-vocal ad hoc machine that sought to cope with the competing and divergent demands being made by the local Northern Irish political parties. It also sought to balance those demands with international opinion and, at various times (1972, 1975–6) opened negotiations with the PIRA. The fact that no single British government policy existed is, therefore, not the same as saying that there were no discernible policies. On the contrary, successive British governments sought to cope with the changing political environment in such a way as to avoid making the situation any worse. Several broad proposals existed, ranging from Wilson's 'nuclear option' of total withdrawal to power-sharing devolution. Yet, as the evidence shows, British policy-makers recognised that imposing – even 'coercing' – a settlement would be perceived as undermining one political party or community to the benefit of the 'other side'. Any ambiguity that resulted from government intervention occurred due to the opposing conclusions local politicians reached regarding their own prospects for gaining or losing ground. Thus, while state intervention encouraged political entrenchment, there was little Westminster could do to ameliorate the situation.

Historical analysis and the politics of ethnic conflict

This book has used these insights to examine the processes by which pre-existing identities in Northern Ireland were mobilised and maintained by historical events, British state intervention and by the rhetorical and strategic work of local political organisations. It argued that even in an ethnically divided society such as Northern Ireland, ethnic divisions need not be the driving force behind political change and outcome. Instead, historical events, political processes, power disparities and the perception of shifting threats and opportunities may influence developments.

This stands in contrast to consociational and conflict transformation literature, much of which is based on unquestioned and untested assumptions regarding the determinative force and destabilising characteristics of ethno-nationalism.[5] In fact, the resort to ethnicity conflates the historical record with institutional change, allowing dominant interests to 'draw a line under the past' in the pursuit of peaceful transition. In other words, a political culture based on ideas about the necessity of sharing power between 'two traditions' may sideline important historical questions about what actually happened and who made key decisions and why – in the long run, institutional engineering may be less a panacea than a placebo. The outcome, as described by Roy Foster, is that democratic 'transition' in Northern Ireland has meant uncritically institutionalising the legacy of the past in power-sharing structures, which themselves 'denote "separate spheres", not reconciliation'.[6] An emphasis on historical decisions, how they unfold and how they function is this work's main contribution to the debate over the management and regulation of the Northern Ireland conflict. Its key implications may be summarised as follows:

- The tendency to examine political antagonisms merely describes rather than explains ethno-national contention. The prioritisation of ethno-nationalism as a catch-all variable may result in a tendency to use the main features of a conflict as explanations of the conflict rather than of why they are causally important.
- By ignoring primary evidence, key decisions, historical sequencing and long-term perspectives academics may simply perpetuate and reproduce the terms of debate. That is to say, by concentrating on a single explanatory variable, scholars may ignore the effect of long-term processes and equate 'context' with short-term changes or post-hoc rationalisations.
- It is only by studying who benefits from conflicts and by identifying the mechanisms through which conflicts are reproduced – in particular, the highly problematic and fragmentary way in which the past is used, abused and ignored – can we even begin to make any kind of definitive statements about how conflicts emerge and why ethno-national identity proves so resilient.
- Paying attention to empirical details and the endurance of long-term historical patterns may guard against resorting to simplistic notions of change and transition, and against the tendency to accept paramilitaries' and politicians' self-justifying narratives of transformation and 'drawing lines in the sand'.

The primary evidence and the theoretical insights contained in this study, therefore, offer a serious challenge to received wisdom concerning the Northern Ireland conflict. Yet the broad, path-dependent approach utilised in this book has not been offered as a systematic model to replace the ethnic conflict school. By seeking to replace one dominant narrative with another would be to miss the point of historical analysis. Although it is true that 'political stability is endangered when at least two versions of the past exist',[7] a greater danger lies in the processes of forgetting, silencing and manipulation. Again, as Paloma Aguilar points out, 'Amnesia is just as important as memory ... what is not recalled always presents a greater danger than what is'.[8] Second, interpretive models rarely fall due to a sustained campaign to discredit them. Large sections of academic and political elites have vested interests in perpetuating the myth that the Northern Ireland conflict was ethnic – it absolves politicians of the responsibility of examining the links between their present rhetoric and their past actions, and allows some academics to ignore the problems that empirical evidence presents for their prescriptions and analyses. As with the processes described in this work, the demise of the ethnic conflict model may be a long, drawn-out affair. Certainly, the movement away from violence towards constitutionality will precipitate new modes of inquiry and different questions from those dominating much of Irish political studies at present, but the conventional narratives will also be gradually replaced as scholars become more aware of their limitations. The main aim of this book has been to open the ground for a less doctrinaire debate about the meanings of the past. To 'draw a line' under the past or to leave the debate to academics is no longer sufficient because the schematising of politico-historical knowledge tends to serve particular interests and its propagation as a utility merely raises the question of who is using it and for what purpose.

The newly released archival material demands significant reappraisal of some of the conventional claims about Northern Irish political developments and about the role and capacity of the British state during the Troubles. The objective of this work is, therefore, both more modest and more far-reaching than a straightforward critique of the ethno-nationalist model. As such, it stands in line with what Paul Ricoeur identified as a common rationale for all historical inquiries, namely to

> open up the archive by retrieving traces which the dominant ideological forces attempted to suppress ... [and thereby oppose] the manipulation of narratives by telling the story differently and by providing a space for the confrontation between opposing testimonies.[9]

By emphasising the fragmentary ways in which the past affects the present, this book has argued for a nuanced view of the Northern Ireland Troubles and eschewed the view that the conflict was a process of learning, trial and error and steady progress. This vision understandably informs political memoirs,[10] but also underpins some of the more teleological academic analyses.[11] Instead of the view that history is an almost constant accumulation of progress and advantage, Ricoeur calls for a 'kind of parallel history of, let us say, victimisation, which would counter the history of success and victory'.[12] However, the danger is that at this juncture of Northern Irish history, the received wisdom about the past could easily be reproduced for another generation. Even if the present influences the types of questions asked about the past, there is no guarantee that different answers will be given: marginalised narratives will stay marginalised, 'forgotten' voices will continue to be silenced and those who benefited from the past will continue to benefit in the future. Critical reflection on the past instead calls into question received assumptions and in itself involves a questioning of political power. It means asking for the stories and testimonies of those who have been marginalised by conventional narratives; again, it means asking questions about the importance of locale, age, gender and class in people's experience of the Troubles.

This study has attempted to restore a degree of historical and political analysis to the narrative of the Northern Irish conflict and has suggested that any future accounting of what the Troubles meant must also be approached through a nuanced and critical fashion. While there is always the danger that academic and political elites will attempt to frustrate this process and use the historical record to suit their own ends, despite such attempts at to manipulating history, the empirical record will always present strong obstacles to such 'presentist' interests. The opening of the debate about the meanings of the past must be based on these foundations and take into account the narratives and voices that have hitherto been silenced.

Notes

Introduction

1. Eric Hobsbawm, *On History* (London: Weidenfeld & Nicolson, 1997), p. 235; original emphasis.
2. Tony Judt, *Postwar: A History of Europe since 1945* (London: Heinemann, 2005), p. 2.
3. David McKettrick Seamus Kelters, Brian Feeney and Chris Thornton, *Lost Lives: The Stories of the Men, Women, and Children Who Died as a Result of the Northern Ireland Troubles* (Edinburgh: Mainstream, 2004).
4. The idea that 'two factions' drove the Northern Ireland conflict continues to inspire exasperated hand-wringing from some political commentators: 'In a province where they can't yet agree the route of a 300-year-old march, such events [proposals for ceremonial remembrance of victims] present the possiblity [sic] of another thousand years of joyless wrangling at our expense.' (The 'our' in this case appears to refer to citizens of the British mainland.) Melanie Reid, 'Money can't buy reconciliation', *The Times*, 29 January 2009.
5. Adrian Guelke, 'Commentary: truth, reconciliation, and political accommodation', *Irish Political Studies*, 22(3) (2006): 363–6.
6. *Report of the Consultative Group on the Past*, p. 52; available at www.cpgni.org, accessed 29 January 2009.
7. Lawrence Stone, *The Causes of the English Revolution: 1529–1642* (London: Routledge & Kegan Paul, 1972), p. 146.
8. Eamon Phoenix, *Northern Nationalism: Nationalist Politics, Partition, and the Catholic Minority in Northern Ireland, 1890–1940* (Belfast: Ulster Historical Society, 1994), p. 399.
9. Thomas Hennessey, *Northern Ireland: The Origins of the Troubles* (Dublin: Gill & Macmillan, 2005), p. xi.
10. Simon Prince, *Northern Ireland's '68: Civil Rights, Global Revolt, and the Origins of the Troubles* (Dublin: Irish Academic Press, 2007), p. 8.
11. *Disturbances in Northern Ireland: Report of the Cameron Commission*, (Cmnd. 532) (Belfast: Her Majesty's Stationery Office, 1969), para. 11; Brendan O'Leary and John McGarry, *The Politics of Antagonism: Understanding Northern Ireland* (London: Athlone Press, 1997), p. 157.
12. Prince, *Northern Ireland's '68*, p. 67.
13. Paul Bew, Peter Gibbon and Henry Patterson, *Northern Ireland, 1921–2001: Political Forces and Social Classes* (London: Serif, 2002), pp. 131–50.
14. Bob Purdie, *Politics in the Streets: The Origins of the Civil Rights Movement in Northern Ireland* (Belfast: Blackstaff, 1990), pp. 157–8.
15. Thomas Hennessey, *A History of Northern Ireland, 1920–1996* (Dublin: Gill & Macmillan, 1997), p. 121.
16. Henry Patterson and Eric Kaufmann, *Unionism and Orangeism in Northern Ireland since 1945: The Decline of the Loyal Family* (Manchester: Manchester University Press, 2007), p. 72.

17. *Irish News*, 21 June 2008.
18. Paul Bew, *Ireland: The Politics of Enmity, 1789–2006* (Oxford: Oxford University Press, 2007); Marc Mulholland, *Northern Ireland at the Crossroads: Ulster Unionism in the O'Neill Years, 1960–9* (Basingstoke: Macmillan, 2000); Prince, *Northern Ireland's '68*.
19. Bew et al., *Northern Ireland*; Kenneth Bloomfield, *The Tragedy of Errors: The Government and Misgovernment of Northern Ireland* (Liverpool: Liverpool University Press, 2007).
20. Hennessey, *Northern Ireland*; Niall Ó Dochartaigh, *From Civil Rights to Armalites: Derry and the Birth of the Irish Troubles* (Basingstoke: Palgrave Macmillan, 2005).

Chapter 1

1. Among others, see Steve Bruce, *God Save Ulster: The Religion and Politics of Paisleyism* (Oxford: Clarendon Press, 1986); John Darby, *Scorpions in a Bottle: Conflicting Cultures in Northern Ireland* (London: Minority Rights Publications, 1997); Michael Hughes, *Ireland Divided: The Roots of the Modern Irish Problem* (Cardiff: University of Wales Press, 1994); John McGarry and Brendan O'Leary, *Explaining Northern Ireland: Broken Images* (Oxford: Blackwell, 2000); Jeremy Smith, *Making the Peace in Ireland* (London: Longman, 2002); John Whyte, *Interpreting Northern Ireland* (Oxford: Clarendon Press, 1991); Stefan Wolff, 'From Sunningdale to Belfast, 1973–98', in Jörg Neuheiser and Stefan Wolff (eds.) *Peace at Last? The Impact of the Good Friday Agreement on Northern Ireland* (Oxford: Berghan Books, 2003).
2. 'Peace' Work, BBC Radio 4, 24 March 2009 (http://www.bbc.co.uk/iplayer/console/b00j6xxx), accessed 25 March 2009); Michael Kerr, *Imposing Power-Sharing: Conflict and Co-existence in Northern Ireland and Lebanon* (Dublin: Irish Academic Press, 2006); Brendan O'Leary, John McGarry and Khaled Salih, *The Future of Kurdistan in Iraq* (Philadelphia: University of Pennsylvania Press, 2006).
3. Among others, Bew, *Politics*; Aaron Edwards, *A History of the Northern Ireland Labour Party: Democratic Socialism and Sectarianism* (Manchester: Manchester University Press, 2009); Richard English, *Irish Freedom: The History of Nationalism in Ireland* (London: Macmillan, 2007); Hennessey, *Northern Ireland*; Henry Patterson, *Ireland Since 1939: The Persistence of Conflict* (Dublin: Penguin, 2006); Prince, *Northern Ireland's '68*; Jonathan Tonge, *The New Northern Irish Politics* (Basingstoke: Palgrave Macmillan, 2005); Graham Walker, *A History of the Ulster Unionist Party: Protest, Pragmatism, and Pessimism* (Manchester: Manchester University Press, 2004).
4. Fidelma Ashe, 'Gendering ethno-nationalist conflict in Northern Ireland', in Colin Coulter and Michael Murray (eds.) *Northern Ireland After the Troubles: A Society in Transition* (Manchester: Manchester University Press, 2008); Lorenzon Cañás Bottos and Nathalie Rougier, 'Generations on the border: changes in ethno-national identity in the border area', *Nationalism and Ethnic Politics*, 12 (2006): 617–42; Colin Coulter, 'The absence of class politics in Northern Ireland', *Capital and Class*, 69 (1999): 77–101; Cillian McGrattan, 'Explaining Northern Ireland? The limitations of the ethnic conflict model',

National Identities (forthcoming, 2010); Nick Vaughan-Williams, 'Towards a problematisation of the problematisations that reduce Northern Ireland to a problem', in Marysia Zalewski and John Barry (eds.) *Intervening in Northern Ireland: Critically Re-thinking Representations of the Conflict* (Abingdon: Routledge, 2008).
5. Donald L. Horowitz, *Ethnic Groups in Conflict* (London: University of California Press, 2000 [1985]), p. xv.
6. Arend Lijphart, *Democracy in Plural Societies: A Comparative Exploration* (London: Yale University Press, 1977), p. 238.
7. Anthony D. Smith, 'The ethnic sources of nationalism', in Michael E. Brown (eds.) *Ethnic Conflict and International Security* (Princeton, NJ: Princeton University Press, 1993), p. 40.
8. Among others, see Ian O'Flynn and David Russell, 'Democratic values and power sharing', in O'Flynn and Russell (eds.) *Power Sharing: New Challenges for Divided Societies* (London: Pluto Press, 2005); Wolff, 'From Sunningdale'.
9. Among others, see Walker Connor, *Ethno-Nationalism: The Quest for Understanding* (Princeton, NJ: Princeton University Press, 1994), p. 73; Horowitz, *Ethnic Groups*; and John McGarry and Brendan O'Leary, 'Five fallacies: Northern Ireland and the liabilities of liberalism', *Ethnic and Racial Studies*, 18(4) (1995): 837–61.
10. Terry M. Moe, 'Power and political institutions', in Ian Shapiro, Stephen Skowronek and Daniel Galvin (eds.) *Rethinking Political Institutions: The Art of the State* (London: New York University Press, 2006).
11. Ian Kershaw, *Fateful Choices: Ten Decisions that Changed the World, 1940–1941* (London: Penguin, Allan Lane, 2007); Paul Pierson, *Politics in Time: History, Institutions, and Social Analysis* (Oxford: Princeton University Press, 2004).
12. Doug McAdam, Sidney Tarrow and Charles Tilly, *Dynamics of Contention* (Cambridge: Cambridge University Press, 2001); Andreas Wimmer, *Nationalist Exclusion and Ethnic Conflict: Shadows of Modernity* (Cambridge: Cambridge University Press, 2002); Stefan Wolff, *Ethnic Conflict: A Global Perspective* (Oxford: Oxford University Press, 2006).
13. Rogers Brubaker *Ethnicity Without Groups* (Oxford: Harvard University Press, 2004).
14. Ibid., p. 9.
15. Rogers Brubaker, *Nationalist Politics and Everyday Ethnicity in a Transylvanian Town* (Oxford: Princeton University Press, 2007), p. 7.
16. Ibid., p. 10; see also V. P. Gagnon, *The Myth of Ethnic War: Serbia and Croatia in the 1990s* (London: Cornell University Press, 2004), pp. xv–xxi.
17. Joseph Ruane and Jennifer Todd, 'The roots of intense ethnic conflict may not in fact be ethnic: categories, communities, and path dependence', *Archives européenes de sociologie*, 45 (2004): 216–17.
18. Kanchan Chandra, 'What is ethnic identity and does it matter?' *Annual Review of Political Science*, 9 (2006), p. 398.
19. Ibid., p. 420; see also Rawi Abdelal, Yoshiko M. Herrera, Alastair Iain Johnston and Rose McDermott, 'Identity as a variable', *Perspectives on Politics*, 4(4) (2006): 695–711.
20. John R. Gillis, 'Memory and identity: the history of a relationship', in John R. Gillis (eds.) *Commemorations: The Politics of National Identity*

(Chichester: Princeton University Press, 1994); Ian McBride, 'Memory and national identity in modern Ireland', in Ian McBride (eds.) *History and Memory in Modern Ireland* (Cambridge University Press: Cambridge, 2001).
21. Charles Tilly, 'Social boundary mechanisms', *Philosophy of the Social Sciences*, 43(2) (2004): 211–36.
22. O'Leary and McGarry, *Politics of Antagonism*, p. 3.
23. See Peter Hart, *The IRA at War, 1916–1923* (Oxford: Oxford University Press, 2003), pp. 3–29.
24. Among others, see Bruce, *God Save Ulster*; Bruce, *The Edge of the Union: The Ulster Loyalist Political Vision* (Oxford: Oxford University Press, 1994); Christopher Farrington, *Ulster Unionism and the Peace Process in Northern Ireland* (Basingstoke: Palgrave Macmillan, 2006); Gladys Ganiel, ' "Preaching to the choir?" an analysis of DUP discourses about the Northern Ireland peace process', *Irish Political Studies*, 22(3) (2007): 303–20; Katy Hayward, 'The politics of nuance: Irish official discourse on Northern Ireland', *Irish Political Studies*, 19(1) (2004): 18–38; Kerr, *Imposing*; McGarry and O'Leary, *Explaining Northern Ireland*; Claire Mitchell, *Religion, Identity and Politics in Northern Ireland: Boundaries of Belonging and Belief* (Aldershot: Ashgate, 2006); Paul Mitchell, Brendan O'Leary and Geoffrey Evans, 'Northern Ireland: flanking extremists bite the moderates and emerge in their clothes', *Parliamentary Affairs*, 54 (2001): 725–42; and Brendan O'Duffy, *British-Irish Relations and Northern Ireland: From Violent Politics to Conflict Regulation* (Dublin: Irish Academic Press, 2007).
25. Wolff, 'From Sunningdale'.
26. Wolff, *Ethnic Conflict*, p. 5.
27. Peter Shirlow and Kieran McEvoy, *Beyond the Wire: Former Prisoners and Conflict Transformation in Northern Ireland* (London: Pluto Press, 2008), p. 4.
28. Fidelma Ashe, 'From paramilitaries to peacemakers: the gender dynamics of community-based restorative justice in Northern Ireland', *The British Journal of Politics and International Relations*, 11(2) (2009): 298–314.
29. McGarry and O'Leary, *Explaining*.
30. Wolff, 'From Sunningdale', p. 3; see also McGarry and O'Leary, *Explaining*, ch. 8; and Whyte, *Interpreting*, ch. 9.
31. McGarry and O'Leary, 'Five fallacies', p. 848.
32. Bernadette Hayes and Ian McAllister, 'Ethno-nationalism, public opinion, and the Good Friday agreement', in Joseph Ruane and Jennifer Todd (eds.) *After the Good Friday Agreement: Analysing Political Change in Northern Ireland* (Dublin: University College Dublin Press, 1999), p. 37.
33. O'Leary and McGarry, *Politics of Antagonism*, pp. 135–47. O'Leary and McGarry, (and Paul Arthur) impute unionist 'motivations' from (a) the desire of nationalists for reunification (see O'Leary and Arthur, 'Northern Ireland as the site of state- and nation-building failures', in John McGarry and Brendan O'Leary (eds.) *The Future of Northern Ireland* (Oxford: Clarendon Press 1990), p. 25); and (b) from unionist politicians' ethnically oriented 'justifications' of discrimination such as that offered by Major Curran in 1946 that the best way to protect Northern Ireland was to 'disenfranchise' those who 'had no stake in the country and had not the welfare of the people of Ulster at heart'; quoted in O'Leary and McGarry, *Politics of Antagonism*, p. 120. This, however, amounts to no more than a discursive sleight-of-hand

that prioritises ethnic fears over nuanced political realities and underlying historical context. William Craig, for instance, told Secretary of State for Northern Ireland William Whitelaw in 1972 that despite his hard-line rhetoric, he was in danger of losing any kind of moderating, political influence over loyalist paramilitaries that he could exert given the extent of their radicalism. 'Note of a meeting between the Secretary of State and William Craig, 24 May 1972', NA CJ 4/340.
34. Jenny Edkins, 'The local, the global, and the troubling', in Zalewski and Barry (eds.) *Intervening*; see also Vaughan-Williams, 'Towards'.
35. Paul Dixon, *Northern Ireland: The Politics of War and* Peace (Basingstoke: Palgrave Macmillan, 2008 [2001]); Ganiel ' "Preaching" '.
36. Kerr, *Imposing*; O'Duffy, *British-Irish Relations*.
37. For example, Dixon, *Northern Ireland*; Cathy Gormley-Heenan, *Political Leadership and the Northern Ireland Peace Process: Role, Capacity and Effect* (Basingstoke: Palgrave Macmillan, 2006).
38. Paul Dixon, 'Political skills or lying and manipulation? The choreography of the Northern Ireland peace process', *Political Studies*, 50(4) (2002): 725–41.
39. Ganiel ' "Preaching" '.
40. Fergal Cochrane, *Unionist Politics and the Politics of Unionism since the Anglo-Irish Agreement* (Cork: Cork University Press, 2001); Farrington, *Ulster Unionism*; Hayward, 'Politics of nuance'; Gareth Ivory, 'Revisions in nationalist discourse among Irish political parties', *Irish Political Studies*, 14 (1999): 84–103; M. L. R. Smith, *Fighting for Ireland? The Military Strategy of the Irish Republican Movement* (London: Routledge, 1995); Jennifer Todd, 'Two traditions in unionist political culture', *Irish Political Studies*, 2 (1987): 1–26.
41. Katy Hayward and Claire Mitchell, 'Discourses of equality in post-agreement Northern Ireland', *Contemporary Politics*, 9(3) (2003): 293.
42. Arthur Aughey, 'The art and effect of political lying in Northern Ireland', *Irish Political Studies*, 17(2) (2000): 1–16.
43. Paloma Aguilar, *Memory and Amnesia: The Role of the Spanish Civil War in the Transition to Democracy* (Oxford: Berghahn, 2002).
44. G. K. Peatling, *The Failure of the Northern Ireland Peace Process* (Dublin: Irish Academic Press, 2004), p. 96.
45. Hayward and Mitchell, 'Discourses'; Mark McGovern ' "The old days are over": Irish republicanism, the peace process, and the discourse of equality', *Terrorism and Political Violence*, 16(3) (2004): 622–45; Roger MacGinty, 'Irish republicanism and the peace process: from revolution to reform', in Michael Cox, Adrian Guelke and Fiona Stephen (eds.) *A Farewell to Arms? Beyond the Good Friday Agreement* (Manchester: Manchester University Press, 2006).
46. Gerard Murray, *John Hume and the SDLP: Impact and Survival in Northern Ireland* (Dublin: Irish Academic Press, 1998).
47. Cillian McGrattan, 'Dublin, the SDLP, and the Sunningdale agreement: maximalist nationalism and path-dependency', *Contemporary British History*, 23(1) (2009): 61–78.
48. The two most recent studies are Steve Bruce, *Paisley: Religion and Politics in Northern Ireland* (Oxford: Oxford University Press, 2007); and Mitchell, *Religion*.
49. Mitchell, *Religion*, p. 20.

50. Paul Pierson, 'Public policies as institutions', in Ian Shapiro, Stephen Skowronek and Daniel Galvin (eds.) *Rethinking Political Institutions: The Art of the State* (London: New York University Press, 2006).
51. Sara McDowell, 'Commemorating the Troubles: unravelling the representation of the contestation of memory in Northern Ireland since 1994', unpublished PhD thesis, University of Ulster, 2006, pp. 55–6.
52. Liam Clarke, 'Did Adams "sign" their death warrants?', *Sunday Times*, 5 April 2009; Clarke, 'Why Adams sticks to his hunger strike myth', *Sunday Times*, 12 April 2009; '*Sunday Times* H-Block story backfires', *An Phoblacht*, 9 April 2009; '*Sunday Times* refuses to publish answers', www.bobbysandstrust.com, accessed 21 April 2009.
53. Bruce, *God Save Ulster*, pp. 90–2.
54. Ibid., p. 248.
55. Kerr, *Imposing*, p. 41.
56. Roger MacGinty and John Darby, *Guns and Government: The Management of the Northern Ireland Peace Process* (Basingstoke: Palgrave, 2002), p. 21; see also Brendan O'Leary, 'The conservative stewardship of Northern Ireland, 1979–97: sound-bottomed contradictions or slow learning?' *Political Studies*, XLV (1997): 663–76; Etain Tannam, 'Explaining the Good Friday agreement: a learning process'. *Government and Opposition*, 43(4) (2001): 493–518.
57. Among others, see MacGinty and Darby, *Guns*; O'Leary and McGarry, *Politics of Antagonism*; Tannam, 'Explaining'.
58. Paul Dixon, 'Why the GFA in Northern Ireland is not consociational', *The Political Quarterly*, 76(3) (2006): 357–67; Rupert Taylor, 'The Belfast agreement and the politics of consociationalism: a critique', *The Political Quarterly*, 77(2) (2006): 217–26; Rick Wilford and Robin Wilson, 'Northern Ireland: a route to stability?' http://cain.ulst.ac.uk/dd/papers/dd03agreview.pdf (2003), accessed 15 May 2008.
59. John McGarry and Brendan O'Leary, 'Proving our points on Northern Ireland (and giving reading lessons to Dr Dixon)', *Irish Political Studies*, 11 (1996): 142–54.
60. Ibid., p. 152.
61. Kerr, *Imposing*; McGarry and O'Leary, 'Consociational theory'; O'Duffy, *British-Irish Relations*.
62. Hay, *Political Analysis*, pp. 145–50.
63. Paul Mitchell, 'Party competition in an ethnic dual party system', *Ethnic and Racial Studies*, 18(4) (1995): 773–93; Mitchell et al., 'Northern Ireland'.
64. Peter McLoughlin 'John Hume and the revision of Irish nationalism', unpublished PhD thesis (Belfast: Queen's University, 2006); Gerard Murray and Jonathan Tonge, *Sinn Féin and the SDLP: From Alienation to Participation* (London: Hurst, 2005).
65. Farrington, *Ulster Unionism*; Hayward, 'Politics of Nuance'.
66. Katherine Side, 'Women's civil and political citizenship in the post-Good Friday agreement period in Northern Ireland', *Irish Political Studies*, 24(1) (2009): 67–87.
67. The record of women's representation in the Northern Ireland Assembly is woeful when placed against the devolved institutions in Scotland and Wales. For example, while women have constituted between 33 and 39 per cent of the Scottish Parliament and between 40 and 50 per cent of the

Welsh Assembly, the Assembly's figure presently stands at a high of 16.7 per cent. Aaron Edwards and Cillian McGrattan, *The Northern Ireland Conflict: A Beginner's Guide* (Oxford: Oneworld, 2010 forthcoming), table 7.1.
68. Ashe, 'Gendering'; see also Marysia Zalewski, 'Gender ghosts in McGarry and O'Leary and representations of the conflict in Northern Ireland', *Political Studies*, 53(3) (2005), 201–21.
69. Thomas Hennessey, *The Evolution of the Troubles, 1970–72* (Dublin: Irish Academic Press, 2007); Catherine O'Donnell, *Fianna Fáil, Irish Republicanism, and the Northern Ireland Troubles, 1968–2005* (Dublin: Irish Academic Press, 2006); Patterson and Kaufmann, *Unionism*; Prince, *Northern Ireland's '68*.
70. Cillian McGrattan, 'Learning from the past or laundering history? Consociational narratives and state intervention in Northern Ireland', *British Politics* (forthcoming, 2010).
71. Kerr, *Imposing*, p. 59, emphasis added.
72. O'Duffy, *British-Irish Relations*, p. 75.
73. Tannam, 'Explaining'; Eamonn O'Kane, *Britain, Ireland, and Northern Ireland since 1980: The Totality of Relationships* (Abingdon: Routledge, 2007), p. 193.
74. Pierson, *Politics in Time*.
75. Paul Pierson and Theda Skocpol, 'Historical institutionalism in contemporary political science', in Ira Katznelson and Helen V. Milner, *Political Science: The State of the Discipline* (London: W. W. Norton, 2002).
76. Pierson, 'Public policies'.
77. See James Mahoney, 'Path-dependence in historical sociology', *Theory and Society*, 29 (2000): 507–48; and Pierson, *Politics in Time*. For Mahoney, path-dependence describes those deterministic sequences that occur through either incremental or reactive changes. Pierson, on the other hand, tends to emphasise the former version. Perhaps the most concise definition of the concept is Douglass North's 'Path-dependence is not "inertia"; rather it is the constraints on the choice set in the present that are derived from historical experiences of the past'; *Understanding the Process of Economic Change* (Oxford: Princeton University Press, 2005), p. 52.
78. Kershaw, *Fateful Choices*; Pierson and Skocpol, 'Historical institutionalism'; Charles Tilly, 'How (and what) are historians doing?' *American Behavioural Scientist*, 33(6) (1990): 685–711.
79. Jacob S. Hacker, *The Divided Welfare State: The Battle over Public and Private Social Benefits in the United States* (Cambridge: Cambridge University Press, 2002), p. 54.
80. Pierson, *Politics in Time*, pp. 36–7.
81. Tilly, 'How (and what) are historians doing?'
82. Pierson, 'Public policies'.
83. Kershaw, *Fateful Choices*, p. 481.
84. Niall Ferguson, 'Virtual history: towards a "chaotic" theory of the past', in Niall Ferguson (ed.) *Virtual History: Alternatives and Counterfactuals* (London: Macmillan, 1998); Hay, *Political Analysis*; Kershaw, *Fateful Choices*; Pierson, *Politics in Time*.
85. Ferguson, 'Virtual history', p. 85.
86. Kershaw, *Fateful Choices*, p. 7.
87. Pierson, *Politics in Time*, pp. 54–78.

196 Notes

88. Sidney Tarrow, *Power in Movement: Social Movements, Collective Action and Politics* (Cambridge: Cambridge University Press, 1998), p. 18.
89. Doug McAdam, *Political Process and the Development of Black Insurgency, 1930–1970* (London: University of Chicago Press, 1999).
90. Doug McAdam, 'Conceptual origins, current problems, future directions', in Doug McAdam, John D. McCarthy and Mayer N. Zald (eds.) *Comparative Perspectives on Social Movements: Political Opportunities, Mobilising Structures, and Cultural Framings* (Cambridge: Cambridge University Press, 1996), p. 27.
91. Charles Tilly, *From Mobilization to Revolution* (London: Addison-Wesley, 1978), p. 8.
92. Jack Goldstone and Charles Tilly, 'Threat (and opportunity): popular action and state response in the dynamics of contentious action', in Ron Aminzade et al. (eds.) *Silence and Voice in the Study of Contentious Politics* (Cambridge: Cambridge University Press, 2001), p. 193.
93. Ibid., p. 183; see also McAdam et al., *Dynamics of Contention*, pp. 111–14.
94. Mahoney, 'Path-dependence'; Pierson, *Politics in Time*; William Streeck and Kathleen Thelen, 'Institutional change in advanced political economies' in William Streeck and Kathleen Thelen, *Beyond Continuity: Institutional Change in Advanced Political Economies* (Oxford: Oxford University Press, 2005).
95. Streeck and Thelen, 'Institutional change', p. 24.
96. Hacker, 'Privatizing', p. 246.
97. Hacker employs the explanatory analogy of the pluralist debate in American political science: although pluralist scholarship identified multiple, overlapping centres of power, it ignored the ways in which elites may determine policy agendas and block or facilitate change; Hacker, 'Privatizing'. See also Peter Bacharch and Morton S. Baratz, 'Two faces of power', *American Political Science Review*, 56(3) (1962): 947–52.
98. Pierson, *Politics in Time*, p. 37.
99. Kershaw, *Fateful Choices*, pp. 480–1.
100. Ruane and Todd, 'Ethnic conflict', p. 226.
101. Aguilar, *Memory*; Elizabeth Jelin, *State Repression and the Struggles for Memory* (London: Latin American Bureau, 2003); Barbara Misztal, *Theories of Social Remembering* (Maidenhead: Open University Press, 2003).
102. Aguilar, *Memory*, p. 21.
103. Pierson, *Politics in Time*, pp. 124–6.
104. Cillian McGrattan, 'Modern Irish nationalism: ideology, policymaking, and path-dependent change', in Adrian Guelke (ed.) *The Challenges of Ethno-Nationalism: Case Studies in Identity Politics* (Basingstoke: Palgrave, 2010 forthcoming).
105. Ronan Fanning, 'Playing it cool: the response of the British and Irish governments to the crisis in Northern Ireland, 1968–9'. *Irish Studies in International Affairs*, 2 (2001), p. 58.
106. Murray, *John Hume*; McLaughlin, 'John Hume'.
107. Among others, see John Coakley, 'The Belfast agreement and the Republic of Ireland', in Rick Wilford (ed.) *Aspects of the Belfast Agreement* (Oxford: Oxford University Press, 2001); Christopher Farrington, 'Reconciliation or irredentism? The Irish government and the Sunningdale communiqué of 1973', *Contemporary European History* 16(1) (2007): 89–107; Hayward, 'The

politics of nuance'; Ivory, 'Revisions'; Jennifer Todd, 'Nationalism, republicanism and the Good Friday agreement', in Ruane and Todd (eds.) *After the Good Friday Agreement.*
108. Hay, *Political Analysis*; Pierson, *Politics in Time.*
109. See Farrington, 'Reconciliation'; and Hayward, 'Politics of nuance'.
110. McLoughlin, 'John Hume'.
111. Ibid.
112. English, *Irish Freedom*, p. 9, original emphasis.
113. Ó hUiginn, quoted in Eamon Delaney, *An Accidental Diplomat: My Years in the Irish Foreign Service, 1987–1995* (Dublin: New Island, 2001), p. 305.
114. McLaughlin, 'John Hume'.
115. Gordon Gillespie, 'The Sunningdale agreement: lost opportunity or an agreement too far?' *Irish Political Studies*, 13 (1998): 100–14.
116. Murray and Tonge, *Sinn Féin*, pp. 54–60.
117. Arthur Aughey, *Under Siege: Ulster Unionism and the Anglo-Irish Agreement* (London: Hurst, 1991); Cochrane, *Unionist Politics*, p. viii; Farrington, *Ulster Unionism*, p. 7; Dean Godson, *Himself Alone: David Trimble and the Ordeal of Unionism* (London: HarperCollins, 2004).
118. For example, Bew et al., *Northern Ireland*; Dixon, *Northern Ireland.*
119. David McKittrick and David McVea, *Making Sense of the Troubles* (London: Penguin, 2001), p. 26; Simon Prince, 'Mythologising and movement: Northern Ireland's '68', *History Ireland*, September/October 2008.
120. O'Leary and McGarry, *Politics of Antagonism*, pp. 181–219.
121. Ibid., pp. 242–76.
122. Though see Bew et al., *Northern Ireland* for a discussion of Britain's influence over Stormont's policy-making from the foundation of the Northern state.
123. Paul Dixon, 'Northern Ireland and the international dimension: the end of the Cold War, the USA, and European integration', *Irish Studies in International Affairs*, 13 (2002): 105–20; O'Kane, *Britain*, pp. 7–8.
124. Cillian McGrattan, ' "Order out of chaos": the politics of transitional justice', *Politics*, 29(3) 2009: 164–72; Henry Patterson, 'Truth and reconciliation in Northern Ireland? not much hope of either', *Parliamentary Brief*, February 2009.
125. Michael Kerr, *Imposing Power-Sharing: Conflict and Co-existence in Northern Ireland and Lebanon* (Dublin: Irish Academic Press, 2006).
126. McGrattan, 'Explaining Northern Ireland?'
127. O'Leary, 'Conservative stewardship'; Tannam, 'Explaining'; CPGNI, *Report*; Patricia McBride, 'We must turn to the future and break the cycle of hatred', *Belfast Telegraph*, 30 January 2009.

Chapter 2

1. Hennessey, *Northern Ireland*; Prince, *Northern Ireland's '68.*
2. See Purdie, *Politics in the Streets*; and Prince, *Northern Ireland's '68* for the most authoritative academic histories of the Northern Ireland civil rights movement.
3. O'Leary and McGarry, *Politics of Antagonism*, ch. 3; see also O'Leary and Arthur, 'Northern Ireland'.

4. Patterson and Kaufmann, *Unionism*.
5. O'Leary and McGarry, *Politics of Antagonism*, p. 175.
6. Paul Bew, 'Historical background to Bloody Sunday: report to the Bloody Sunday tribunal by Professor Paul Bew, 24 November 2000, Expert Report E7'; available at www.bloody-sunday-inquiry.org, accessed 12 November 2007.
7. Bew, *Ireland*, p. 489.
8. Ibid., p. 493.
9. Mulholland, *Northern Ireland*, p. 192.
10. O'Dochartaigh, *From Civil Rights*, p. 53.
11. Henry Patterson, *Ireland since 1939: The Persistence of Conflict* (London: Penguin, 2007), p. 210; Paul Bew and Henry Patterson, *The British State and the Ulster Crisis: From Wilson to Thatcher* (London: Verso, 1985), pp. 7–38.
12. Bloomfield, *Tragedy*, p. 21.
13. Simon Prince, 'The global revolt of 1968 and Northern Ireland', *The History Journal*, 49(3) (2006): 874.
14. Bew, *Ireland*, pp. 489–93.
15. Hennessey, *The Evolution*, p. 99.
16. Ferguson, 'Virtual history'; Pierson, *Politics in Time*.
17. Prince, *Northern Ireland's '68*, p. 163.
18. Ferguson, Virtual history', pp. 86–7.
19. *Irish News*, 22 August 1970. Those reforms included a minimum wage, economic development of rural areas, the established of state industries and 'cooperation in all fields between North and South'.
20. Paddy Devlin, *Straight Left: An Autobiography* (Belfast, Blackstaff, 1993), p. 155.
21. *Irish News*, 3 March 1971.
22. *Irish Press*, 21 March 1971.
23. Ivan Cooper, quoted in the *Irish News*, 1 May 1971.
24. Cooper called on the party to 'step out of our entrenched position' and tackle sectarian divisions; ibid.
25. Hume, interview with the author, 14 June 2002.
26. Hume's biographer, Paul Routledge, comments that a mass rally organised by the Provisionals coincided with the meeting of four of the six SDLP MPs who made the decision. Those MPs were John Hume, Paddy O'Hanlon, Austin Currie and Ivan Cooper; the two Belfast MPs, Paddy Devlin and Gerry Fitt, were absent; Routledge, *John Hume: A Biography* (London: HarperCollins, 1997), p. 102.
27. The *Sunday Times Insight* team concluded that shootings such as those in Derry 'were becoming so frequent in Ulster as to constitute the ordinary risks of politics'; *Ulster*, p. 59.
28. Murray, *John Hume*, p. 11.
29. Ian McAllister, *The Northern Ireland Social Democratic and Labour Party: Political Opposition in a Divided Society* (London: Macmillan, 1977); McLoughlin, 'John Hume'; Murray, *John Hume*; Murray and Tonge, *Sinn Féin*.
30. Farrington, 'Reconciliation'; Hayward, 'Politics of nuance'.
31. O'Dochartaigh, *From Civil Rights*, p. 198.
32. 'Draft working document on proposals relating to the present situation in Northern Ireland, September 1971', PRONI D/3072/1/30/1.

33. 'Draft working document on proposals relating to the present situation in Northern Ireland, September 1971, Second Draft, 17 September 1971', ibid.
34. Fanning, 'Playing it Cool', p. 58.
35. Lynch to Heath, 19 August 1971, PRONI D/3072/1/43/1.
36. McLoughlin, 'John Hume'.
37. 'Draft working document on the Assembly of the Northern Irish People, 9 December 1971', PRONI D/3072/1/30/3 (henceforth cited as 'Draft document, December 1971').
38. *Irish News*, 2 January 2002.
39. Draft document, December 1971.
40. Ibid.
41. *Irish Times*, 21 December 1971.
42. 'Civil disobedience, 10 December 1971', PRONI D/3072/1/30/1.
43. McLoughlin, 'John Hume', p. 106; Murray, *John Hume*, pp. 12–21.
44. 'Some notes on future SDLP policy, March 1972', PRONI D/3072/1/30/3. In addition, the paper suggests that, given the changed circumstances and new ground rules, the party need no longer consider itself bound by its previous pledge not to negotiate.
45. To this end, Faulkner sounded a note of intent by assuming responsibility for the Ministry of Home Affairs and establishing a new security branch in the Cabinet Office to liaise with the British army personnel and the RUC; Patterson and Kaufmann, *Unionism*, p. 130.
46. Faulkner described his motivations as being to counteract the IRA's campaign, which he saw as aimed against Northern Ireland's political institutions. If the IRA won, he argued, 'democratic politics would be discredited and violence would spread like a disease'; *Memoirs of a Statesman* (London: Weidenfeld & Nicolson, 1978), p. 98. See also Walker, *A History of the Ulster Unionist Party*, p. 190.
47. PRONI CAB/9R/238/6, 'Note of a meeting at 10 Downing Street, 1 April 1971'.
48. These policy, or 'functional' committees would be designed to 'cover wide areas and not shadow particular departments'; Kenneth Bloomfield, 'Report of working party on parliament, 14 May 1971', PRONI CAB/9J/30/3. However, as Faulkner took pains to explain to his cabinet, the committees' remit would 'not usurp the government's ultimate authority in the determination of policy and …that Bills would only go to a committee if that was the will of the House'. Cabinet conclusions, 18 June 1971, PRONI CAB/4/1602.
49. Henry Kelly, *How Stormont Fell* (Dublin: Gill & Macmillan, 1972), p. 36.
50. Northern Ireland House of Commons Debate (hereafter cited as NIHCD), vol. 82, col. 269 (23 June 1971).
51. Ibid., col. 53 (22 June 1971).
52. Ibid., col. 95 (23 June 1971).
53. Ibid. col. 97 (23 June 1971).
54. Ibid. col. 54 (22 June 1971).
55. Faulkner, *Memoirs*, p. 99.
56. Bew et al., *Northern Ireland*, pp. 149–50.
57. See Hume in NICHD, Vol. 82, col. 101 (23 June 1971).
58. Devlin, *Straight Left*, p. 154; Kelly, *Stormont*, pp. 43–4.
59. Kelly, *Stormont*, pp. 45–6; J. J. Lee, *Ireland, 1912–1985: Politics and Society* (Cambridge: Cambridge University Press, 1995), p. 436.

60. Routledge, *John Hume*, p. 102.
61. Patterson and Kaufmann, *Unionism*, p. 132.
62. Hennessey, *The Evolution*, pp. 345–9.
63. 'Report by working party on membership of unlawful organisations, 2 August 1971', PRONI CAB 9R/238/6.
64. See, for example, Craig's Motion of Censure on 25 January 1972 in which he complained that not only was the ban impractical, but that it equated Orange marches with nationalist civil disobedience; ibid., vol. 83, cols. 1864–70. For the fractious relationship between Faulkner and the Order itself during the latter half of 1971, see Patterson and Kaufmann, *Unionism*, pp. 143–5.
65. Clifford Smyth, *Ian Paisley: Voice of Protestant Ulster* (Edinburgh: Edinburgh University Press, 1987), pp. 31–2.
66. Mulholland, *Northern Ireland*, pp. 154–5.
67. 'Visit of the Prime Ministers of the Irish Republic and of Northern Ireland, 26–27 September 1971', NA PREM 15/487.
68. UUP, *Towards the Future: A Unionist Blueprint* (Belfast: Unionist Publicity and Research Department, 1972).
69. Ibid. See also Faulkner, *Memoirs*, p. 176.
70. Faulkner to Heath, 1 March 1972, NA CJ 4/189.
71. Bew, 'Historical background', p. 38; see also, Hennessey, *The Evolution*, p. 345.
72. *Newsletter*, 10 August 1971.
73. *Irish News*, 8 October 1971.
74. *Newsletter*, 3 September 1971.
75. See Craig in NICHD, vol. 82 col. 1278 (13 October 1971). Craig suggested that if Faulkner was 'not prepared to do what is necessary then I would be prepared to take up this role'; *Newsletter*, 8 November 1971.
76. 'Notes of a meeting held at Chequers, 19 August 1971,' PRONI CAB/4/1607/19.
77. Northern Ireland Cabinet conclusions, 14 September 1971, PRONI CAB/4/1615.
78. Trend, cited in Bew, 'Historical Background', p. 18.
79. Northern Ireland Cabinet conclusions, 14 September 1971, PRONI CAB/4/1615.
80. Bloomfield, 'Meeting of permanent secretaries held at Stormont Castle, 12 October 1971', PRONI CAB/9J/83/1.
81. 'Record of a discussion with the Prime Minister of Northern Ireland, 7 October 1971', NA PREM 15/1034. William Whitelaw (later the first Northern Ireland Secretary of State) was present at this meeting in his capacity as Lord President of the Council, together with Heath and the core cabinet ministers (Reginald Maudling, Sir Alec Douglas-Home and Lord Carrington), and General Tuzo, General Officer Commanding and Director of Operations Northern Ireland.
82. Faulkner to Heath, 16 February 1972, NA CJ 4/189.
83. *Newsletter*, 16 February 1972.
84. *Newsletter*, 3 March 1972.
85. Hennessey, *The Evolution*, p. 345.
86. See, for example, 'An assessment of proposed or possible "political initiatives"', [September] 1971', PRONI CAB 9R/238/7. The memorandum claims that a 'restructured state' could facilitate the operation of a minority council

or even 'an executive compromising not only unionists and republicans, but also extreme Protestants – a daunting if not impossible task'. It also claims that 'a purely consultative economic [Council of Ireland] would be a fairly harmless organisation if set up in the right atmosphere'.
87. Bew et al., *Northern Ireland*, pp. 175–7.
88. 'Note of a meeting held at Downing Street on 7 October 1971', PRONI CAB/9R/238/7.
89. Ibid.
90. D. C. B. Holden, 'Note on political initiatives, 17 August 1971', PRONI FIN/30/R/1/6.
91. D. C. B. Holden, 'Cabinet memorandum on proposals for a political settlement', 18 February 1972, PRONI FIN/30/R/1/7.
92. 'Permanent secretaries' committee meeting, 8 December 1971', PRONI FIN/30/R/1/6.
93. 'Study Group – Final Report' ([September] 1971), in ibid. (hereafter 'Study Group').
94. The group's task was to produce policy proposals to deal with the increasing inter-communal division, the deteriorating security situation and the general escalation of civil disobedience. As an ad hoc body of junior or lower-level officials, there was an obvious feeling that the group's suggestions were too radical and that 'what they have produced may not be quite what was expected in some quarters'. J. H. Parkes to Harold Black, October 1971, ibid.

Chapter 3

1. These risks included doubts over the cooperation of the Northern Ireland police, civil service and judiciary and the fact that the IRA would now see itself as involved in a 'direct confrontation with the British Government'. In addition, the cabinet did not believe that Maudling's 'community government' could function in a territory where no 'general agreement upon the broad objective of preserving the integrity of the State' existed. Further, ministers were fearful that such measures would reduce 'the prospect of retaining adequate Parliamentary support' for the European Community legislation, and likewise, they could not count on such a scheme meeting with support from Dublin. Cabinet conclusions: confidential annex, 7 March 1972, NA CAB 128/48/3.
2. Ibid.
3. Ibid.
4. These risks included doubts over the cooperation of the Northern Ireland police, civil service and judiciary and the fact that the IRA would now see itself as involved in a 'direct confrontation with the British Government'. In addition, the cabinet did not believe that Maudling's 'community government' could function in a territory where no 'general agreement upon the broad objective of preserving the integrity of the State' existed. Further, ministers were fearful that such measures would reduce 'the prospect of retaining adequate Parliamentary support' for the European Community legislation, and likewise, they could not count on such a scheme meeting with support

from Dublin. Cabinet conclusions: confidential annex, 7 March 1972, NA CAB 128/48/3.
5. Cabinet conclusions, confidential annex, 9 March 1972, ibid.
6. Cabinet conclusions, confidential annex, 14 March 1972, ibid.
7. D. J. Trevelyan to P. J. Woodfield, 16 March 1972, NA CJ 4/189. Faulkner's expendability is underlined in the Home Office official, Philip (P. J.) Woodfield's memorandum to the Downing Street official P. L. Gregson, in which he states that 'it is the total of his [Faulkner's] package – his views of what is adequate to the situation and the general attitude of mind disclosed – which is more disturbing than [the] individual proposals, some of which have merit in themselves'; Woodfield to Gregson, 20 March 1972, NA CJ 4/189.
8. 'Northern Ireland – Mr Faulkner's letters', ibid.
9. Ibid.
10. Woodfield to Norbury, 17 March 1972, ibid.
11. Cabinet conclusions, confidential annex, 23 March 1972, NA CAB 128/48/3.
12. Walker, *A History*, p. 212.
13. Patterson and Kaufmann, *Unionism*, p. 153.
14. In this regard, James Kilfedder was admonished by the County Armagh Unionist Association: 'The members of the executive committee of this association ... were appalled at press reports about dissention among unionist members at Westminster and call upon you all to get together and form a united front so that the other Westminster members, including the government, will have some confidence in what you say'. J. K. Truman to Kilfedder MP, 6 July, 1972, PRONI D/4127/1.
15. *Guardian*, 20 May 1972.
16. *Irish Times*, 27 July 1972.
17. Patterson and Kaufmann, *Unionism*, pp. 154–5.
18. Martin McGuiness, quoted in the *Sunday News*, 9 April 1972.
19. 'Some notes on future SDLP policy, March 1972', PRONI D/3072/1/33/2 (henceforth, 'Notes').
20. The memo continues: 'If the SDLP refuse absolutely to enter in negotiations ... it is very likely that the Westminster government will decide on complete integration as the only possible solution. It should, therefore, be borne in mind throughout that our decision on the question of negotiation may well influence the nature of that eventual solution'.
21. 'Report of meeting of policy sub-committee, held on Wednesday, April 26 1972', PRONI D/3072/1/30/1.
22. *Irish Independent*, 25 May 1972. See also Cooper in the *Irish Times*, 23 May 1972: 'it is necessary for us to face up to the political realities...that there are elements in this community who are determined, in order to maintain their position, to provoke a sectarian confrontation ...'
23. 'Meeting of the standing committee, 18 July 1972', PRONI D/3072/1/32/1.
24. The press release claimed that: 'The Provisional IRA do not seem to place the same importance as do the people on internment and seem to want its continuation in order to hold public sympathy for its methods ... [Its] recent actions seem designed to provoke both a Protestant backlash and strong Brit military actions against Catholic areas in order to provoke a

widespread emotional uprising in the whole island behind them'. *Irish Times* 27 July 1972.
25. See Ivan Cooper, 'Northern Ireland – a condominium? August 1972' (henceforth, Cooper, 'Condominium'); and Ben Caraher, 'Condominium – a suggestion to the policy committee of the SDLP, August 1972'; 'Commentary on "Condominium" ' 25 August 1972 (henceforth Caraher, 'Commentary'). See PRONI D/3072/1/30/1.
26. See Caraher, 'Commentary'.
27. Cooper, 'Condominium'.
28. This point was acknowledged by British officials at the beginning of August: 'Mr Lynch believes he has to be seen to be persuading the SDLP to taking part in talks in order to strengthen the party's credibility in the ghettos and to reinforce the confidence of the Northern minorities generally ... They [Dublin] genuinely believe that a public role will help rally the minorities behind the SDLP.' Peck to Steele, 3 August 1972, NA FCO 87/80.
29. 'First meeting with William Whitelaw on Monday 7 August 1972', PRONI D/3027/1/30/1. See also the British report of the meeting, 'Note of meeting between the Secretary of State and the SDLP, 7 August 1972', NA FCO 87/80.
30. 'Note of a meeting between the Prime Minister and the SDLP, 12 September 1972', ibid.
31. 'Visit of Dr Hillery to London, 4 August 1972', ibid.
32. On 20 September, Hume reiterated the SDLP's rejection of Whitelaw's invitation, which, he argued, 'is much too limited to produce a solution to the North's present problems, but for wide ranging discussions which must of necessity involve the Republic', NAI DFA 2003/17/319.
33. Devlin, *Straight Left*, p. 183.
34. John Duffy, 'Some notes on Caraher's and Cooper's papers on the condominium proposal', PRONI D/3072/1/30/1.
35. SDLP, *Towards a New Ireland: Proposals by the Social Democratic and Labour Party* (Belfast: SDLP, 1972).
36. 'SDLP proposals, 21 September 1972', NAI DFA/2004/7/2698. See also 'Briefing note for Taoiseach: meeting with SDLP members, 28 September 1972', NAI DFA/2003/16/466.
37. Walker, *A History*, p. 214.
38. Faulkner to McIvor, 22 December 1982, PRONI D/2962/1/8.
39. 'Note of a meeting between the Secretary of State and the Ulster Unionist Party, 12 December 1972', PRONI CAB/9J/90/10.
40. See also Faulkner's testimony to the Northern Ireland Committee at Westminster in March 1973, in which he argued that while 'power sharing was necessary', any executive must consist of 'people of like minds' as it was 'impossible to expect those on either side of the political divide to agree to have sufficient common ground'. Northern Ireland Committee, 1 March 1973, NA CJ 4/514.
41. 'Note of a meeting between the Secretary of State and the United Loyalist Council, 19 December 1972', PRONI CAB/9J/90/10.
42. 'Note of a meeting between the Secretary of State and the Democratic Unionist Party, 19 December 1972', ibid.
43. 'Note of a meeting between the Secretary of State and the Unionist Party', 15 March 1973. NA CJ 4/514. Kilfedder made his comment in response to

a suggestion by Captain Orr that perhaps a 'British Islands Council dealing solely with social and economic matters' would be acceptable. Orr also rejected a straightforward North-South council.
44. 'Joint statement by the Parliamentary leaders of the Ulster Unionist Party and the Ulster Democratic Unionist Party at Westminster, 12 March 1973', ibid.
45. HMSO, 'Northern Ireland Constitutional Proposals'.
46. *Newsletter*, 28 March 1973.
47. *Belfast Telegraph*, 2 April 1973.
48. Faulkner, *Memoirs*, p.193.
49. *Newsletter*, 22 March 1973.
50. *Newsletter*, 24 March 1973.
51. *Newsletter*, 9 May 1973.
52. Patterson and Kaufmann, *Unionism*, p. 161. Paisley's DUP won eight seats; Vanguard, seven; and independent loyalists, three; see Bew and Gillespie, *Northern Ireland*, p. 65.
53. *Newsletter*, 4 July 1973.
54. *Newsletter*, 3 October 1973.
55. *Newsletter*, 10 October 1973. The following day, the paper warned that Faulkner's position was so precarious that 'SDLP "overplay" is the new danger'; *Newsletter*, 11 October 1973.
56. The meeting itself took place on 26 October. See 'Report of a meeting between D. Nally and B. Faulkner, 26 October 1973', NAI DT/2004/21/625. Faulkner won a Standing Committee vote (132:105) on the question of entering into talks regarding a power sharing executive (*Irish Times*, 24 October 1973).
57. Another revealing aside occurred towards the end of the meeting in which Faulkner supplied the Irish delegation with his copy of the 'Constitution and Rules of the UUC', in response to an inquiry to enlighten them as to the party's procedures.
58. *Newsletter*, 3 November 1973.
59. *Irish Times*, 23 November 1973.
60. See, for example, its support for Paisley's calls for enhanced security initiatives at the beginning of October. Paisley's condemnation of the IRA, it argued, 'summed up the situation perfectly. There are those who, for their own ends and to cover up their own deplorable deficiencies, would put it aboard that the establishment of a new, artificial form of government is the answer to the ghastly problem of violence'. *Newsletter*, 5 October 1973.
61. *Newsletter*, 9 November 1973.
62. *Newsletter*, 21 and 22 November 1973. *The Times* reported that the narrowness of Faulkner's victory meant that his decisions would continue to be called into question, and quoted a Faulknerite Assembly member: 'It is a victory of a sort, I suppose, but where is our power base? In the long run, this could prove disastrous'. *The Times*, 21 November 1973.
63. *Newsletter*, 28 November 1973.
64. Faulkner, *Memoirs*, pp. 192–3.
65. *Newsletter*, 29 November 1973.
66. 'Council of Ireland, Paper 1, N.D. [December 1972]', NAI DT/2003/16/430.

67. 'Report on discussion between the Taoiseach and the Prime Minister, 24 November 1972', NAI DT/2003/16/468.
68. *Newsletter*, 15 January 1973.
69. *Irish News*, 23 March 1973.
70. O'Brien to Cosgrave, 26 March 1973, 'Northern Ireland assembly', NAI AG/2004/1/254.
71. Cabinet Minutes, 12 June 1973, NAI DT/2004/21/624; see also Garret FitzGerald, *All in a Life: An Autobiography* (London, Macmillan, 1991), p. 202.
72. 'Memorandum on the conference proposed by the British government's white paper, "Northern Ireland constitutional proposals", 24 May 1973,' NAI DT/2004/21/624.
73. 'Inter-Departmental Unit on Northern Ireland: "Interim Report on Council of Ireland," 12 June 1973', ibid. (hereafter 'IDU Report, June 1973').
74. Costello to Cosgrave, 30 May 1973, NAI AG/2004/1/254.
75. 'Report on meeting between the Irish government and the SDLP, 12 July 1973', NAI DT/2003/21/467.
76. Bew and Patterson, *The British State*, pp. 57–8.
77. 'Report of conversations with the SDLP, 27 September 1973', NAI DT/2004/21/624.
78. Austin Currie, *All Hell Will Break Lose* (Dublin: O'Brien, 2004), pp. 222–3.
79. 'Minutes of a meeting between the SDLP and the Irish government, 2 November 1973', NAI DT/2005/7/649.
80. O'Brien to Cosgrave, 5 November 1973, ibid.
81. Whelan to Nally, 'Council of Ireland – observations on organisation and structural matters', 1 November 1973, ibid.
82. FitzGerald to Cosgrave, 9 November 1973, NAI DT/2004/21/625.
83. 'Council of Ireland: executive functions – agreed presentation document following consultations with the delegations of the Alliance, SDLP and Unionist Parties', nd (12 November 1973?), ibid.
84. In addition to Carrington's briefing, 'Individual SDLP men were taken aside by ... senior army officers from their areas and given more detailed information than they had ever before been given about the security situation in their localities'. The effect on the SDLP seems to have been to suppress their internment demands - Ivan Cooper, for one was 'frighteningly impressed' with the army's intelligence. Donlon to Nally, 20 November 1973, NAI DT/2004/21/625.
85. 'Summary of outcome of talks with the British at official level on 28 and 29 November 1973', NAI DT/2004/21/627.
86. 'Summary of government decisions, December 1973', NAI DT/2004/21/627.
87. Devlin claimed that the SDLP approach was 'get all-Ireland institutions established which, with adequate safeguards, would produce the dynamic that would lead ultimately to an agreed united Ireland. SDLP representatives thus concentrated their entire efforts on seeking a set of tangible powers for the council which in the fullness of time would create and sustain the evolutionary process. All other issues were governed by that approach, and the need to reduce loyalist resistance to the concepts of a Council of Ireland and a power-sharing Executive'; Devlin, *Straight Left*, p. 205.
88. 'Status of Northern Ireland, December 1973', NAI DT/2004/21/627.

89. *Newsletter*, 7 December 1973.
90. Faulkner argued that 'the Irish government has fully accepted the status of Northern Ireland and has solemnly declared that it cannot be changed until a majority of Ulster people wish to change it'. 'Speech to the Junior Chamber of Commerce, 14 December 1973', NAI DT/2004/21/678.
91. The *Newsletter* (11 December 1973) raised the question, 'Is there any reason why the setting up of a Council of Ireland is needed as a prelude for the implementation of what should be normal peaceful cooperation – unless an opportunity is being sought under duress, to establish the first essential institutions of a united Ireland'.
92. Bew and Gillespie, *Northern Ireland*, p. 76. The Ulster Unionist Council remained the highest body in the Unionist Party during this time despite the policy differences between the pro-Sunningdale Faulknerites and those party members who followed Harry West in lending support to the umbrella coalition of the UUUC
93. 'Note of a meeting between the Secretary of State and Mr Brian Faulkner, 2 January 1974', NA CJ 4/470. McLachlan, in a separate meeting with Northern Ireland officials 'implie[d], gloomily, it is now not a question of a defeat but of how large it is'. Allan to Trevelyan, 2 January 1974, ibid.
94. Ibid. Faulkner expressed similar sentiments before the power-sharing executive, claiming that 'views were divided as to whether the result of the vote at Friday's meeting of the Unionist Council accurately expressed Unionist opinion in the country', PRONI OE/2/1a, 'Meeting of the Northern Ireland executive, 8 January 1974, Note of discussions'.
95. 'Peter McLachlan telephone call, 4 January 1974', NAI DT/2005/7/624.
96. Bew and Gillespie, *Northern Ireland*, pp. 76–7.
97. 'Note of meeting between the Taoiseach and the Chief Executive, 16 January 1974', NAI DT/2005/7/653.
98. 'Council of Ireland: Memorandum by the Chief Minister, EXMEMO 1/74', 17 January 1974, PRONI OE/2/3.
99. Murray and Tonge, *Sinn Féin*, p. 59; Murphy, 'Gerry Fitt', p. 187.
100. McIvor, *Hope Deferred*, p. 100.
101. *Irish Press*, 21 December 1973.
102. 'Visit to Belfast, 9 January 1974', NAI DT/2005/7/649.
103. Devlin expanded on the point, describing how Fitt's room at Stormont adjoined Faulkner's and that since he had no executive responsibilities, 'he simply has his room, a secretary, and a cabinet of liquor – he has plenty of time to develop a relationship with Faulkner, which will work mainly to Faulkner's advantage'. Ibid.
104. 'Report of a meeting between the All-Party Committee on Irish Relations and a delegation from the SDLP, 18 January 1974', NAI DT/2005/7/621.
105. *Irish Times*, 19 January 1974.
106. *Irish News*, 22 January 1974.
107. 'A meeting between representatives of the Northern Ireland executive and the government of the Irish Republic, 1 February 1974', NA CJ/4/527.
108. 'Summary of tactics in post-Sunningdale situation, 9 January 1974', NAI DT/2005/7/624.
109. 'Visit to Northern Ireland, 13/14 February 1974', NAI DT/2005/7/649.
110. Ibid.

111. 'Note for the record, meeting between Brian Faulkner and Frank Cooper', 5 March 1974, NA CJ 4/786.
112. Rees also expressed his view of the results vis-à-vis Westminster and Northern Ireland. Although there was still inter-party support for the 'Whitelaw approach', Rees detected a 'tendency towards disinterest'. However, he said this could change due to the views of some 'right-wing moderates in the Labour Party who looked a Northern Ireland in an essentially historical context'. This group, Rees said, believed that 'it was impossible to go on indefinitely' and favoured 'home rule for Ireland on the Gladstone pattern'. A response by Faulkner to this news is not included in the minutes.
113. 'Speech by Bradford to the Victoria Unionist Association Executive meeting, 13 March 1974', PRONI D/4211/1/10/25.
114. 'Record of a meeting between the Secretary of State and the leaders of the UUUC, 18 March 1974', NA CJ4/785. The responsibilities of the Dublin government were a common thread linking these matters, which included the shipment of guns across the border and the ability of terrorists in the Crossmaglen area to seek refuge in the South.
115. *Newsletter*, 20 March 1974.
116. 'Note of a meeting between the Secretary of State and Mr Brian Faulkner, 19 March 1974', NA CJ 4/786.
117. 'Prime Minister's meeting with Rt. Hon Brian Faulkner, 1 April 1974', NA PREM 16/163.
118. 'Record of a conversation between the Prime Minister and the Chief Executive of Northern Ireland, 1 April 1974', ibid.
119. 'Meeting of the Northern Ireland executive, 2 April 1974', PRONI OE/2/15.
120. Reid to Woodfield, 12 April 1974, 'Further talk with Mr Faulkner', NA CJ 4/473.
121. Reid to Woodfield, 16 April 1974, 'Discussion with the SDLP: Sunningdale', ibid.
122. FitzGerald, *All in a Life*, p. 234.
123. Reid to Allen, 30 April 1974, NA CJ 4/492. Fitt explained to Rees and Faulkner that he had avoided the meeting because he did not wish to be 'in a minority of one'.
124. See Faulkner to Fitt, 12 April 1974, NAI DT/2005/7/649.
125. Rees to Wilson, 8 April 1974, NA CJ 4/473.
126. Ministers of the following departments sat on the group: Foreign and Commonwealth, Home Office, Defence, the Chancellor and the Attorney-General. The remit suggested that the officials 'should do their work on a personal basis and with the absolute minimum of consultation with their departments'. John Hunt to Wilson, 11 April 1974, 'Northern Ireland contingency planning', NA PREM 16/145.
127. Allan, 'Pro-Assembly Unionist opinion – following a discussion with McLachlan, 30 April 1974', NA CJ 4/786. McLachlan intimated his 'amazement' at the 'naivety of the Department of Foreign Affairs', which repeatedly sent him invitations to social functions. He said that to have accepted would have meant committing 'political suicide'.
128. 'Unionist objectives, April 1974', PRONI D/1327/5/33.

129. The Portrush blueprint included the proposal that the RUC and its reserves 'should return to their pre-Hunt role, the better to enable them to deal with the special problems of riot and subversions'.
130. 'Sunningdale: alternative courses of action following results of recent Westminster general election, 26 March 1974', NAI DT/2005/7/658 (hereafter 'Sunningdale: alternative courses of action, March 1974').
131. Ibid. The Irish government was effectively prevented from voicing any support for the Sunningdale Communiqué while the 'Boland case' was under judicial consideration. Although the Irish High Court ruled in the government's favour in March, the hiatus did little to bolster Faulkner's claims for the feasibility of the Communiqué's proposals.
132. Sunnningdale: alternative courses of action, March 1974.
133. Don Anderson, *Fourteen May Days: The Inside Story of the Loyalist Strike of 1974* (Dublin: Gill & Macmillan 1994), p. 103.
134. Currie, *All Hell will Break Lose*, p. 277.
135. 'SDLP, draft statement, 21 May 1974', NAI DT/2005/7/649.
136. 'Northern Ireland situation, 21 May 1974', ibid.
137. 'Meeting of the Northern Ireland executive, 22 May 1974', PRONI OE/2/26. The meeting, scheduled for 12.00 pm, postponed to allow for party consultation until 1.10pm. It quickly adjourned at 1.40 pm and at 2.10 pm Fitt reported that his party remained unchanged. Following a vote to issue a statement, which passed by seven votes to four, Fitt stated that his party could no longer 'regard themselves as bound by the principle of collective responsibility'. However, the SDLP reported at 4.20 pm to agree to the staged approach. For the SDLP's meeting with NIO minister Stanley Orme, see 'Note for the record, 22 May 1974', NA PREM 16/147.
138. Cosgrave to Wilson, 23 May 1974, NA PREM 16/147.
139. 'Statement issued after today's discussions at Chequers, 24 May 1974', PRONI D/4211/4/1/28.
140. *Newsletter*, 20 May 1974. Bradford's supporters had previously demanded that he 'adhere to party policy. A Council of Ireland with executive powers is against this policy, and we herewith register our strong objection to our elected members supporting the Council of Ireland as envisaged in the Sunningdale agreement'. 'Knock and Ballyhackamore branch of the Bloomfield Unionist Association to Bradford, Agnew, and Cardwell, 1 May 1974', PRONI D/4211/4/1/30.
141. 'Meeting of the Northern Ireland executive, 28 May 1974', PRONI OE/2/32.
142. Richard Bourke, *Peace in Ireland: The War of Ideas* (London: Pimlico, 2003), p.217; Gillespie, 'Sunningdale'; Hennessey, *A History*, p. 227; Kerr, *Imposing*; O'Duffy, *British-Irish Relations*; Jonathan Tonge, 'From Sunningdale to the Good Friday Agreement: Creating Devolved Government in Northern Ireland'. *Contemporary British History*, 4(3) (2000); Walker, *A History*, p. 204.
143. Devlin, *Straight Left*, p. 225; Faulkner, *Memoirs*, p. 222; Maurice Hayes, *Minority Verdict: Experiences of a Catholic Public Servant* (Belfast: Blackstaff, 1995), p. 203; Basil McIvor, *Hope Deferred: Experiences of an Irish Unionist* (Belfast: Blackstaff, 1998), p. 100; Merlyn Rees, *Northern Ireland: A Personal Perspective* (London: Methuen, 1985), pp. 33, 90.
144. R. F. Foster, *Luck and the Irish: A Brief History of Change c. 1970-2000* (London: Allen Lane, 2007), p. 118.

145. See Brian Faulkner to Reginald Magee, 18 February 1976, reprinted in Faulkner, *Memoirs*, p. 287.
146. Farrington, 'Reconciliation'.

Chapter 4

1. Bruce, *Edge of the Union*; Hughes, *Ireland Divided*; McGarry and O'Leary, *Explaining*.
2. O'Leary and McGarry, *Politics*, p. 209. O'Leary and McGarry claim that British 'arbitration' in Northern Ireland was 'structurally biased' in favour of the Union; however, they fail to consider what the implications of an alternative policy – possibly weighted in favour of joint sovereignty, or executive power-sharing – might have been.
3. Kerr, *Imposing*, p. 66.
4. O'Duffy, *British-Irish Relations*, pp. 169–70; see also, Kerr, *Imposing*, p. 59.
5. O'Leary, 'Conservative Stewardship'; Tannam, 'Explaining'.
6. Kerr, *Imposing*, p. 59; emphasis added.
7. McGrattan, 'Explaining Northern Ireland?'
8. O'Leary and Arthur, 'Northern Ireland'.
9. Kerr, *Imposing*, p. 59; O'Duffy, *British-Irish Relations*, p. 101.
10. Bernard Donoughue, *The Heat of the Kitchen: An Autobiography* (London: Politico's, 2003), pp. 135–8. Donoughue admits that his advice was coloured by his emotional attachment to the "'green" and Catholic side'.
11. Pierson, *Politics in Time*.
12. Aguilar, *Memory*, pp. 21–2; Tonkin, *Narrating*, p. 1.
13. O'Leary and McGarry, *Politics of Antagonism*, p. 197.
14. O'Leary and McGarry, *Politics of Antagonism*, pp. 183–5, 197.
15. Bernard Donoughue, *Prime Minister: The Conduct of Policy under Harold Wilson and James Callaghan* (London: Jonathan Cape, 1987), p. 132.
16. Bourn to Cooper, 3 June 1974: 'Political arrangements, the next steps', NA CJ 4/492.
17. Bourn to Cooper, 6 June 1974, 'Future political arrangements in Northern Ireland', ibid. Bourn points out: 'I have been wondering whether there is anything to learn from the arrangements in other countries who have faced somewhat similar problems ... like Belgium and Holland .... If you think that there is anything in this idea, we could consider how best it could be followed up.'
18. Hayes, *Minority Verdict*, p. 212.
19. Bloomfield, 'The Northern Ireland executive: some retrospective conclusions, 19 July 1974', PRONI CENT/1/3/24.
20. Bloomfield tied both these points together: 'There was always a conflict between conventional ideas of cabinet or executive confidentiality and the need to make sure one's party came along.'
21. Hayes, 'Catholics and the SDLP, 26 June 1974', NA FCO 87/347.
22. Cooper to Rees, 19 July 1974, NA 87/347.
23. 'The Northern Ireland Constitution' (Cmnd. 5675) (London: Her Majesty's Stationery Office, 1974).

24. Allan: 'Northern Ireland: the future', NA CJ 4/492 (henceforth, 'Northern Ireland: the future').
25. See 'Note of a meeting between permanent secretaries and Cooper, 9 July 1974', and 'Note by the NIO: "Community wardens" 12 August 1974', for further details on plans to introduce a form of 'community policing', PRONI CENT/1/4/1.
26. 'Northern Ireland: the future'. See also the conclusion of the Foreign and Commonwealth Office in December 1974 that 'While the form of expression used to give effect to [the Irish dimension] might be a matter of negotiation, the continuing validity of the aspiration must not be ignored'; Harding to Arthur, 'Discussions with the Department of Foreign Affairs, 12 December 1974', PRONI CONV/7/19.
27. Bourn to Trevelyan, 5 September 1974, 'The political situation in Northern Ireland: brief for Prime Minister's meeting', NA CJ 4/492.
28. Trevelyan to Cooper, 2 October 1974, PRONI CENT/1/3/24.
29. Wyatt to Cooper, 'Northern Ireland: the next few months', 9 October 1974, NA CJ 4/492.
30. Bew and Gillespie, *Northern Ireland*, pp. 98–9; for more details on the talks, see below.
31. Sean Hollywood, the spokesperson for the SDLP's anti-internment 'Motion Number One Committee', claimed that the leadership had allowed the party 'to be hoodwinked by a British government which … was more interested in capitulating to the loyalists at the expense of its allies in the power-sharing coalition', *Sunday News*, 9 June 1974. The committee took its name from the SDLP's original decision to boycott talks with the government while internment continued.
32. 'Minutes of a meeting between the government and the SDLP, 22 August 1974', NAI DT/2005/7/649.
33. Geróid Ó Brion, 'Note on SDLP [Assembly Party] conference, 24–25 August 1975,' in ibid.
34. Ibid.
35. *Irish Press*, 26 June 1974.
36. Lindsay Diary, 20 January 1975, PRONI D/4175/3/7.
37. 'Note of a meeting between the Secretary of State and a deputation led by Mr West and Dr Paisley, 3 February 1975', PRONI CENT/1/3/40.
38. Burns to Blackburn, ND [April 1975], PRONI CONV/7/19.
39. Hayes: 'Note for the record, 21 April 1975: Meeting between Blackburn and West, 11 April 1975', PRONI CONV/7/19. Powell joined the Unionist Party in October 1974 following a prolonged estrangement from Edward Heath and his leadership of the Conservative Party; see Simon Heffer, 'Enoch Powell', *Oxford Dictionary of National Biography*, 2008.
40. West to Lowry, 10 May 1975, PRONI CONV/1/4.
41. Bew and Gillespie, *Northern Ireland*, p. 101.
42. For Maurice Hayes, one of the Convention's team of officials, the Convention 'was an entirely insignificant and ineffective interlude. Nobody except a few politicians, and those mainly in the UUUC, was in the least interested, and the papers could have been scattered to the winds without the least loss to scholarship'; *Minority Verdict*, p. 230.
43. Ibid., pp. 227–31; Smyth, *Ian Paisley*, pp. 101–2.

44. McAllister, *The SDLP*, pp. 154–5; Murray and Tonge, *Sinn Féin*, p. 54.
45. 'Meeting between Lowry and West, 7 July 1975', PRONI CONV/1/1.
46. J. A. Oliver, 'Note for the record: Meeting with Mr Harry West, 7 July 1975', in ibid. Ken Bloomfield originally turned down West's request for assistance before Oliver agreed to provide 'some inkling of the thinking that underlay the proposal'. Although Oliver reports that West 'was obviously embarrassed by his own way of going about this problem of getting advice', it did not stop him from asking for an another paper on the issue of the return of the governor.
47. Maurice Hayes, for example, explained that 'The turning point in Dutch political life was the German occupation ... which provided all parties with an external enemy to unite against', Hayes to Oliver, 7 July 1975, PRONI CONV/1/3.
48. 'UUUC policy position, 26 August 1975', PRONI CONV/1/11; see also 'Northern Ireland Constitutional Convention Report' (London: Her Majesty's Stationery Office, 1975), pp. 171–2.
49. Smyth, *Ian Paisley*, pp. 100, 101.
50. 'Chairman's meeting with UUUC leaders, 27 August 1975', PRONI CONV/1/1.
51. 'Chairman's meeting with Mr Fitt, 25 August 1975', ibid.
52. See 'Note for the record: talks with Messrs Devlin and Hume, 27 August 1975', PRONI CONV/1/1 (hereafter 'Meeting, 27 August'). See also PRONI CONV/7/93 for the material supplied on request to Trimble on the Westminster and Congressional committee systems.
53. McLoughlin, 'John Hume'; Murray, *John Hume*.
54. 'Meeting, 27 August'.
55. Among numerous other incidents, two children died following a shoot-out between the IRA and the British army after an anti-internment rally escalated into a riot on 10 August. On 13 August, the IRA killed five people in a shooting in a bar on the Shankill Road. In addition, the Provisionals killed four people during an attack on an Orange hall in Newtownhamilton on 1 September; Bew and Gillespie, *Northern Ireland*, p. 104. See David McKettrick Seamus Kelters, Brian Feeney and Chris Thornton, *Lost Lives: The Stories of the Men, Women, and Children Who Died as a Result of the Northern Ireland Troubles* (Edinburgh: Mainstream, 1999), pp. 567–9, for a record of the activities of the IRA's 'Balcombe Street gang'. These provided a catalyst for the steep rise in killings from August onwards. Between 1 August and 1 September, republicans killed 20, while loyalist paramilitaries killed 17 (including the 'Miami Showband' massacre on 31 July), ibid.
56. *Protestant Telegraph*, 29 August 1975.
57. *Belfast Telegraph*, 29 August 1975. Following initial denials by the army and the Secretary of State as to the document's veracity, the army later admitted that it was genuine; *The Times*, 10 September 1975.
58. *Belfast Telegraph*, 4 September 1975.
59. Patterson and Kaufmann, *Unionism*, p. 180.
60. 'Chairman's meeting with Dr Paisley, 6 September 1975', PRONI CONV/1/2.
61. Bew and Gillespie, *Northern Ireland*, p. 106.
62. Eamon Phoenix, 'Paisley and Powell wrecked hopes of voluntary coalition', *Irish News*, 29 December 2005.

63. Smyth, *Paisley*, p. 101.
64. Murray, *John Hume*, pp. 34–8; Murray and Tonge, *Sinn Féin*, pp. 53–8.
65. McLoughlin, 'John Hume', p. 171.
66. 'Chairman's meeting with SDLP, 9 September 1975', PRONI CONV/1/2.
67. O'Leary and McGarry, *Politics of Antagonism*, pp. 185–93; Mitchell, 'Party Competition'; Mitchell et al., 'Northern Ireland'.
68. McLoughlin, 'John Hume'; see also O'Leary and McGarry, *Politics of Antagonism*, p. 200.
69. 'Discussions between OUP and SDLP, March-September 1976', NA CJ 4/1441.
70. Ibid.
71. 'SDLP-OUP talks, 2 July 1976', ibid.
72. B. C. Cubbon, 'Note for the record', 11 May 1976, ibid.
73. Cubbon to Janes, 22 June 1976, NA CJ 4/1440.
74. See, for example, the conclusions reached at a meeting of officials in December 1976: 'Although the SDLP remained disunited and depressed ... there was no immediate justification for HMG's taking any measures which might help or change the present state of affairs within the party'. 'Note of a meeting on Northern Ireland politics held by the permanent under-secretary, 21 December 1976', ibid.
75. Murray, *John Hume*; Todd, 'Nationalism'.
76. Michael Cunningham, 'The Political Language of John Hume', *Irish Political Studies*, 1997, Vol. 12: 13–22.
77. FitzGerald, *All in a Life*, pp. 662–3.
78. McLoughlin, 'John Hume', p. 171.
79. Seamus Deane, quoted in 'Interview with John Hume', *The Crane Bag*, 4(2) (1980): 41.
80. Murray, *John Hume*, pp. 91–5; Todd, 'Nationalism', pp. 53–5.
81. John Hume, 'The Irish question: a British problem', *Foreign Affairs*, 58 (1980): 303–4.
82. 'New Ireland Forum Report' (Dublin: The Stationery Office, 1984).
83. FitzGerald, *All in a Life*, p. 463.
84. Jackson, *Home Rule*, p. 284.
85. Patterson and Kaufmann, *Unionism*, pp. 205–6.
86. Bew and Gillespie, *Northern Ireland*, p. 137.
87. Jackson, *Home Rule*, pp. 288–9.
88. *Irish Times*, 23 March 1983.
89. Jim Prior, *A Balance of Power* (London: Hamish Hamilton, 1986), pp. 190, 192.
90. Ibid., p. 197.
91. Jackson, *Home Rule*, p. 296; see also Aughey, *Under Siege*; Farrington, *Ulster Unionism*; Patterson and Kaufmann, *Unionism*.
92. Aughey, *Under Siege*; Cochrane, *Unionist Politics*; Farrington, *Ulster Unionism*.
93. Bew et al., *Northern Ireland*, p. 210.
94. Farrington, *Ulster Unionism*, pp. 50–1.
95. See also O'Kane, *Britain*.
96. See Bacharch and Baratz, 'Two Faces of Power'.
97. Bernard Donoughue, *Downing Street Diary: With Harold Wilson in No. 10* (London: Jonathan Cape, 2005), p. 129.

98. Wilson, 'Apocalyptic note for the record, 10 January 1976', NA CJ 4/1358.
99. Hunt to Wilson 16 January 1976, NA PREM 16/960.
100. Cabinet Official Committee on Northern Ireland (hereafter NIC), 'Note by the Northern Ireland Office', February 1975, NA CJ 4/753.
101. NIC, 'Machinery of government, Note by the NIO', 29 April 1975, NA CJ 4/755.
102. Official working group on Northern Ireland, 'Distancing, Note by the NIO', July 1975, NA CJ 4/756.
103. Official working group on Northern Ireland, 'Distancing, Note by the NIO', 21 October 1975, ibid.
104. NIC, Minutes of a meeting, 31 October 1975, ibid.
105. Official working group on Northern Ireland, 'Majority rule, Note by the NIO, October 1975', NA CJ 4/754.
106. Note of a meeting of senior civil servants, 7 October 1975, NA CJ 4/759.
107. On this point, see NIC, 'Future policy, Note by the NIO', 28 October 1975, NA CJ 4/754.
108. Janes to Cooper, 4 August 1975, 'Distancing', NA CJ 4/1352.
109. Donoughue to Wilson, 'Northern Ireland: future policy options, 21 September 1975', NA PREM 16/520.
110. Donoughue, *Heat of the Kitchen*, p. 136.
111. O'Leary and McGarry, *Politics of Antagonism*, p. 202.
112. John Bowman, 'Britain opts for a "firm hand" on the North', *Irish Times*, 30 December 2006.
113. Rees to Wilson, 'The Provisionals', 29 November 1975, NA PREM 16/958.
114. Ibid.
115. *Guardian*, 18 March 2008, 'Talking to the enemy: the secret intermediaries who contacted the IRA'.
116. Robert W. White, *Ruairí O Bradáigh: The Life and Politics of an Irish Revolutionary* (Chesham, IN: Indiana University Press, 2006), p. 220.
117. Note of a meeting, 18 December 1974, 'Church leader's meeting with the IRA', NA CJ 4/860.
118. Ibid.
119. White, *O Bradáigh*, p. 235; original emphasis.
120. Ibid., p. 241. See also Bew and Gillespie, *Northern Ireland*, p. 98.
121. Two versions of the 'terms' exist – those that republicans say the British agreed to, and those that the British say the IRA agreed to. Both are reprinted in White, *O Bradáigh*, pp. 228, 230.
122. Peter Taylor, 'Disobeyed orders and a dangerous message', *Guardian*, 18 March 2008.
123. Meeting with representatives of Provisional Sinn Féin, 10 February 1976, NA PREM 16/960.
124. John Bew, 'Power-sharing on backburner, but don't tell Dublin', *Irish Times*, 28 December 2007.
125. Rees advised Wilson that 'we should avoid major initiatives in the near future and should concentrate on positive and even-handed government', Rees to Wilson, 22 April 1976, NA PREM 16/962.
126. Cabinet conclusions, 4 March 1976, NA CAB 128.
127. Abbot to Burns, 24 February 1976, NA CJ 4/1427.

128. 'Note of a seminar on constitutional developments held at Hillsborough Castle, 6 May 1976', NA CJ 4/1352.
129. Margaret Thatcher, *Downing Street Years* (London: HarperCollins, 1993), p. 385.
130. FitzGerald, *All in a Life*, p. 463.
131. Bew, *Ireland*, pp. 531–7; Henry Patterson, *Ireland since 1939: The Persistence of Conflict* (London: Penguin, 2006), p. 213.
132. O'Kane, *Britain*, p. 40.
133. John A. Farrell, *Tip O'Neill and the Democratic Century*. (Boston, MA: Little, Brown, 2001), pp. 222–4.
134. O'Leary and McGarry, *Politics of Antagonism*, p. 235.
135. Ibid., p. 236; see also O'Kane, *Britain*, p. 62.
136. O'Leary and McGarry, *Politics of Antagonism*, p. 238.
137. Jackson, *Home Rule*, p. 299.
138. J. Henderson, 'Political future of Northern Ireland', 10 August 1976, NA CJ 4/1427.
139. Gilliland, 'Discussion paper', October 1976, ibid.
140. Burns, 'Political strategy', 29 October 1976, ibid.

Chapter 5

1. Darby and MacGinty, *Guns*, pp. 20–5.
2. Farrington, *Ulster Unionism*, p. 182.
3. Gerry Adams, *Hope and History: Making Peace in Ireland* (Dingle: Brandon, 2004); John Hume, *Personal Views: Politics, Peace and Reconciliation in Ireland* (Dublin: Town House, 1996).
4. Eamon Mallie and David McKittrick, *The Fight for Peace: The Secret Story Behind the Irish Peace Process* (London: Heinemann, 1996); Peter McLoughlin, 'John Hume'; Jeremy Smith, *Making the Peace*.
5. Ed Moloney, *A Secret History of the IRA* (London, Allen Lane, 2002), p. 224.
6. Kevin Bean, *The New Politics of Sinn Féin* (Liverpool: Liverpool University Press, 2007), p. 6.
7. G. K. Peatling, *The Failure of the Northern Ireland Peace Process* (Dublin: Irish Academic Press, 2004), p. 10.
8. Edwards and McGrattan, *The Northern Ireland Conflict*. For a recent exposition of the importance of inclusivity see Powell, *Great Hatred*.
9. Among others, see Darby and McGinty, *Guns*; O'Leary, 'The Conservative Stewardship'; Tannam, 'Explaining'.
10. Richard English, 'The Northern Ireland Peace Process Reconsidered', *Éire-Ireland*, 1996, 31(3 & 4): 270–6; Henry Patterson, *The Politics of Illusion: A Political History of the IRA* (London: Serif, 2002), p. 225.
11. McGrattan, 'Explaining Northern Ireland?'
12. Ruane and Todd, 'Path-Dependence'.
13. McDowell, 'Commemorating the Troubles'.
14. Hume believed that the Agreement had, in his words, 'lanced the unionist boil'; quoted in Patterson, *Ireland*, p. 313.
15. FitzGerald, *All in a Life*, pp. 528–32.
16. English, *Irish Freedom*, p. 383.

17. Delaney, *An Accidental Diplomat*, pp. 289–90. Delaney also points out that the British reluctance to implement reforms was, in fact, counterproductive: 'by the time [a reform] trickled down it was accepted in the same [begrudging] spirit, and replaced by some new demand'; ibid., p. 290.
18. Murray, *John Hume*, p. 175.
19. Delaney, *Accidental Diplomat*, p. 303.
20. Currie, *All Hell will Break Lose*, p. 364. Currie concludes that the failure of the talks in ending the violence 'convinced me more than ever of the necessity of finding a way of opening talks with the unionists', ibid., p. 370. See also Sean Farren, 'Trying to persuade Sinn Féin', *SDLP: 1970–1990* (Belfast: SDLP, 1990), NIPC 4505.
21. Dixon, *Northern Ireland*, p. 228.
22. Chilcott quoted in Eamonn O'Kane, 'Anglo-Irish relations and the Northern Ireland peace process: from exclusion to inclusion', *Contemporary British History*, 18(1) (2004): 80–1.
23. Sinn Féin, 'The Sinn Féin/SDLP Talks: January-September, 1988' (Dublin: Sinn Féin, nd) available at www.sinnfein.ie, accessed 29 May 2009; Murray and Tonge, *Sinn Féin*, p. 166. The documents submitted by each party to the talks were first published in the *Irish Times* in September 1988.
24. Brian Feeney, *Sinn Féin: A Hundred Turbulent Years* (Dublin: Gill & Macmillan, 2000), p. 344.
25. Sinn Féin, 'A Scenario for Peace' (Dublin: Sinn Féin, 1987) available at www.sinnfein.ie, accessed, 29 May 2009.
26. *Irish Times*, 13 September 1988.
27. *Irish Times*, 19 September 1988; original emphasis.
28. McGrattan, 'Northern Nationalism', p. 158.
29. Hume, *Personal Views*, p. 46.
30. The most comprehensive account of the talks is Currie, *All Hell will Break Lose*, pp. 356–62.
31. John Hume, 'Speech by John Hume to the SDLP's 18th Annual Conference, 25–27 November 1988', Linenhall Library, Belfast, Northern Ireland Political Collection (hereafter NIPC) P3212.
32. Ibid.
33. John Hume, 'Speech by John Hume to the SDLP's 19th Annual Conference, 3–5 November 1989' NIPC P4323.
34. John Hume, 'Shaping the Future: Address by John Hume to the 20th Annual Conference of the SDLP, 16–18 November 1990', NIPC P4503.
35. John Hume, 'Address to the 23 Annual Conference, 26 November 1993', NIPC P5798.
36. For example, Hayward and Mitchell, 'Discourses'; Henry McDonald, *Gunsmoke and Mirrors: How Sinn Féin Dressed up Defeat as Victory* (Dublin, Gill & Macmillan, 2008), p. viii; McGovern, ' "The Old Days are Over" '; McLoughlin, 'John Hume'; Murray and Tonge, *Sinn Féin*, p. 263.
37. Clare O'Halloran, *Partition and the Limits of Irish Nationalism: An Ideology Under Stress* (Dublin: Gill & Macmillan, 1987).
38. McGrattan, 'Dublin'.
39. 'The SDLP Analysis of the Nature of the Problem, May 1991: Submission to the Brooke Talks', NIPC P5769.
40. Cited in Murray, *John Hume*, p. 163.

41. Tom Hartley, 'Towards a Broader Base, Belfast Six-County Internal Conference, June 25 1988', NIPC PH1566.
42. Ibid.
43. Martin Ó Muilleor, 'Real Politics, Belfast Six-County Internal Conference, 25 June 1988', NIPC PH1566.
44. Bean, *The New Sinn Féin*.
45. Adams, *Hope and History*; Mallie and McKittrick, *The Fight for Peace*.
46. Paul Dixon, 'Political Skills or Lying and Manipulation? The Choreography of the Northern Ireland Peace Process', *Political Studies*, 2002, 50(4): 725–41. The charge of duplicity is not peculiar to Ulster unionists, the SDLP's Seamus Mallon has been particularly critical of Blair's Northern Ireland policy: 'This [was] a man with a moral dimension to everything, who applied morality to nothing. I got increasingly to the point where I wouldn't have taken his word for anything … It was around that period leading up to the GFA that I think we all came to the conclusion this guy would buy anybody – and if he will buy anybody he will sell anybody'; *Guardian*, 14 March 2007.
47. For example, Roger MacGinty, 'Irish Republicanism and the Peace Process: From Revolution to Reform' in Michael Cox, Adrian Guelke and Fiona Stephen (eds.) *A Farewell to Arms? Beyond the Good Friday Agreement* (Manchester: Manchester University Press, 2006); McLoughlin, 'John Hume'.
48. Farrington, *Ulster Unionism*, p. 83; see also Aughey, *Under Siege*.
49. O'Kane, 'Anglo-Irish Relations', p. 80.
50. Cillian McGrattan, 'Northern Nationalism and the Belfast Agreement', in Brian Barton and Patrick J. Roche (eds.) *The Northern Ireland Question: The Peace Process and the Belfast Agreement* (Basingstoke, Palgrave Macmillan, 2009), p. 156; Patterson, *Ireland*, p. 319.
51. Farrington, *Ulster Unionism*, p. 56; see also Arthur Aughey, *Under Siege: Ulster Unionism and the Anglo-Irish Agreement* (Belfast: Blackstaff, 1989).
52. McKittrick et al., *Lost Lives*, p. 1526.
53. Patterson and Kaufmann, *Unionism*, p. 220.
54. 'The Task Force Report: An End to Drift, 16 June 1987', available at www.cain.ulster.ac.uk, accessed 18 June 2007.
55. Patterson and Kaufmann, *Unionism*, p. 221.
56. Ulster Political Research Group, 'Common Sense: Northern Ireland – An Agreed Process' (Belfast: UPRG, 1987), available at www.cain.ulst.ac.uk, accessed 21 June 2007.
57. Steve Bruce, 'Terrorism and Politics: The Case of Northern Ireland's Loyalist Paramilitaries', *Terrorism and Political Violence*, 13(2) (2001): pp. 34–5.
58. Margaret Thatcher, *The Downing Street Years* (London: HarperCollins, 1993), p. 415.
59. Brooke, quoted in Henry Patterson, *The Politics of Illusion: A Political History of the IRA* (London: Serif, 1997), p. 228.
60. Ibid.; also Maloney, *A Secret History*, p. 282.
61. Sinn Féin, 'Setting the Record Straight', 1994; available at www.sinnfein.ie, accessed 31 May 2009.
62. Tonge, *The New Northern Irish Politics*, p. 244.
63. Patterson, *Ireland*, p. 324.
64. Brooke, cited in Bew and Gillespie, *Northern Ireland*, p. 245.

65. Stephen King cited in Farrington, *Ulster Unionism*, p. 125.
66. Murray, *John Hume*, p. 192.
67. Delaney, *Accidental Diplomat*, p. 344.
68. McGrattan, 'Northern Nationalism', p. 160.
69. Sections of the documents are reprinted in Mallie and McKittrick, *The Fight for Peace*, pp. 411–20.
70. Ibid., p. 420.
71. Bew, *Ireland*, p. 541.
72. Murray and Tonge, *Sinn Féin*, p. 183.
73. 'Joint Declaration on Peace: The Downing Street Declaration, 15 December 1993'; available at www.cain.ulst.ac.uk, accessed 6 March 2008.
74. Major's private secretary replied that 'there can be no question of renegotiation' and that the Declaration provided 'a balanced framework for peace and democracy', Bew and Gillespie, *Northern Ireland*, p. 287.
75. Mitchell McLaughlin, 'Unionists and the Irish Peace Debate: Speech at the 1994 Ard Fheis', NIPC P5685.
76. Ibid.
77. Gerry Adams, 'Presidential Address to Sinn Féin Ard Fheis, 1994', available at www.sinnfein.ie, accessed 1 June 2009.
78. TUAS Document, 1994; reprinted in Mallie and McKittrick, *The Fight for Peace*, pp. 422–3. Although not specified in the document, 'TUAS' has been understood as being either an acronym for 'Totally Unarmed Strategy', or 'Tactical Use of the Armed Struggle'.
79. *Newsletter*, 1 September 1994.
80. *Belfast Telegraph*, 1 September 1994.
81. Lindy McDowell, 'Questions the victims couldn't ask', *Belfast Telegraph*, 1 September 1994.
82. *Irish Times*, 1 September 1994.
83. *Irish News*, 7 September 1994.
84. *Newsletter*, 7 September 1994.
85. Bew and Gillespie, *Northern Ireland*, p. 287. The most comprehensive analysis of the decommissioning issue is Eamonn O'Kane, 'Decommissioning and the peace process: where did it come from and why did it stay so long', *Irish Political Studies*, 22(1) (2007): 81–101.
86. *Irish News*, 30 January 1995.
87. *Irish News*, 23 February 1995.
88. Alvin Jackson, *Home Rule*, pp. 306–7.
89. The Framework Documents, 22 February 1995', available at www.cain.ulst.ac.uk, accessed 6 March 2008.
90. Henry Patterson, 'Response from both sides has been predictable', *Irish Times*, 23 February 1995.
91. Adams, for example, claimed the Frameworks Document represented 'a clear recognition that partition has failed, that British rule in Ireland has failed, and that there is no going back to the failed policies and structures of the past ... It could be argued that these issues need careful management, that they are part of the give and take, the evolution of a peace process', *Irish Times*, 23 February 1995; see also Murray and Tonge, *Sinn Féin*, p. 189.
92. *Newsletter*, 23 February 1995.

93. *Irish News*, 27 February 1995.
94. Ibid.
95. John Major, *John Major: The Autobiography* (London: HarperCollins, 1999), p. 474.
96. Dominic Bryan, 'Drumcree: marching towards peace in Northern Ireland?' in Jörg Neuheiser and Stefan Wolff (eds.) *Peace at Last? The Impact of the Good Friday Agreement on Northern Ireland*, (Oxford: Berghahn, 2003), p. 94.
97. Dominic Bryan, *Orange Parades: The Politics of Ritual, Tradition, and Control* (London: Pluto Press, 2000).
98. Bryan, 'Drumcree', p. 107.
99. Eric P. Kaufmann, *The Orange Order: A Contemporary Northern Irish History* (Oxford: Oxford University Press, 2008), p. 155.
100. Ibid.
101. Godson, *Himself Alone*, pp. 129–30.
102. Malachi O'Doherty, *The Trouble with Guns: Republican Strategy and the Provisional IRA* (Belfast: Blackstaff Press, 1995), pp. 129–30.
103. Godson, *Himself Alone*, p. 130.
104. Ibid., p. 131; see also Chris Ryder and Vincent Kearney, *Drumcree: The Orange Order's Last Stand* (London: Methuen, 2001).
105. O'Doherty, *The Trouble with Guns*, p. 176.
106. *Newsletter*, 2 July 1995.
107. Bew and Gillespie, *Northern Ireland*, p. 308.
108. *Irish Times*, 4 July 1995.
109. *Newsletter*, 8 July 1995.
110. *Newsletter*, 10 July 1995.
111. The head of the Orange Order, Martin Smyth, for example, called on Orange supporters not to accompany the Ormeau parade so that 'those bent on causing problems would not have the cover of peaceful bystanders'. *Newsletter*, 11 July 1995.
112. *Irish News*, 12 July 1995.
113. *Newsletter*, 11 July 1995.
114. *Newsletter*, 12 July 1995.
115. *Irish News*, 12 July 1995.
116. *Irish Times*, 12 July 1995.
117. *Irish News*, 15 July 1995.
118. Ibid.
119. Godson, *Himself Alone*, p. 142.
120. Patterson, *Ireland*, p. 329.
121. Godson, *Himself Alone*, pp. 169–70.
122. *Irish Times*, 9 July 1995.
123. *Irish News*, 9 September 1995.
124. *Irish Times*, 9 September 1995.
125. *Newsletter*, 9 September 1995.
126. *Belfast Telegraph*, 9 September 1995.
127. *Irish Times*, 9 September 1995.
128. Ibid.
129. *Newsletter*, 23 September 1995.
130. Bew and Gillespie, *Northern Ireland*, p. 314.

131. *Irish News*, 29 November 1995.
132. *Irish News*, 2 December 1995.
133. *Newsletter*, 2 December 1995.
134. *Belfast Telegraph*, 24 January 1996.
135. Bew and Gillespie, *Northern Ireland*, pp. 318–19.
136. *Irish News*, 25 January 1996.
137. Bew and Gillespie, *Northern Ireland*, p. 323.
138. *Newsletter*, 5 February 1996.
139. *Irish News*, 12 February 1996.
140. *Belfast Telegraph*, 14 February 1996.
141. *Irish News*, 12 February 1996.
142. *Irish Times*, 13 February 1996.
143. *Belfast Telegraph*, 12 February 1996.
144. Henry Patterson, 'From insulation to appeasement: the Major and Blair governments reconsidered', in Rick Wilford (ed.) *Aspects of the Belfast Agreement* (Oxford: Oxford University Press, 2001), p. 174.
145. Bew and Gillespie, *Northern Ireland*, p. 326.
146. Ibid., p. 328.
147. *Irish News*, 15 July 1996; see also Bew and Gillespie, *Northern Ireland*, pp. 330–1.
148. *Newsletter*, 4 July 1996.
149. *Irish Times*, 8 July 1996.
150. Ibid.
151. *Irish Times*, 10 July 1996.
152. Martin Smyth, quoted in the *Newsletter*, 7 July 1996.
153. *Newsletter*, 9 July 1996.
154. Ibid..
155. Ibid.
156. *Newsletter*, 10 July 1996.
157. *Irish Times*, 10 July 1996.
158. Ibid.
159. *Irish Times*, 11 July 1996.
160. *Irish News*, 10 July 1996.
161. *Belfast Telegraph*, 12 July 1996.
162. *Irish News*, 12 July 1996.
163. *Belfast Telegraph*, 13 July 1996.
164. *Newsletter*, 17 July 1996.
165. *Irish News*, 13 July 1996.
166. *Irish Times*, 13 July 1996.
167. *Irish News*, 15 July 1996.
168. Speech by John Hume to the SDLP's 26th Annual Conference, 8–10 November 1996', NIPC P7361.
169. Tony Blair, quoted in Hennessy, *The Northern Ireland Peace Process*, p. 104.
170. Bew and Gillespie, *Northern Ireland*, p. 341.
171. Ibid., p. 344.
172. *Irish Times*, 7 July 1997.
173. *Irish News*, 7 July 1997.
174. *Newsletter*, 4 July 1997.
175. *Belfast Telegraph*, 7 July 1997.

176. *Newsletter*, 8 July 1997.
177. The document is reprinted in the *Irish Times*, 8 July 1997.
178. *Irish News*, 8 July 1997.
179. *Irish News*, 17 July 1997. On 19 July, the paper printed two pages of readers' letters on the Drumcree crisis under the headline: 'Shocking sense of disbelief'.
180. Paul Bew, 'The unionists have won, they just don't know it', *Sunday Times*, 17 May 1998.

Chapter 6

1. See, for example, Ken Maginnis, 'Prisoners and the Stormont agreement', *Newsletter*, 12 May 1998.
2. See Robert McCartney, ' "No" can be the only verdict on this Agreement', *Newsletter*, 19 May 1998.
3. See Sean Farren, 'The SDLP and the roots of the Good Friday Agreement', in Cox et al. (eds) *A Farewell to Arms?*
4. Adams, *Hope and History*.
5. O'Leary, 'The nature of the Agreement', p. 92.
6. Peter Shirlow and Colin Coulter, 'Enduring problems: The Belfast Agreement and a disagreed Belfast', in Marianne Elliot (ed.) *The Long Road to Peace in Northern Ireland: Peace Lectures from the Institute of Irish Studies at Liverpool University* (Liverpool: Liverpool University Press, 2007).
7. Paul Dixon, *Northern Ireland: The Politics of War and Peace* (Basingstoke: Palgrave Macmillan, 2008), p. 288.
8. Hennessey, *The Northern Ireland Peace Process*, p. 109.
9. *Irish Times*, 19 July 1997.
10. Trimble, quoted in Hennessey, *The Northern Ireland Peace Process*, p. 110.
11. *Irish Times*, 19 July 1997.
12. Bew and Gillespie, *Northern Ireland*, p. 348.
13. On the negotiations, see Hennessey, *The Northern Ireland Peace Process*; on the institutional details of the Agreement, see Brendan O'Leary, 'The nature of the Agreement', *New Left Review*, 233 (1999): 66–96.
14. See O'Leary and McGarry, *Politics*, pp. 322–5.
15. English, 'The Northern Irish peace process', p. 274.
16. O'Leary and McGarry, *Politics*, p. 323.
17. Henry Patterson, 'From insulation to appeasement: the Major and Blair governments reconsidered', in Rick Wilford (ed.) *Aspects of the Belfast Agreement* (Oxford: Oxford University Press, 2001), p. 173.
18. McGrattan, 'Learning'.
19. Aughey, *Politics*, p. 83.
20. 'The Agreement: agreement reached in multi-party negotiations' (Belfast: NIO, 1998).
21. John Hume, 'A Future Together: Address by John Hume to the 28th Annual SDLP Conference, 14 November 1998', NIPC P9091.
22. John Hume, 'Address to the SDLP Party Conference, 6 November 1999', NIPC P10095.
23. MacGinty, 'Irish Republicanism and the peace process', p. 126.

24. See also Brendan O'Leary, 'Mission accomplished? Looking back at the IRA', *Field Day Review*, 1 (2005): 217–29.
25. Stephen Hopkins, 'Comparing revolutionary narratives: Irish republican self-presentation and considerations for the study of communist life-histories', *Socialist History*, 34 (2009): 52–69; John A. Murphy, 'Republicans: the ones rewriting history', *Irish Independent*, 7 September 2003.
26. Henry Patterson, 'The republican movement and the legacy of the Troubles', in Iseult Honohan (ed.) *Republicanism in Ireland: Confronting Theories and Traditions* (Manchester: Manchester University Press, 2008), p. 149.
27. *Guardian*, 12 September 2007.
28. Adams, quoted in *An Phoblacht/Republican News*, 23 April 1998.
29. McDonald, *Gunsmoke*, p. 121.
30. Claire Mitchell, 'From victims to equals? Catholic responses to political change in Northern Ireland', *Irish Political Studies*, 18(1) (2003): 51–71. Mitchell's unproblematic reiteration of 'Catholic responses' ignores the wider political and historical context in which nationalist understanding occurs. The empirical reality of continued commemoration fundamentally questions the assertions of a transformative culture within nationalism or unionism; see McDowell, 'Commemorating the Troubles', p. 55.
31. 'Speech by Councillor Tom Hartley on Council Commemorations and Ceremonies, 20 September 2002', NIPC P12321.
32. Tom Hartley, 'Oration at the unveiling of a mural for Nora McCabe', 9 July 2000, NIPC P10540.
33. Sara McDowell, 'Selling conflict heritage through tourism in peacetime Northern Ireland: transforming conflict or exacerbating difference?' *International Journal of Heritage Studies*, 14(3) (2008): 405–21.
34. *Newsletter*, 11 May 1998.
35. *Newsletter*, 12 May 1998.
36. *Newsletter*, 14 May 1998.
37. *Newsletter*, 15 May 1998.
38. *Newsletter*, 18 May 1998.
39. Ibid.
40. Ibid.
41. Ibid.
42. *Newsletter*, 13 May 1998.
43. *Newsletter*, 15 May 1998.
44. Ibid.
45. *Newsletter*, 15 May 1998.
46. Ibid.
47. *Newsletter*, 16 May 1998.
48. Patterson and Kaufmann, *Unionism and Orangeism*, p. 223.
49. *Newsletter*, 23 May 1998.
50. *Newsletter*, 27 May 1998.
51. Bew, *Ireland*, p. 550.
52. Bew and Gillespie, *Northern Ireland*, p. 368.
53. *Newsletter*, 3 July 1998.
54. The children were the three Quinn brothers: Richard (aged 11), Mark (10) and Jason (9); Bew and Gillespie, *Northern Ireland*, pp. 371–2.
55. *Newsletter*, 13 July 1998.

222 *Notes*

56. According to his biographer Dean Godson, Trimble believed that nationalists saw Patten 'as something they have already got' and that they were unlikely to 'give back' the concession of police reform; *Himself Alone*, p.489.
57. Bew, *Ireland*, p.550.
58. Patterson and Kaufmann, *Unionism and Orangeism*, p. 253.
59. BBC, *Hearts and Minds* poll, 17 October 2002; cited in Dixon, *Northern Ireland*, p. 288.
60. Dixon, *Northern Ireland*, p. 294.
61. O'Kane, *Britain, Ireland and Northern Ireland*, p.167.
62. Sinn Féin's emphasis on security force collusion with loyalists underpinned its arguments. However, the moral high ground looks less secure when the fact that republicans accounted for 58.8 per cent of the killings is taken into account. The statistics are taken from the 1999 edition of McKittrick et al., *Lost Lives*.
63. Dixon, *Northern Ireland*, pp. 294–5; Patterson, *Ireland*, p. 343.
64. Godson, *Himself Alone*, p. 472.
65. Patterson, *Ireland*, p. 342.
66. The logical extrapolation from this – that the IRA campaign had solidified Protestant opposition to a united Ireland and made reunification a less likely prospect than it had been in 1970 – was denied by Adams in a long interview with Nick Stadlen QC in the *Guardian*. The fact that republicans ended up with less than was on offer at Sunningdale was not a defeat, claimed Adams; the campaign had been worth it. *Guardian*, 12 September 2007; see also McGrattan, 'Northern Nationalism', p. 163. See Timothy Shanahan, *The Provisional Irish Republican Army and the Morality of Terrorism* (Edinburgh: Edinburgh University Press, 2009), pp. 130–2 for a critical deconstruction of republicans' 'consequentialist morality'.
67. O'Kane, *Britain, Ireland and Northern Ireland*, p. 163.
68. Ibid., p. 164.
69. Dixon, *Northern Ireland*, p. 297.
70. O'Kane, *Britain, Ireland and Northern Ireland*, p. 168.
71. Patterson, *Ireland*, p. 344.
72. See Fidelma Ashe, 'Gendering the Holy Cross school dispute: women and nationalism in Northern Ireland', *Politics*, 54(1) (2006): 147–64.
73. Dixon, *Northern Ireland*, p. 298; Patterson, *Ireland*, p. 345.
74. O'Kane, *Britain, Ireland and Northern Ireland*, p. 170.
75. Northern Ireland Office and the Department of Foreign Affairs, 'Implementation plan issued by the British and Irish governments on 1 August 2001', available at www.cain.ac.uk, accessed 10 June 2009. Mandelson, later described Blair's policy as being 'basically about conceding and capitulating in a whole number of different ways to republican demands … the Sinn Féin shopping list'; *Guardian*, 14 March 2007.
76. Bew, *Ireland*, p. 551.
77. *Guardian*, 18 October 2002.
78. Patterson, *Ireland*, pp. 349–50.
79. Trimble also failed to ask for republican commitments prior to the IRA's announcement, believing not only that they would not be 'transparent', but also that he would be 'blamed by London' for scuppering the deal; Godson, *Himself Alone*, p. 795.

80. O'Kane, *Britain, Ireland and Northern Ireland*, p. 172.
81. Timothy Shanahan, *The Provisional Irish Republican Army and the Morality of Terrorism* (Edinburgh: Edinburgh University Press, 2009), p. 2.
82. In the event, Adams' disastrous TV performances in the Republic's 2007 elections contributed to the party's reduction to four seats. Their marginality was seemingly confirmed in the Socialist Party's victory over Adams' protégé and party vice-president Mary-Lou McDonald in Dublin in the 2009 European elections; *Irish Times*, 9 June 2009.
83. Patterson, *Ireland*, p. 353.
84. *Guardian*, 8 May 2007.
85. *Belfast Telegraph*, 5 June 2007.
86. *Irish Times*, 8 May 2007.
87. *Guardian*, 14 March 2007.
88. Anthony McIntyre, *Good Friday: The Death of Irish Republicanism* (New York: Ausubo Press, 2008). The former hunger striker Brendan Hughes railed against the vacant symbolism of Sinn Féin's post-Agreement politics: 'Painting murals on walls to commemorate blanketmen after they have died a slow and lonely death from alcohol abuse is no use to anyone'; *Irish News*, 7 October 2006.
89. Ronan Bennett, 'In a British fairyland', *Guardian*, 17 March 2007.
90. 2008 Sinn Féin Ard Fheis Clár, available at www.ardfheis.com, accessed 17 May 2008.
91. *Irish Times*, 9 March 2008.
92. Neil Jarman, *No Longer a Problem? Sectarian Violence in Northern Ireland* (Belfast: Institute for Conflict Research, 2005).
93. Robin Wilson, *The Northern Ireland Experience of Conflict and Agreement: A Model for Export* (Manchester: Manchester University Press, 2010); PSNI, 'Security-related incidents: 1990/91-31 March 2009', available at www.psni.police.uk/security_related_incidents_fy.pdf, accessed 10 June 2009.
94. Christine Bell, 'Dealing with the past in Northern Ireland', *Fordham International Law Journal*, 26(4) (2003): 1095–147.
95. *We Will Remember Them: Report of the Northern Ireland Victims' Commissioner, Sir Kenneth Bloomfield KCB* (Belfast: NIO, 1998).
96. Kirk Simpson, 'Untold stories: unionist remembrance of political violence and suffering in Northern Ireland', *British Politics*, 3(4) (2008): 465–89.
97. See, for example, the discussion by former prisoners on 'victims' reproduced in Peter Shirlow and Kieran McEvoy, *Beyond the Wire: Former Prisoners and Conflict Transformation in Northern Ireland* (London: Pluto Press, 2008), pp. 115–17.
98. *Observer*, 9 December 2007.
99. Dáil Éireann, Parliamentary Debates, Official Report, 608(5), 27 October 2005, cols. 1491–4; *Belfast Telegraph*, 18 January 2007.
100. *Belfast Telegraph*, 22 June 2007.
101. Northern Ireland Office, 'Hain announces group to look at the past', 22 June 2007; available at www.nio.gov.uk, accessed 11 June 2009.
102. Report of the Consultative Group on the Past, available at www.cpgni.org, accessed 28 January 2009.

103. Edwards and McGrattan, *The Northern Ireland Conflict*, ch. 8.
104. Henry Patterson, 'Truth and reconciliation in Northern Ireland? Not much hope of either', *Parliamentary Brief*, February 2009.
105. Ibid.
106. *Irish Times*, 29 January 2008.
107. *Belfast Telegraph*, 29 January 2008.
108. Northern Ireland Office, 'A shared future: policy and strategic framework for good relations in Northern Ireland' (NIO: Belfast, 2005).
109. Ashe, 'From paramilitaries to peacemakers'.
110. See Edwards and McGrattan, *Northern Ireland*.
111. Aughey, *Politics*, p. 128.
112. See, for example, Christine Bell, *On the Law of Peace: Peace Agreements and the Lex Pacifatoria* (Oxford: Oxford University Press, 2008), pp. 300–1; McGarry and O'Leary, 'Proving our points', p. 152.
113. Marie Breen-Smyth, *Truth Recovery and Justice after Conflict: Managing Violent Pasts* (London: Routledge, 2007).
114. EPIC, 'Truth recovery: a contribution from loyalism' (Belfast: EPIC, 2004).
115. Sinn Féin, 'Truth: a Sinn Féin discussion document' (Belfast: Sinn Féin, 2003).
116. Gerry Kelly, 'Speech delivered to the Sinn Féin Ard Fheis, 21 February 2009', available at www.ardfheis.com, accessed 1 May 2009.
117. Northern Ireland Affairs Committee, 'Ways of dealing with Northern Ireland's past: Interim Report – Victims and Survivors' (London: The Stationery Office, 2005).
118. Kieran McEvoy, 'Making peace with the past: options for truth recovery regarding the conflict in and about Northern Ireland' (Belfast: Healing Through Remembering, 2006), p. 80.
119. See, for example, Catherine Nash, 'Local histories in Northern Ireland', *History Workshop Journal*, 60 (2005): 45–68.
120. Grainne Kelly, 'Storytelling audit' (Belfast: Healing Through Remembering, 2005); Brandon Hamber and Richard A. Wilson, 'Symbolic closure through memory: reparation and revenge in post-conflict societies', *Journal of Human Rights*, 1(1) (2002): 35–53.
121. McGrattan, ' "Order out of chaos" '.

Conclusion

1. Javier Cercas, *The Speed of Light*, trans. Anne McLean (Edinburgh: Bloomsbury, 2007), p. 214.
2. Kerr, *Imposing*, p. 67.
3. *Newsletter*, 5 October 1973.
4. Aughey, *Under Siege*; Cochrane, *Unionist Politics*; Farrington, *Ulster Unionism*.
5. Among others, Bell, *Law of Peace*; Kerr, *Imposing*; McGarry and O'Leary, *Explaining*; Shirlow and McEvoy, *Beyond*.
6. Roy Foster, 'Partnership of loss: "Ireland: The Politics of Enmity 1789–2006" by Paul Bew', *London Review of Books*, 13 December 2007; original emphasis.
7. Paloma, *Memory*, p. 31.
8. Ibid., p. 15.

9. Richard Kearney and Mark Dooley, 'Imagination, testimony and trust: a dialogue with Paul Ricoeur', in Richard Kearney and Mark Dooley (eds.) *Questioning Ethics: Contemporary Debates in Philosophy*, (London: Routledge, 1999), p. 16.
10. Adams, *Hope and History*.
11. MacGinty and Darby, *Guns*.
12. Paul Ricoeur, 'Memory and forgetting', in Kearney and Dooley, p. 10.

Index

abstentionism 39–41, 44, 51, 56, 62, 87, 158
Adair, Johnny 132
Adams, Gerry 14–15, 122, 125–9, 135–40, 143, 145, 148, 152–3, 160–1, 172–3, 184
Aguilar, Paloma 25, 187
Ahern, Bertie 153
Allan, James 115
Allen, Harry 150–1
Alliance Party 50, 61
Anglo–Irish Agreement (1985) 17, 31, 103, 107–8, 117–18, 124–6, 129–34, 183
Annesley, Hugh 148
Armstrong, Robert 108
Aughey, Arthur 159

Baird, Ernest 96, 106
Balcombe Street Gang 163
Ballymoney arson attack 166–7
Barr, Glenn 96
Bean, Kevin 122, 130
Beattie, Desmond 40
Belfast Agreement (1998) *see* Good Friday Agreement
Belfast Telegraph 67, 138, 178
Best, William 63
Bew, Paul 36–8, 117
Bingham, William 167
Blair, Tony 152–3, 158, 162–5, 168–73, 179
Bloody Friday 61
Bloody Sunday 41, 44, 46, 58, 175
Bloomfield, Kenneth 93–4, 163, 175
Boland, Kevin 78, 84
Border Campaign (1956–62) 4
Bradford, Roy 80–1, 86
Breen–Smyth, Marie 179
British Army 6, 17, 27, 34–9, 48, 53, 64, 85, 150, 170, 174
British–Irish Council 159
Brooke, Peter 128, 134–5, 139

Brown, Gordon 163
Brubaker, Rogers 11
Bruce, Steve 15–16, 134
Bruton, John 138, 145–6, 152
Bryan, Dominic 140–1
Burnside, David 150

Canary Wharf explosion 148
Canavan, Michael 80
Caraher, Ben 63, 65
Carrington, Lord 76
Castlereagh barracks raid 171
Cercas, Javier 181
de Chastelain, John 158
Chichester-Clark, James 45, 51
Chilcott, John 125, 136
Churchill, Winston 141
civil disobedience 43–4
civil rights movement 4–6, 17, 24, 35–40, 55, 58, 128
Clegg, Lee 143
Clinton, Bill 135, 147, 164
coalition, voluntary 98–101, 109, 174, 183
Cold War, ending of 135
conflict transformation literature 11, 185
'consent' principle 136–7, 152, 155, 158
consociationalism 11, 17–18, 33, 90, 92, 108, 113, 118, 123, 159, 162, 185
Constitutional Convention 92–104, 107, 111–12, 116, 183
Consultative Group on the Past in Northern Ireland 176–7
Cooper, Frank 93–4, 96, 109, 112
Cooper, Ivan 63–5
Cosgrave, Liam 72, 78, 80, 86
Costello, Declan 73
Council of Ireland 42, 44, 47, 51, 57, 65–88, 96, 103

Craig, William 28, 30, 47–51, 61, 66–7, 77, 81, 87–8, 93, 96–102, 182–3
Cubbon, Brian 104
Cunningham, Michael 104
Currie, Austin 4, 6, 29, 47, 74–5, 79, 85, 124–5
Cusack, Seamus 40

decommissioning of arms 139–40, 147–9, 152–5, 158–9, 163–4, 167–72, 175
Democratic Unionist Party (DUP) 106–7, 122–4, 133, 166, 170–4, 178
Derry 6, 35–40, 46
Devlin, Paddy 29, 39–40, 45, 72, 75, 79, 82, 100, 103
direct rule 24, 35–6, 48, 58, 84, 106–12, 116–17, 120, 167
'distancing' policy 110–13, 117
Dixon, Paul 13, 17, 157
Donaldson, Jeffrey 150
Donlon, Seán 69, 73–4, 79–80
Donoughue, Bernard 91–3, 108, 112–13
Downing Street Declaration (1993) 136
Drumcree dispute 123, 141–5, 149–54, 158, 160, 166–7, 183
Duffy, John 65
'Dungiven assembly' (1971) 43

Eames, Robin 144, 151, 153, 164
Eksund incident 125
elites, political 13–14, 19–20, 119, 174, 184
English, Richard 29, 158
Enniskillen bombing 125
entrenchment, political 2–3, 8, 26–8, 34, 38, 47, 55, 57–8, 89–92, 95– 9, 102–4, 116–17, 120–1, 123, 130, 174–5, 181–4
Ervine, David 132, 149
ethnic conflict and the 'ethnic conflict model' 7–13, 16–21, 26, 31, 35–6, 90–2, 114, 118–20, 128, 185–7

Faulkner, Brian 2, 6, 28–30, 35–41, 45–57, 59–62, 66–71, 74–88, 93, 96, 181–3
Ferguson, Niall 23
Fianna Fáil 172
Fine Gael 57
Finucane, Patrick 180
Fitt, Gerry 4, 29, 39–40, 45, 47, 64, 73–5, 79–83, 96, 100, 103
FitzGerald, Garret 68, 72, 75, 79, 105, 116–18, 152
Flanagan, Ronnie 153, 166
Foster, Roy (R.F.) 86, 186

Goldstone, Jack 24
Good Friday Agreement 1, 19, 108, 122–3, 156–69, 173–5
  referendum on 162–5
Good, Harold 164
Gracey, Harold 149
Grogan, Dick 146

Hacker, Jacob 25
Haddock, Mark 176
Hain, Peter 176, 178
Haines, Joe 108
Hartley, Tom 129–30, 161–2, 178
Hayes, Bernadette 12
Hayes, Maurice 94
Hayward, Katy 13
Heads of Agreement document (1998) 158
Healing Through Remembering 180
Heath, Edward 43–52, 59–60, 64, 69–72, 87
Hendron, Joe 124
Hennessey, Thomas 38
Hillery, Patrick 64
Historical Inquiries Team (HET) 176–7
  see also Police Service of Northern Ireland
Holden, David 52–3
Horowitz, Donald 8
House of Commons Northern Ireland Affairs Committee 179–80
Hughes, Brendan 173
human rights 151, 159, 171

Hume, John 4, 29, 32, 39–41, 45–6, 63, 73–6, 79, 82, 96, 100–5, 118–19, 122–8, 132, 135–9, 145–8, 152, 154, 159–60
hunger strikes 15
Hunt, John 108–9, 111

Ingram, Adam 164, 175
Inquiries Act (2005) 180
Inter-Departmental Unit on Northern Ireland (IDU) 71–3
inter-governmentalism 17, 20, 47–8, 62, 67, 69, 73, 91, 117–18, 133, 136
international relations theory 33
internment 32, 36, 41, 44–9, 58–60, 63–5, 79–80, 96
Ireland Act (1949) 4
'Irish dimension' 21, 27, 30, 34, 42, 47, 50–1, 56, 62, 66, 79, 85–6, 90, 94–6, 102–8, 113, 117, 132, 146, 182, 184
Irish News 138–40, 145–8, 151–5
Irish Republican Army (IRA) 17, 27, 32, 45, 48, 59, 61, 66, 68, 80, 86, 89, 94, 96, 100–1, 106, 113–17, 126–30, 136, 139, 146, 148–9, 152, 160, 167–74, 182
see also Provisional IRA
Irish Times 79, 138, 146, 148, 151–4, 163

Jackson, Alvin 106–7, 119
Judt, Tony 1

Kaufmann, Eric 68, 141–2
Kerr, Michael 20, 90–1
Kershaw, Ian 22–3
Kilfedder, James 66
King, Martin Luther 5

Laitin, David 11
Legacy Commission 177
Lemass, Sean 5
Lijphart, Arend 8–9
Lillis, Michael 139
Lindsay, Kennedy 70
lock-in effects 22

Logue, Hugh 79
Lowry, Robert 96–100
Loyalist Volunteer Force (LVF) 132, 166
Lynch, Jack 43, 47–8, 72

McAdam, Doug 24
McAllister, Ian 12
McAteer, Eddie 47
McBride, Alan 164
McCabe, Jerry 149
McCartney, Robert 122–3, 157, 172
MacCionnaith, Brendan 142–3, 150
McDonald, Henry 161
McDougal, Bertha 178
McDowell, Sara 15, 162
McEvoy, Kieran 11
McGarry, John 11, 17–18, 20, 31, 35–6, 108, 113–14, 118–19, 158
McGeown, Pat 140
MacGinty, Roger 160
McGoldrick, Michael 149
McGrady, Eddie 124
McGuinness, Martin 14, 153–4, 160, 172–3, 178, 184
McIntyre, Anthony 173
McIvor, Basil 66, 79
McKee, Billy 116
McLachlan, Peter 78, 83
McLaughlin, Mitchell 137
McLoughlin, Peter 102
'Macrory Gap' 111
Maginnis, Ken 148
Major, John 140, 147, 149
Mallon, Seamus 41, 103, 138, 166, 173
Manchester bombing 149
Mandelson, Peter 169, 173
Mason, Roy 113–14
Maudling, Reginald 59, 62–3
Mayhew, Patrick 140
Mitchell, Claire 13–15, 161
Mitchell, George 147–9, 170
'Mitchell principles' 147, 158
Moloney, Ed 107, 122
Molyneaux, James 106, 133, 145–6

Mowlam, Mo 153–4
Mulholland, Marc 37

Nally, Dermot 69
New Ireland Forum 105, 117
Newe, G.B. 60
The Newsletter 48, 50, 67–71, 77, 123, 138–40, 143–7, 150, 153–4, 162–6, 183
North Atlantic Treaty Organisation (NATO) 135
North-South Ministerial Council 159, 170
Northern Bank robbery 172
Northern Ireland Assembly 76, 159, 165–6, 169–73, 178
Northern Ireland Office (NIO) 91, 103–4, 109–12, 147, 154, 174–5, 183

Oatley, Michael 115
Ó Brádaigh, Ruairí 114–16
O'Brien, Conor Cruise 72, 75
Ó Conaill, Dáithí 114, 116
Ó Dochartaigh, Niall 37
O'Doherty, Malachi 143, 148–9
O'Duffy, Brendan 20, 91
O'Hanlon, Paddy 85
Ó hUiginn, Seán 29
O'Kane, Eamonn 20, 117–18, 169, 172
O'Leary, Brendan 11, 17–18, 20, 31, 35–6, 91, 108, 113–14, 118–19, 158
Omagh bombing (1998) 160
Ó Muilleor, Martin 130
O'Neill, Terence 5, 16, 31, 47
O'Neill, Tip 118
Orange Order 5, 46–7, 106, 142–4, 149–55, 163–7
Orr, William 66

Paisley, Ian 5, 15–16, 28–31, 35, 46–53, 61, 66–7, 70, 77, 81, 87–8, 93, 96, 99–106, 133, 144, 146, 151, 157, 165, 173, 178, 182
Parades Commission 166

parades disputes 15, 47, 141–4, 154, 158
paramilitarism 37, 46, 56, 106, 114–15, 119, 132, 147, 149, 159, 162, 170, 174–80, 184
path-dependence 21–8, 56, 88, 98, 186
Patten, Chris 169
Patten Report (1999) 167–70, 176
Patterson, Henry 68, 117
Patton, Joel 132
peace process 121–3, 130–1, 142, 147, 149, 158, 160, 163, 171–3, 184
People's Democracy 37
Pierson, Paul 22
police ombudsman 176
Police Service of Northern Ireland (PSNI) 169
'political opportunity structures' 24
Powell, Enoch 97, 101–2
power-sharing 1, 16–33, 34–5, 42–4, 47–57, 66–88, 90–113, 117–18, 121, 126–7, 132–3, 156, 165, 168–70, 173–4, 182–6
Prince, Simon 37–8
Prior, James 107
prisoner release 163–5, 175
Progressive Unionist Party (PUP) 166
proportional representation 17, 42, 49, 54–5, 65–6, 115, 159
Provisional IRA (PIRA) 6, 30, 34–5, 38–46, 54–5, 62–3, 95, 102, 114–16, 124, 134–7, 163, 172, 185
'punishment' attacks 143

Reagan, Ronald 117–18
Real IRA 160
Rees, Merlyn 80–3, 93–6, 99–101, 114–16
Reid, Alex 125
religious differences 14–16
rent and rates strike 44, 79
restorative justice schemes 174, 178
Reynolds, Albert 138–9

Index

Rice, Gerard 142
Ricoeur, Paul 187–8
Robinson, Peter 107, 174
Rose, Paul 6
Royal Ulster Constabulary (RUC) 123, 141–4, 150, 166, 169, 176
Ruane, Joseph 123

St Andrews Agreement (2006) 172–3
Second World War 4
Secretary of State for Northern Ireland 59, 67–8, 76, 83, 103, 159
sectarianism 35, 40, 46, 56, 63, 151, 157, 170, 174–9, 183
Shirlow, Peter 11
Sinn Féin 14–15, 114, 117, 122–30, 134–43, 149, 153, 155, 157–74, 179
Smith, Anthony 9
Smyth, Clifford 98–9, 102
Smyth, Martin 103, 149–50, 170
Social Democratic and Labour Party (SDLP) 2, 6, 14, 21, 27–30, 34–46, 49–57, 61–88, 92–107, 111, 118–19, 123–37, 141, 146, 152, 157, 159, 166, 172, 179–84
Spirit of Drumcree group 132
Spring, Dick 145
Stone, Lawrence 3
'storytelling' movement 180
Sunningdale Agreement 77–85, 88

Tannam, Etain 20, 91, 118–19
Tarrow, Sidney 24
Taylor, John 146, 148–9
Taylor, Rupert 17
Thatcher, Margaret 107, 117–18, 122, 134
Tilly, Charles 24
'tipping points' 23
Todd, Jennifer 123
Tonge, Jonathan 135
Trend, Burke 49

Trimble, David 100, 132, 141, 144–54, 158, 162–73, 184
truth recovery process 179–80
Tughan, Fred 83
Twomey, Seamus 101, 116

UK Unionist Party 123, 157, 166
Ulster Defence Association (UDA) 115
Ulster Political Research Group 134
Ulster Unionist Council (UUC) 168, 170, 182
Ulster Unionist Party (UUP) 3–4, 21, 27, 60–2, 68, 102–7, 124, 133, 156–7, 162–5, 168, 171–2, 176, 183
Ulster Volunteer Force (UVF) 149
Ulster Workers Council strike 85–6, 94
unification of Ireland 54–5, 62, 68, 71, 75–6, 79, 108, 117, 122, 125–7, 136–7, 141, 155, 161, 182–3
Unionist Assembly Party 80
United Nations 111
United Ulster Unionist Council (UUUC) 24, 77, 80–3, 92, 95–102, 106, 111

Vanguard Unionist Progressive Party (VUPP) 106
Victims Liaison Unit 175, 178

West, Harry 28, 30, 70, 77–8, 83, 87–8, 93, 96–9, 182
Whitelaw, William 61–7, 74, 93
Wilford, Rick 17
Wilson, Harold 69–72, 80, 83, 86, 91, 96, 108–9, 112, 114, 185
Wilson, Robin 17
Wolff, Stefan 10–11
Wright, Billy 132, 154